THE WALL STREET JOURNAL ON MARKETING

THE WALL STREET JOURNAL ON MARKETING

Ronald Alsop
Bill Abrams

DOW JONES-IRWIN
Homewood, Illinois 60430

ISBN 0-87094-896-2

Library of Congress Catalog Card No. 86-71213

Printed in the United States of America

1 2 3 4 5 6 7 8 9 0 MP 3 2 1 0 9 8 7 6

Introduction

The Wall Street Journal began publishing a weekly column
about marketing in 1980, amid the growing recognition
that marketing was the single biggest challenge facing almost any enterprise. Whether for Procter & Gamble and
McDonald's, or dentists and religious groups, marketing is
simply the vital task of determining consumers' needs and
then finding ways to satisfy them.

This book is a collection of the *Journal's* weekly columns
about marketing, supplemented by other, longer features.
All are drawn from case studies and real-world examples
rather than abstract theory. Each selection is intended for a
broad audience of marketing professionals, nonmarketing
executives, and consumers alike.

We hope this book will be a guide through an era that is
perplexing even for the most experienced marketers—as
shown by Coca-Cola's bungled attempt to introduce a new
version of its flagship brand. Practitioners in a wide array
of businesses might find a lesson in General Electric's use of
toll-free telephone numbers to stay in touch with consumers. Advertisers mulling whether to use Hollywood
stars or real consumers in their next campaign might want
to study the articles on advertising credibility. And new-
product planners might find a cautionary tale in the story of
how Hanes got snagged when it tried to translate the ideas
that worked so well for L'eggs pantyhose to the market for
eye shadow and lipstick.

We wrote most of the articles included in this book and
have been responsible for the marketing column since its
inception. The remaining selections were written by other

Wall Street Journal reporters, including George Anders, Ed Bean, Amanda Bennett, Lee Berton, Hank Gilman, Janet Guyon, Paul Ingrassia, John Koten, Julie Salamon, Gregory Stricharchuk, Steve Swartz, Steve Weiner, and David Wessel. We appreciate their contributions, and we also would like to thank Roger May, the talented and patient editor of the *Journal's* marketing column.

Ronald Alsop
Bill Abrams

Contents

3   Advertising Styles

4   Advertising Campaigns

8   The World Market

9   Corporate Strategies

1

Changing Consumers

What Do Working Women Want?

Insurance agent Jerry Maxwell thinks his next sale will be a cinch. Calling on a young prospect named Diane Foster, he bumbles into her office 10 minutes late and doesn't even bother shaking hands. He further insults the businesswoman by calling her Miss instead of Ms. and assuming that as a single person she couldn't possibly have any dependents.

"I'm expecting my sister in 20 minutes," she tells the salesman. "That's nice," he replies. "A bite to eat, maybe a little shopping." Actually, she and her sister are business partners about to close on a big real estate deal. It takes just a few seconds more for Ms. Foster to lose all patience and usher Mr. Maxwell out of her office.

Is this for real? Well, not quite. It's part of a videotape Metropolitan Life Insurance Co. produced this year to try to make its agents more sensitive to the feelings of working women. Sample suggestions: Don't ask for the man of the house if a woman answers the telephone, and don't assume a single woman's main destination in life is the altar.

The very need to teach such elementary lessons shows how far behind the times marketers are in their understanding of working women. "Women in focus groups tell us that the days of depending on others for their financial and material needs are over," says Maree Waters, market director for personal-insurance sales at Metropolitan. "But they can't find anyone to take them seriously and patiently explain insurance to them."

Today, more than 54 percent of women work, according to the U.S. Department of Labor, and even though they still trail men in earnings and purchasing power, they make many of the buying decisions in two-income households. In fact, Metropolitan expects working wives to contribute nearly 40 percent of family income by 1990.

It's not surprising, then, that a growing number of companies are taking off the blinders. But in trying to promote their products to working women, marketers are finding more challenges than they bargained for. Many companies still don't know how to communicate intelligently with women through advertising or in face-to-face sales pitches.

What marketers too often fail to see is that the working-woman market has many facets. The tendency is to classify women as either cute and sexy or stiff and businesslike. Jane Fitzgibbon, senior vice president and director of research development at the Ogilvy & Mather ad agency, says two of the most popular stereotypes are "the Betty Crocker woman" and "the Mary Cunningham woman," who acts just like a man except for the skirt. "Marketers love to find easy handles," she says, "rather than try to get into the heads and hearts of women."

Companies have blundered most in their advertising. Ogilvy & Mather found in a 1985 survey that 76 percent of career women believe most ads insult the intelligence of the average consumer, and 46 percent feel most ads are in poor taste.

Certainly, fewer ads today treat women as mindless drudges, but it takes only a little television viewing to discover that some women in adland are stuck in a time warp. They still fret hysterically about water spots on their crystal and about dingy toilet bowls. Household-product companies have been slow to progress out of the 1950s, partly because they fear they might offend traditional homemakers.

The ad agency Young & Rubicam considered it nothing short of a milestone recently when it persuaded Colgate-Palmolive Co. to run a commercial with the tag line: "There's more to life than laundry." The ad, for Fresh Start detergent, shows a young woman searching for her red dress so she can go out on the town with her husband. She finally finds it on her rouge-covered little girl who is playing dress up.

"The client was courageous in going along with this," says John Ferrell, executive vice president and creative director at Young & Rubicam. "We felt that women's priorities have changed and that you shouldn't make detergent seem any more important than it is."

Underwear ads usually rank right up there with household-product ads as most offensive to working women. Maidenform Inc., for example, ran a series of ads depicting women as stockbrokers and doctors, but they were in their undies in the presence of fully dressed men. "All hell broke loose," recalls Beatrice Coleman, Maidenform's president. "We were trying to show women in positions of authority, but it was misread as showing them as sex objects."

Jockey International Inc. is using real professional women in its underwear ads this year, and that approach is under fire, too. "They're career women, but look like little girls saying, 'Peek-a-boo, look at my panties,'" complains Carol Nathanson-Moog, a psychologist and advertising consultant. "It's very denigrating."

But at least one of the underwear models doesn't understand all the fuss: "What's wrong with a doctor modeling underwear if she's got a good physique?" asks Lynne Pirie, a Phoenix, Arizona, osteopath. "If Jim Palmer can do it, so can I."

Some advertisers seem to think the sure-fire way to appeal to working women is to show a woman in bow tie and business suit. That's about all Schieffelin & Co. has done in a recent Hennessy cognac ad in which a businesswoman lifts her glass to toast and flirts with a man across the aisle of an airplane. Even worse are the ads that play on the superwoman image. Some marketing consultants, for example, criticize a Spiegel Inc. ad in which a woman holds a small child next to an airplane and brags: "I've successfully managed one aviation company, two children, and three languages."

"There's this cooling out among women, but most marketers are missing it," says Carol Colman, a partner at Inferential Focus, a firm that specializes in trend spotting. "Women are saying there are other things in life besides racing on the fast track."

A few companies have picked up on such subtleties and won praise from fellow marketers. Last year, a commercial for Ford Motor Co.'s Lincoln-Mercury division followed a young female reporter as she turned in her press badge and sped off in her Cougar to the beach to begin writing a novel. All the while, the rock song "Proud Mary" played. "A lot of women don't want to give up their personal identity the way men have," says Susan Gianinno, senior vice president and director of research services at Young & Rubicam. "We tried to capture that feeling of confidence and freedom of choice in the Cougar commercial."

But ads can do only so much. Marketers say women like a softer, more personal sell than men. So a few companies are trying informational seminars.

A former stage actress named Ann Benson has been putting on investment seminars geared to women for Merrill Lynch & Co. for about 10 years, but just in the past year have such marketers as General Motors Corp.'s Chevrolet division and Apple Computer Inc. gotten into the act.

"Seminars give you a captive audience for several hours and allow you to fully demonstrate your products," says Peter Lycurgus, a manager of sales development at Apple. "Women tell us they want the bottom line on what computers can do for them. They tell us not to try dazzling them with gimmicks." But rival International Business Machines Corp. doesn't plan any similar programs. "The corporation firmly believes men and women should be treated equally in all IBM practices and programs," a spokeswoman says.

Auto companies have been using women in ads and have been buying space in such magazines as *Working Woman* for a few years now. But Chevrolet is making a much more aggressive push in 1986 to deal with some of the continuing complaints women have about automobile marketing. For one thing, the company is including credit applications in two magazines—*Cosmopolitan* and *Women's Sports and Fitness*—so that women can mail them in and get their financing approved before they ever walk into a showroom. Research showed that, for women, the credit process was one of the most intimidating aspects of buying a car.

The car maker also is sponsoring "Strategies for Success" conferences in about 10 cities in 1986 and 20 more in 1987. It will dispense tips on resumé preparation, stress management, and other career topics, and will use celebrity speakers, including Diahann Carroll, Barbara Walters, and Sally Ride, as lures. "We wanted to do something useful, not just something symbolic like a women's golf or tennis tournament," a Chevrolet spokeswoman says. "Hopefully, down the line, women will remember us in a positive light when they go car shopping."

But that positive memory may turn sour once women enter the dealer showroom. Women claim that many dealers either ignore them or act as if they care only about the color of the upholstery. Never mind that Chevrolet's research shows that about a third of new cars are bought by women and that the female share of the market will jump to about 50 percent by 1990.

Marketing consultants say auto companies need to do the same kind of sensitivity training with dealers as Metropolitan Life is conducting with its sales force. "I don't think you can find many sexist car ads anymore," says Rena Bartos, a senior vice president at J. Walter Thompson, the ad agency for Ford cars and trucks. "But there's corporate schizophrenia. The men at the top have begun to understand working women, while dealers still wonder: 'When are you going to bring a man in with you, honey?'"

Putting American Express Cards into Purses

It's hard to find advertising more popular than American Express Co.'s "Do you know me?" campaign. Johnny Carson and "Saturday Night Live" have parodied it affectionately. Hundreds of people have written to American Express and its ad agency asking to be in the ads. Most significantly, in the campaign's nine years on TV, the number of American Express cardholders in the United States has quadrupled to 12 million.

Why then is Jerry Welsh, the American Express senior vice president in charge of marketing the card, talking about changing the commercials even as they help bring in record numbers of applicants? "We're trying to redecorate our apartment," he explains, "while the cocktail party is still going on."

The problem is that, after 25 years of pursuing affluent, frequent-traveling businessmen, American Express has won over about 40 percent of those it considers worthy of its card. The financial-services company needs to find new prospects.

That has Mr. Welsh contemplating the changing nature of prestige, which American Express believes is what customers want when they pay $35 a year for its basic green card. The company always has defined prestige as success and attainment and, in 60 commercials produced since 1974, personified it with famous but not familiar entertainers (Mel Blanc, Benny Goodman, Luciano Pavarotti), athletes (Jesse Owens, Pele, Rusty Staub), executives (George Gallup, Roy Jacuzzi), politicians (Sam Ervin, William Miller), and others.

But many people, especially women and younger men, aren't thinking of prestige that way any longer, Mr. Welsh suspects. Instead, he says, they're defining it as "leading an interesting, varied, unexpectedly rich life."

His theory holds that many of those outside American Express's usual customers see prestige attached to those who have interesting hobbies or skills, have lived in several places, or have had more than one career. Brain surgeons have prestige by the old definition; brain surgeons who also ride motorcycles, by the new one.

Mr. Welsh (who has a motorcycle, used to be a professor of Russian and lived in Tennessee until joining American Express in New York in 1975) comes to these conclusions as a result of American Express's attempts to sign up more women cardholders.

The company had been wooing women for years. A magazine ad in the early 1970s showed a cigar-smoking man, described as a "former male chauvinist pig," saying: "It's time women got their own American Express card and started taking me to dinner." More women (actress Barbara Feldon, conductor Sarah Caldwell) were shown in "Do you know me?" commercials.

Such efforts accomplished little. American Express estimates that its 2½ million female cardholders represent only about 20 percent of the women that meet its financial, occupational, and life-style criteria. Male cardholders outnumber women 4 to 1.

Some reasons why became clearer to American Express executives as they listened to a group of Atlanta women, participants in a market-research panel, discuss credit cards. "What absolutely floored me," recalls Mr. Welsh, "was the irony that they were so familiar with American Express and laudatory about it, yet they didn't see the American Express card as something for them." The sort of prestige promoted in "Do you know me?" ads appealed mostly to men.

So Ogilvy & Mather, the company's ad agency, was assigned to write ads geared to women. The result is a campaign that is running in 16 national women's magazines and on TV in seven cities—San Francisco, Houston, New York, Philadelphia, Boston, Chicago, and Washington, D.C.—that make up about one fourth of the U.S. population. Although "Do you know me?" continues to dominate the advertising there, it is accompanied by a campaign that does away with celebrities.

Instead, the TV commercials feature confident, independent women using their American Express cards. In one ad, a briefcase-toting woman takes her husband to dinner to celebrate her first American Express card. In another, a mother—her marital status undisclosed—trades wisecracks with her kids in a restaurant. A third ad shows a young woman in a bookstore playfully fending off a flirtatious man. The American Express card, a female announcer says in each spot, is "part of a lot of interesting lives."

That slogan also is carried in the print ads; all other copy has been eliminated. One shows a woman cross-country skiing, her infant in a carrier on her front. Another features a dress-for-success woman leaving a sporting goods shop, carrying her briefcase in one hand and a lacrosse stick in the other.

In cities where the commercials have been shown, American Express has found, the number of women who say they feel the company is interested in them has nearly tripled. The number who plan to apply for a card has doubled, surprising the company and ad agency. "We were hoping to change attitudes, not behavior," explains Mayling Dodgin, the Ogilvy account supervisor.

The success of the "Interesting Lives" campaign, as American Express calls it, has led Mr. Welsh to ask his associates at the company and agency to consider ways of tying the new campaign's definition of prestige with the one in "Do you know me?" His goal is to keep up with sociological trends and to be ready in case the appeal of "Do you know me?" starts to wear out.

Although "Interesting Lives" will be used more extensively, American Express won't abandon its main campaign anytime soon. "You simply don't walk away," says Mr. Welsh, "from one of the most successful campaigns in the history of advertising."

Courtesy American Express

Finding the Best Approach to Black Buyers

When the U.S. Army hired Lockhart & Pettus Advertising in 1984, the black-owned agency wasted no time in getting an Army commercial pulled off the air. The spot showed a black enlisted man checking the gyroscope of a helicopter. "That's it, Frye," the white pilot says when the work is completed. "That's what I'm here for, sir," the black man responds.

To many people, the ad seemed perfectly harmless. But not to Ronn Harris, senior vice president of the ad agency. "The black was shown in a very subordinate role," he says.

Such subtleties often elude advertisers, who are still grappling with how to relate to black consumers some 20 years after the civil rights movement first hit Madison Avenue. Stereotypes live on in some ads. And too often, black characters are excluded altogether. "Blacks are sensitive to any signs of racism," says George Edwards, president of the National Black Network, a radio network. "We notice how many seconds blacks are on the screen and whether they're center-stage or not."

The stereotypes, though, are far less offensive than in the 1930s and 1940s. A toothpaste ad circa 1930 showed a black boy eating a watermelon and declared, "Go right ahead, Sambo! Sink those ivories in that luscious watermelon." In another ad from that era, a black mammy exclaimed: "Lawsee! Folks sho' whoops with joy over Aunt Jemima pancakes."

Only a few big advertisers, such as Burger King Corp. and Coca-Cola Co., are praised consistently for their use of blacks as central characters in believable and positive situations. At stake is a market of about 25 million black Americans with annual disposable income estimated at more than $150 billion. But some companies fret that they might offend white customers by showing blacks in prominent roles in their ads. Judith Langer Associates, a New York market-research firm, tested two commercials for an Alabama department store and found white consumers uncomfortable while watching the black version.

People disagree over whether blacks are more or less visible in ads these days. A 1980 study at Amherst College found that blacks appeared in only 9 percent of TV commercials featuring live actors and that they interacted with whites in less than 2 percent. "You still see a lot of black faces stuck in the background of white ads," says Carol Nathanson-Moog, a psychologist and advertising consultant in Bala-Cynwyd, Pennsylvania. "It comes off as tokenism."

What offends many blacks is advertisers' insistence that minority characters add some swing to their sales pitch. Some advertising executives criticize a Domino brown sugar ad in which a black housewife dances up a storm in her kitchen. "Black women don't act hip and boogie around their kitchens," complains Caroline Jones, executive vice president of Mingo-Jones Advertising Inc.

Then there is the "right-on school of advertising." Some companies can't resist injecting black slang into their ads—phrases like "hey, brother" and "oooh child." Ads for Accent food seasoning received low marks from some blacks for such lines as, "Honey, when I use Accent, I'm always cookin'."

Los Angeles actress Saundra Sharp is often asked to "sound blacker" when she does radio and TV commercials. For a political candidate's radio commercial in Texas, she was told to adopt a Southern accent and street-style of speaking. "It's as if white ad agencies think all blacks talk alike," she says.

Advertisers are also accused of relying on such black celebrities as Bill Cosby and O. J. Simpson, instead of depicting ordinary black consumers washing their clothes or barbecuing in the backyard. Marketing executives say that there seems to be an obsession, too, with showing blacks dancing, singing, and playing basketball. More effective are ads that capitalize on the close family ties that are common in the black community. The American Telephone & Telegraph Co. commercial that showed a mother talking about a surprise phone call from her son Joey scored highly with blacks. So did the humorous MCI Communications Corp. take-off of the ad.

Stereotypes linger partly because few blacks hold positions of power at big ad agencies. "It's pathetic," says Noel Hankin, chairman of the equal opportunity committee of the American Association of Advertising Agencies. "You can count the blacks in authority at general ad agencies on one hand." He exerted his influence once at a major agency by threatening to leave the set for a beer ad if a black actor had to "be-bop" across the stage.

Blacks are also rare in the marketing departments of big corporations even though their input can be helpful. Naylor Fitzhugh recalls that as an executive for PepsiCo Inc., he once censured an ad for Mountain Dew. Blacks were shown in the corporate boardroom, but they were barefoot.

Marketers that do the best job of advertising to blacks typically employ a minority-owned ad agency. McDonald's Corp., for example, uses Leo Burnett Co. for its major national campaigns and assigns minority projects to Burrell Advertising, a black-owned agency in Chicago. Some of the award-winning Burrell spots have shown black children jumping rope "double-dutch" style and a young black man escorting his grandmother to McDonald's.

Procter & Gamble Co. and Wendy's International Inc. have jumped on the bandwagon and hired agencies that specialize in marketing to blacks. "Blacks have a higher propensity to eat out than whites," a Wendy's spokesman says. "We want the black community to know they're important to us."

In Pursuit of the Gray Market

Germaine Monteil Cosmetiques Corp. has broken the age barrier. A recent ad for one of its skin-care products features a 45-year-old interior designer and mother of three from Nashville, Tenn. "We and others in the cosmetics business had long been guilty of using 22-year-old models for products bought primarily by older people," says Stewart Rohr, president.

In a national search for a spokeswoman over 40, the company was deluged with 7,000 glossies, some of them from women in their 50s and 60s. But Germaine Monteil didn't want to be overly realistic in its portrayal of the "mature woman." The winner, Tish Hooker, has gray hair, but it's long and flowing like—well—a 22-year-old model's. Mr. Rohr reasons: "It's easier for a 65-year-old woman to relate down to a 45-year-old than the other way around."

Germaine Monteil's gingerly approach seems typical these days as more companies try to come to grips with the aging trends in America. "There's growing interest in understanding and marketing to the 50-plus consumer, but it's not taking off as much as it should be," says Paula Drillman, executive vice president of the McCann-Erickson USA ad agency. "There's been such an emphasis by ad agencies on the youth market that it's hard to change even when you're aware the world around you is changing."

There was a proliferation of market research about five years ago predicting steady growth in the over-50 popula-

tion well into the 21st century. But the results of that work have been spotty. In 1983, for example, Sears, Roebuck & Co. formed Mature Outlook, a club offering discounts to people over 55. Selchow & Righter Co. brought out a version of the game Scrabble with letter tiles 50 percent larger than normal. And General Foods Corp. won the first commendation given out by 50 Plus magazine for its use of realistic and cheerful older couples in Jell-O ads. For the first time in 1984, the magazine also attracted such advertisers as Procter & Gamble, Nestlé, and Eastern Air Lines.

"But there's a long way to go," says publisher John Pres-

IT'S EASY TO MAKE
A BANANABERRY BLAST.

1 package (3 oz.) JELL-O
Brand Gelatin, any flavor
2½ cups of your favorite
fresh fruits, sliced
1½ cups thawed COOL WHIP
Whipped Topping

1. Prepare gelatin as directed on package. Chill until slightly thickened. Fold in ½ cup of the fruits. If desired pour into individual glasses. Chill until set.

2. Spread whipped topping evenly over gelatin.

3. Top with remaining fruit. Makes 6 servings.

strawberry
ARTIFICIAL FLAVOR
JELL-O
gelatin dessert

CREATE A SENSATION.

© Copyright 1983 General Foods Corporation. Jell-O and Cool Whip are registered trademarks of the General Foods Corporation.

Courtesy General Foods Corporation

cott. "More companies need to recognize that older people aren't saving their money the way they once did to leave behind a big inheritance." Market researchers estimate that consumers over 55 account for more than $400 billion of income annually and have about twice the discretionary funds of people under 35.

The gray market isn't easy to crack, though. Which is why some companies aren't yet taking it to heart. "People over 50 aren't a monolithic group," says Rena Bartos, an expert on older consumers at the J. Walter Thompson ad agency. "There is a sizable segment below the poverty line who won't be taking cruises on the QE2." She segments the market into "the active affluents, housewives, and active retireds."

One of the stickiest marketing problems is how to single out older people without insulting them. Age-perception studies indicate that most people feel 5 to 10 years younger than they actually are. "Older people tell us they don't want special treatment, just equal treatment," says Gail Brewer, director of specialty markets for Ramada Inns Inc.'s hotel group.

Ramada found its senior-citizen discounts didn't work very well when desk clerks were calling older customers "sweet little old ladies" and were allowing businessmen to push ahead of them in line. So, Ramada employees are taking classes to learn to be sensitive without being condescending. They're receiving tips on how to address people with impaired hearing (don't shout, just speak distinctly); which words to avoid (golden-ager and fuddy duddy, to name a couple); and what kind of photographs to use in promotions (people jogging or gardening; no knitters or bakers).

Johnson & Johnson is taking a gamble with a special new shampoo formulated for people over 40. Promotions bluntly state that Affinity is for "brittle, hollowed out" older hair, and the spokeswoman for the product is 51. Pfizer Inc. failed in the late 1970s to sell a shampoo for the over-50 set, but consumer research for Johnson & Johnson indicates that fewer women nowadays "hide from their age."

Faith Popcorn, president of BrainReserve, a New York marketing consulting firm, is skeptical nonetheless. "Even if they feel more pride in getting older, women don't want an identification of their age sitting on the bathroom shelf," she asserts. "They don't want to think they're drying up. There's a death fear in people."

Creating ads that please older people continues to be a thorny issue for marketers, as evidenced by the fuss in 1984 over the three old women in the Wendy's "Where's the Beef?" commercials. Ads that aren't carefully planned may not pass muster at some of the magazines targeted at people over 50. *Modern Maturity,* for example, appeals to some advertisers because it has a circulation of more than 9 million. But it won't accept what it deems to be downbeat ads or promotions for products such as diapers for incontinent adults. It also censors words like "pain" and "suffer" from headlines.

Even a seemingly tasteful ad for Eastern Air Lines' special travel discounts for older people drew frowns from some of the magazine's staff. It showed a couple literally jumping for joy. "We ran it but thought it was silly and undignified," says Treesa Drury, advertising standards manager. Now, Eastern ads show tourist-style snapshots of an attractive gray-haired couple simply posing in front of the Manhattan skyline and the Golden Gate Bridge.

Liquor Firms Court Baby Boomers

Elegant in her stark white gown, the woman caresses her hair and gazes longingly at the young man slouching in the doorway. They flirt across a shadowy blue room that seems suspended in clouds. Both mystical and sexy, the scene looks like another trendy ad for some new fashion design or fragrance.

But the product being pitched in this magazine ad is neither new nor trendy. It's Canadian Club whiskey, a brand that dates back to pre–Civil War days. "Our prime objective was to create something that didn't look like liquor advertising," says Stephen Nadelberg, marketing director for Hiram Walker Inc., importer of Canadian Club. "We're trying to emulate Calvin Klein and Chanel. We believe the liquor business sells image and fashion, too."

Liquor ads typically show a bottle and cocktail glass or some well-dressed people wearing plastic smiles. Such repetition has caused the blurring of brand names in many people's minds. "Liquor advertising definitely needs a whiff of fresh air," says William Tragos, chief executive officer of TBWA Advertising Inc. His agency used surrealistic drawings of oranges, windows, and people floating in space for the Grand Marnier liqueur campaign.

Creative marketing to distinguish one liquor brand from another has probably never been more important. Consumption of distilled spirits has been on a steady slide the past few years, reflecting a major change in U.S. tastes.

Alcoholic beverages are also suffering from the growing emphasis on physical fitness and national concern about drunk driving.

In response to these trends, companies have been concocting lots of sweet, creamy drinks and low-alcohol spirits to attract baby-boom consumers who don't like the bite of bourbon and Scotch. But some marketers hope that through more provocative advertising and promotions, they can also persuade younger consumers to try the established brands they grew up watching their parents drink.

For example, Benedictine Marketing Services Inc., the U.S. distributor of B&B liqueur, increased its ad budget 85 percent to nearly $5 million in 1984 for a campaign that shows a wet-haired young couple nuzzling and sharing a snifter of B&B. Research shows that the wet look is causing people to stop and study the ad.

"The average age of our customers is well over 40, and we'd like to drop that to the late 20s and early 30s, the heart of the baby boomers," says Richard Bland, president of Benedictine. Sales have been flat at about 175,000 cases a year.

Already, a new approach in advertising is transforming stodgy cognac into an "in" drink. Through more stylish ads in popular magazines such as *People* and *Cosmopolitan,* companies that market the premium-priced French brandy are reaching many more 25 to 34-year-olds and more blacks. In 1984 the four major U.S. importers spent a record $30 million in advertising. The intent is to exploit people's desire for status and sophistication.

"The traditional image of a cognac drinker is an old guy in a stuffed leather chair, smoking a cigar," says Kevin Dowling, group marketing manager for the U.S. subsidiary of E. Remy Martin & Co. "But we're trying to appeal to upwardly mobile young professionals who want to make a statement about themselves by the drink they order," adds Mr. Dowling, who used to help market Kool-Aid for General Foods Corp.

While cultivating new customers, Remy Martin also intends to keep its old clientele. It advertises these days in both *Opera News* and *Rolling Stone,* but is careful to use different verbs: "savor" in *Opera News,* "arouse" in *Rolling Stone.*

Hiram Walker's $10 million campaign represents the first major change for its Canadian Club brand since the repeal of Prohibition. The company did run an innovative series of treasure hunt ads a few years back that provided clues about where a case of Canadian Club had been hidden. The gimmick inspired plenty of free publicity, "but we got so wrapped up in selling the hunt that the product got buried," says Mr. Nadelberg, the marketing director.

The Canadian whiskey market is one of the most intensely competitive, and despite some of the heaviest advertising, Canadian Club has been losing ground. Sales fell 8 percent in 1982 and 3 percent more in 1983, to 3.3 million nine-liter cases. The company thinks the new advertising approach, along with the improving national economy, may signal a turnaround. Canadian Club's May 1984 sales increased from their 1983 levels in most major cities, and, for a change, consumers are talking about Canadian Club ads. Reaction is running about 50-50 for and against the ad that shows the flirting couple in the clouds. Some people are put off by what they perceive to be a woman seducing a younger man.

To instill extra drama in the print ads, Hiram Walker's ad agency, McCaffrey & McCall, draws storyboards and writes scripts just as if the ads were going to be filmed for television. Some story lines are beginning to sound like breathless romance novels: One has a male character with "the blood of peasants and kings bubbling through his veins."

Not all ideas have succeeded. Hiram Walker recently killed an exotic-looking ad because a test group identified the setting as Hawaii and didn't find it very mysterious. Similarly, in the current ad, minarets and palm trees were deleted so that more of the story could be left to the viewer's imagination. Some test panelists thought the ad was set on the moon; others said that the man was a figment of the woman's imagination. Says Mr. Nadelberg: "We want our ads to be Rorschach tests."

Translating a Cigarette into Spanish

When Liggett & Myers Tobacco Co. decided to make a play for the Hispanic market, it looked like a nearly impossible sell. Hispanics tend to be unusually brand loyal; in the case of cigarettes, many are die-hard fans of Philip Morris's Marlboro and R. J. Reynolds Tobacco's Winston brand.

"We were coming from nowhere with little knowledge of Hispanics," concedes Don Fish, Liggett's national director of marketing programs. The company quickly rejected the notion of merely translating ads for its L&M or Chesterfield brands into Spanish. Such a token gesture might only alienate Hispanics. "They already feel like stepchildren," Mr. Fish says, "because manufacturers don't take the time to do research and tailor marketing plans to them."

So Liggett dug in and conducted door-to-door interviews with 477 Hispanic families in New York, Miami, San Antonio, Texas, and Los Angeles to learn more about their smoking habits. The result: not merely an ad campaign, but a recipe for an entirely new cigarette. It had to be a full-flavored blend. Menthols and low-tar products wouldn't do. To convey status and machismo, the package was designed with gold lettering on paper that has a rustic rosewood look. And the brand name? Something with a slight Latin ring. Dorado and L&M Superior turned out to be most popular in Hispanic consumer tests; Liggett is trying out both names.

Such careful courting is important for any company attempting to tap the Hispanic market, which consultants

23

Courtesy Liggett & Myers Tobacco Company, Inc.

estimate has more than 20 million people (including illegal aliens) with buying power of about $60 billion a year.

"Companies can't just rush into this market," warns Castor Fernandez, president of Castor Spanish International, a Hispanic ad agency in New York. "They must study the different cultures and create special marketing campaigns just as if they were entering a foreign country." His agency, for example, departs from the soft-drink advertising norm. Its commercials show Coca-Cola alongside food in a restaurant kitchen rather than as part of a rollicking beach scene or sporting event. Research revealed that a high percentage of Coke consumption by Hispanics occurs at mealtime.

In Albuquerque and Santa Fe, New Mexico, where Dorado was tested, the cigarette garnered a 0.68 percent share of the local cigarette market during 1984. That may sound paltry, but Mr. Fish says that even a 0.5 percent share is considered very successful. L&M Superior has a market share of about 0.45 percent in such Texas cities as Browns-ville and Corpus Christi. The only differences between the two brands are their packaging and advertising slogans: Dorado is "crafted for pleasure"; L&M Superior is "created to satisfy."

Liggett walks a fine line in catering to Hispanics with such a customized cigarette. If it becomes too closely identi-fied with Hispanics, the product could bomb. "Hispanics start fighting to become part of the American mainstream as soon as they cross the border," says Lionel Sosa, president of an advertising and marketing agency in San Antonio. "They want an advertiser to recognize them and reach out to them. But the product must be for everyone."

To try to make its cigarette appeal to Anglos as well as Hispanics, Liggett cautiously chose brand names that didn't sound "too Spanish." The advertising also was designed to be homogeneous, even at the risk of being a bit bland. There aren't any Hispanic people or Spanish themes, only pictures of the cigarette pack, a tobacco leaf, and a wood carving.

The neutral tone of Liggett's ads also will make it easier to introduce Dorado or L&M Superior into new cities. His-panic marketing can be tricky because Western areas of the United States have large pockets of Mexican-Americans, while such cities as Miami and New York are home to many Cubans and Puerto Ricans. Advertisers must be wary of Spanish expressions that could have multiple interpreta-tions or no meaning at all to certain groups.

"If a company wants to do national advertising, it's a matter of using universal Spanish words and pure Hispanic models who don't look obviously Puerto Rican, Cuban, or Mexican," says Mr. Sosa, the San Antonio ad man. "A Ricardo Montalban type would be very acceptable. He could be anything."

The U.S. prohibition on broadcast advertising of ciga-rettes is always a handicap in introducing new brands, but Liggett found that particularly true with Dorado and L&M

Superior because Hispanics rely so much more on TV than on newspapers or magazines. The company tried to compensate with more billboards, ads in Spanish-language publications and marketing at special events. In Santa Fe, it hired a marketing consultant whose connections with Hispanics and other local officials helped get Dorado promotions into the state fair, a hot-air balloon festival, and the annual Santa Fe fiesta.

Ed Delgado, the consultant, also strongly recommended that Liggett hire models in Albuquerque to pass out free samples of Dorado. "I told the company not to bring in flashy blondes with a Northern twang or rednecks ignorant of the Hispanic culture," he says. "Good PR can be more important than advertising in winning the confidence of Hispanic consumers."

Update

Liggett & Myers has dropped L&M Superior, but it continued in 1986 to market Dorado, which proved to be the more popular brand. "We still think the Hispanic market is a viable one for us; it was just more economical to go with Dorado alone," a spokeswoman says.

Teen-Age Girls:
A Hazardous Market

Clement Soffer has always known that his privately owned company is in a perilous line of work. "You can get wiped out in this business if you aren't careful," he says. "You may anyway."

Mr. Soffer isn't involved in drilling for oil, trading commodity futures, or building nuclear plants. His company, Jou Jou Design Inc., sells clothes to teen-age girls.

Unpredictable in their tastes and fickle in their loyalties, teen-age girls can be downright dangerous as customers. They can go through a style faster than a stick of gum, or send sales of a shampoo or snack food soaring or plunging almost overnight. Keeping up with them is a job that can humble even the most sophisticated marketer.

Just ask any of the victimized makers of Frye boots, designer jeans, or Izod shirts. "It's a hazardous market," says Jane Evans, a senior executive at General Mills Inc. "I don't think any responsible public corporation would deliberately go after it."

While heading the Minneapolis-based company's apparel division, Mrs. Evans was horrified to discover that more than a fifth of the division's Izod alligator shirts were being bought by girls under 20 years old. Knowing how unreliable that market can be, she immediately began to worry that a large part of Izod's business could vanish at any time. Not long afterward, it did.

Big business would have little fear, of course, if the young ladies could be shrugged off as only a minor market. But they can't be: There are 12.8 million of them in the United States, and estimates of their spending range as high as $30 billion a year. By some calculations, the average teen-age girl lavishes over $1,000 annually on her wardrobe alone. One third have the use of at least one charge card; one quarter have their own checking account.

"Teen-age girls have more discretionary income than you can believe," says Ron Galante, the marketing manager at Chattem Inc., a Chattanooga-based manufacturer of pharmaceuticals and beauty products. "Most have jobs, a lot have big allowances, and none of them have to pay the mortgage or the gas bill."

Moreover, their sway in consumer markets extends far beyond their personal buying power. In fashion, in cosmetics, and in hair care, teen-age girls are more often than not the ones who set the trends. They also have been taking on an increased share of family grocery shopping as more of their mothers have gone off to work. Even General Motors Corp. has begun advertising in magazines aimed at teen girls.

But it is their tendency to act collectively that, for better or worse, makes them such a volatile market for business. "When one of the young ladies has to have something, they all do," says designer Georges Marciano. "It's like mass hysteria."

Mr. Marciano should know. Since he persuaded New York's Bloomingdale's to carry the first 20 pairs of his Guess? jeans, his stone-washed denims have become one of the hottest new fads among teen-age girls, helping him build the Guess? label into a $200-million-a-year enterprise. (By comparison, Apple Computer Inc., probably the most talked about corporate success story, had annual sales of $117 million in its third year of business.)

Divining the whims of the market, however, may be next to impossible. "Modern marketing techniques are almost useless with teen-age girls," says Leo Shapiro, who owns a market-research firm in Chicago. "By the time you've finished a consumer survey, the picture has already changed." A couple of examples:

—In a 1983 study conducted by Teen-age Research Unlimited of Lake Forest, Illinois, 36 percent of the girls surveyed said the Stray Cats was one of their favorite rock groups, but when the firm repeated the study one year later, the band's fans had all but disappeared.

—In the first study, 44 percent of the respondents said they played video games. In the second, the number plummeted to 23 percent.

Most marketers agree that the reason teen-age girls are so mercurial as customers is that they have only a fragile sense of self-identity. "They are still trying to figure out who they are," says Ellen Plusker, an expert on teen-age marketing at J. Walter Thompson Co. "It's a part of growing up."

Thus, when SRI International of Menlo Park, California, created VALS, its widely used marketing system that classifies consumers by their value-shaped life styles, it had to leave out teen-agers. Its researchers found that teen-agers' personal beliefs aren't well enough established for VALS to work. "They are kind of dizzy," an SRI official says.

As consumers, teen-agers translate their search for self-identity into brand experimentation and fads. Shampoo makers, for instance, say the average teen-age girl tries four different brands a year, compared with 1½ for older women. "It's the biggest part of the business and it's the most unstable," says Robert Thomas, a marketing vice president at Helene Curtis Industries Inc. of Chicago. "No manufacturer has been able to hang on to them as customers for any length of time."

Apparel makers sometimes can get warning about what teen-age girls will want by watching what their counterparts are wearing in Europe or Japan. But increasingly, manufacturers say, trends are originating in the United States. And when that happens, the industry can get caught off guard.

An example was the overnight popularity of the torn-shoulder look for sweaters that was inspired by the 1983 movie "Flashdance." By the time apparel makers could begin meeting the demand, the fad was already ending. "I don't know anyone in the business who didn't regret getting into that 'Flashdance' thing," says Leonard Rubin, a vice president at Perry Ellen Inc. in New York.

To keep up with teen-age girls' changing tastes, John A. Frye Shoe Co. of Marlboro, Massachusetts, alters the styling of boots aimed at the market three times a year. But the company, whose products once enjoyed enormous status among teens, no longer dominates the market the way it once did. "The last big kick we got was from the movie 'Urban Cowboy,'" says Stephen Merriam, the vice president of merchandising. "This business goes up and down. You can't control it."

Record companies are wary of teen-age girls for another reason. "If a group or a musician gets too popular with the girls, the guys won't buy it," says Alan Grunblatt, a marketing executive at RCA Records. "That can be a big deal because teen-age boys purchase four times more records than the girls."

Santa Cruz Imports Inc. believes that the business of selling to teen-age girls "requires a corporate culture that's comfortable with constant change," according to David Hirsch, its president. Among other things, the San Francisco-based company employs a staff of 25 fashion consultants, all young women, who travel from store to store interviewing teen-age customers. When the consultants reported a falling off in a trend toward neon colors, Santa Cruz immediately began making plans to tone down its spring line.

One sales pitch that always has seemed to work with teen-age girls, regardless of fads, is sex. Even though it is read mostly by girls between 13 and 16 years old, *Seventeen* magazine carries more than its share of titillating sales pitches. "For love on the wild side," promises a Jordache ad, showing a couple sprawled on a beach. "Coty: The essence of animal attraction," says another.

"It's the only constant thing you can sell these kids on," says Ken Utech, the director of market research at Chattem, which produces the leading teen-age cologne, Love's Baby Soft.

Teen-age girls' interest in romance, however, doesn't exactly explain their recent rage to buy men's boxer shorts. "We're a little mystified by it," says Donald Ruland, the vice president for merchandising at Jockey International Inc. of Kenosha, Wisconsin. "But then, why did people buy Pet Rocks?"

Although Mr. Ruland asserts that some competitors have capitalized on the development by selling men's shorts in the women's departments of stores for substantially higher prices, he says Jockey hasn't tried to build a business on the trend. "We stay away from fad-type things," he says. "Once you start counting on those sales, you know that's when they'll start to disappear."

2

New Products

For Frito, a New Chip
Is No Picnic

Twenty managers at the Frito-Lay Inc. headquarters in Dallas sit at a conference table, nibbling thick, white tortilla chips. The chips taste good, but the managers aren't here for idle munching.

Small tortilla-chip makers in the West have been winning customers who like corn chips to eat with meals, rather than just as a snack. Their paler, blander chips are hurting sales of two Frito stars, Doritos and Tostitos. The chips the Frito managers are sampling, a proposed new offering called Sabritas, are supposed to put a stop to that.

But there are problems. The marketing people want Sabritas to be made only of white corn so they will be pale, but Frito-Lay plants now use yellow corn or a yellow-white mix. Will a new grain bin have to be built for the white corn?

Another thing: The competing chips have a twist tie around the top of the bag. Twist ties are expensive and are a bother to put on. But shoppers might not think of Sabritas the way they do the others if Sabritas' bag doesn't look the same.

Wayne Calloway, the company's president, gives the objectors a meaningful look. "Jerry, Jim, we need to get with this one," he says. "We're already late." A committee is formed to solve the problems so that test marketing can begin. The product manager for Sabritas has scored a small victory.

This may seem like a rather elaborate approach to a commodity most people just crunch absent-mindedly. But Frito-Lay didn't get where it is by taking tortillas for granted. The PepsiCo Inc. subsidiary takes in $2 billion on snack food a year, easily topping big rivals like Nabisco and Borden, not to mention the regional makers. Frito-Lay's earnings from operations have been growing an average of 23 percent a year, though the pace slowed a bit in recent months. The $311 million Frito earned in 1982 made it the biggest contributor to PepsiCo's profits.

Coming up with new products is essential to keeping this lead, and Frito-Lay is good at it. Company managers consider hundreds of suggestions each year, but their screening process is so tough that only five or six get much past the idea stage. To go from being a gleam in the eye to a bag on the shelf, a new chip has to make it through the test kitchen, consumer taste-testing, naming, package design, ad planning, manufacturing, and test-marketing. A poor grade on one of the tests—or a poor decision about the name or ad theme—can kill a new product.

A successful one, though, can be worth $100 million or more a year in added revenue. So, although Frito-Lay develops certain products to meet specific competitive threats, its researchers are constantly trying to dream up new ideas simply in hopes of selling more snacks.

"The world isn't going to tell you it wants another potato chip," says Willard Korn, the senior vice president for sales and marketing. Hoping to grab the imagination of the noshing public, Frito has tested hash-brown potato chips, batter-fried potato chips, whole-grain chips made of wheat, corn, and oats, and any number of others.

It knows when to throw in the bag. "We've tested carrot chips and we've tested plantain chips," says Brad Todd, the marketing director for new products, referring to the banana-like tropical fruit. "We couldn't even sell plantain chips in Miami."

Inspiring these searchers for the perfect snack is the success of products like Doritos, Tostitos, and Ruffles. Frito-

Lay brought out Ruffles potato chips in 1960, giving them an unusual ridged texture. Twenty-three years later, the company still sells Ruffles and flourishes; it markets $425 million (retail) of them every year. Doubtless there will be rewards for the product manager who can duplicate that success.

"I don't want it on my tombstone that I created the first big potato chip since Ruffles," says George Reynolds, the potato-chip marketing director. "But I do want to get promoted to president."

That spirit has served Frito well since 50 years ago, when a young Texas ice-cream maker named Elmer Doolin paid an unknown Mexican $100 for the recipe to some corn chips he had at lunch in a San Antonio cafe. Mr. Doolin started making the chips with a potato ricer at night in the kitchen of his mother, Daisy Dean Doolin, peddling them by day in his Model-T Ford. Eventually Mr. Doolin hooked up with a fellow in Nashville named Herman Lay who was doing the same sort of thing with potato chips; they merged in 1961 and were snapped up by Pepsi four years later. The original potato ricer, now gold-plated, sits under a glass dome in Mr. Calloway's office.

The chip-maker's trade has undergone quite a refinement in modern times. "It's a lot of art, intuition, experience, and science," Mr. Calloway says. But Mr. Reynolds has his own secret of success: "The first thing I look at is whether the damn thing tastes good."

These days, Frito-Lay has several up-and-coming new chips, chief among them Ta-Tos and O'Gradys. These are both made of potatoes, but they are not to be confused. Around Frito-Lay, Ta-Tos are known as "super-crispy wavy." O'Gradys aren't like that. They are "extra-thick and crunchy."

"Small differences can build big brands," explains Mr. Korn. "Ta-Tos and O'Gradys have different textures, different mouth feel, and potato impact."

What makes Ta-Tos so crispy is that before the potatoes are fried, they are brined, or soaked in a salt solution. Their waviness not only makes them interesting looking but also strengthens them, so they aren't so likely to snap off in the dip. Consumers were given a taste of Ta-Tos; some people found them too hard, but most said they probably would buy some. So Ta-Tos have arrived in supermarkets in several cities for test-marketing.

When super-crispy wavy comes, can extra-thick and crunchy be far behind? That chip, too, has recently made it into test-marketing, but not before overcoming a problem all thick potato chips face: They don't fry well. Their outsides turn brown but their insides stay white. The solution was to make the chip thick mainly in the ridges, and to run the ridges one way on one side and crosswise on the other. When it was cut this way, the chip fried right.

But it still needed a name, so product managers set about finding one that would give the right impression. Mr. Todd explains the thinking: "This product was of the earth, it was thicker, a natural-tasting product." It also would have local competitors. So Frito began screening hearty names that would make the chips sound locally made.

Among the candidates was O'Gradys. Consumers were asked what a person named O'Grady might be like. They replied, variously, that O'Grady would be fun, jovial, male, happy-go-lucky, hearty, and big. It was just the image Frito wanted.

Before naming Sabritas, managers pored over Spanish dictionaries and maps of Mexico and the South, looking for a word that sounded good in English and meant something in Spanish. One strong contender, "Mamacita's," turned out to be trademarked by somebody else. Another, "Captivas," turned out to be the island off Florida where the pirate Gasparilla kept his women prisoners. Next to these two, "Sabritas" looked pretty good; Frito-Lay already owned the trademark on it, and the word means "little tasty ones."

A wrong name can hold back a worthy chip. Tiffles "light corn chips" failed in two test markets, until a different product manager got hold of them and called them Sunchips, the "corn chips for potato-chip lovers." They are in a third test market now, and are selling almost twice as well as before.

Even so, manufacturing needs have to be considered. Sunchips are made of ground corn using a special extrusion process, so if Frito-Lay goes national with them, it probably will have to build new production lines. Similarly, the cutting machines used to make O'Gradys during the current test marketing won't accept potatoes longer than four inches. To make O'Gradys on a large scale, the company would have to either buy bigger cutters or sort its potatoes.

As for Ta-Tos, soaking them in brine adds so much salt that managers were afraid the chips might corrode the machinery. But Ta-Tos got a clean bill of health; an engineering study concluded that the briny chips would shorten the life of machines only a little.

Making chips with "no preservatives"—to please consumers conscious of additives—also requires adjustments. Preservatives keep the frying oil from getting rancid. To prevent oxidation without preservatives, Frito-Lay has to keep oxygen away from the frying oil, so it covers it with a layer of nitrogen gas.

Getting the right package means more decisions. How should it be sealed? What color should it be? Should it say "potato chips" or "potato crisps"? Should the chips show through a window on the package? Frito figures that for a chip sold nationally, a window costs $1 million to $2 million extra a year.

Then, of course, there is the advertising theme, one of the toughest but most important of decisions. Frito-Lay managers spare no effort to get this one right. In the case of Ta-Tos, also known as super-crispy wavy, Frito wanted shoppers to realize that this was "a chip with the crispness of a regular chip, with the potato taste of a ridged chip," explains John Cranor, the marketing vice president. Alas, he adds, "there was no way we could get that idea across in a 30-second commercial."

One of the first proposals had people on camera trying to describe the taste. Then someone from the ad agency, Foote Cone & Belding, wondered whether there wasn't a way to get people to "listen" to the taste. Thus was born the theme

"Listen to the taste of Ta-Tos," with slow-motion film of chips breaking.

If advertisements can't get people to buy potato chips, maybe the deliveryman can. Frito-Lay's 9,500 truck drivers get only a small weekly salary but a 10 percent commission on all the chips they sell. They can earn $40,000 a year if they really deliver.

So the drivers stop to talk with supermarket managers, angling for an extra foot of shelf space. In a small drive-in grocery, where the direction of the flow of shoppers can be gauged, deliverymen may tilt the bags on the shelf to face the oncoming consumer.

And they know a bit about psychology. Some shoppers pass over a half-empty shelf, perhaps thinking the potato chips on it have been there awhile and are getting stale. A smart deliveryman will "fluff" the shelf, laying the rear bags on their sides to fill space so the others reach the front.

For Ta-Tos, Sunchips, Sabritas, and the rest, the final hurdle is the test market. To Frito-Lay, it doesn't matter how crunchy a chip is; if the thing can't sell $50 million to $100 million worth a year, forget it. And that had better not be money the shopper was going to spend on Lay's or Doritos. If a new chip is taking too many of its sales from another Frito product, it probably will never go national.

The company is wrestling with questions like this about Ta-Tos and O'Gradys. Ta-Tos played well in Kansas City at first but then faded; reactions are awaited from three other cities. Mr. Korn, indulging in the lingo of his marketing profession, describes the situation: "We think there's an extra-crispy segment, but we have to see if it has staying power."

O'Gradys, meantime, has just begun its marketing test. Mr. Korn's inclination is to go national with just one new potato-chip brand. When all the figures are tallied, then, it may come down to a difficult choice: Will it be super-crispy wavy, or extra-thick and crunchy?

Update

O'Gradys extra-thick chips, one of the new products that Frito-Lay was testing in 1983, became the company's "most successful new product ever," says a spokesman. It was the seventh Frito-Lay brand ever to reach the $100 million mark in annual sales.

Frito-Lay continues to work on Sabritas, though. Under a new name, Santitas, it still is in test markets. Ta-Tos are distributed in a limited number of markets but haven't become a major national brand. Meanwhile, Frito-Lay has come up with many more new ideas for snack chips. Among recent ones are Kincaid's "hard-bite" chips and a jalapeno-and-cheddar extension to the Lay's potato chip line.

Hitchhiking on Proven Brand Names

Building new brands is tougher than ever. Advertising costs are growing rapidly, as is rivalry for consumers' attention. Technological breakthroughs are harder to find. Top executives are queasier about spending huge sums on products that history warns are likely to fail. Says a marketing executive: "Financial people are putting the squeeze on us."

One way to cope with these pressures is to make better use of brands that already have been created. "Names like Armour, Maxwell House, and Del Monte represent a huge investment over years," says John Diefenbach, president of Landor Associates, a San Francisco design concern. "The incredible cost of introducing new brands points out the need to hitchhike on what already exists."

That technique is called "franchise extension" by Edward Tauber, a University of Southern California marketing professor. "It's a method for a company to enter a new business," he says, "through the leverage of its most valuable asset—the consumer awareness, good will, and impressions conveyed by its brand name."

Some examples: Sunkist orange soda, Minolta copiers, Levi shirts and shoes, Del Monte Mexican food, Woolite rug shampoo, Easy-Off window cleaner, Gerber insurance, and Vaseline Intensive Care skin lotion, bath oil, and baby powder.

Ten years ago Bic Pen's sole U.S. business was making ballpoint pens. Today Bic also puts its name on shavers, lighters, and two other types of pens. Bic's reputation as a manufacturer of inexpensive, disposable products "is a very big plus for us, especially with new products," says Bruno Bich, vice president for sales and marketing.

Bic is spending $11 million to advertise its new Bic Roller pen. Under a different name, says Mr. Bich, the cost would have been higher. In addition, he says, the Roller campaign "helps all Bic products, especially other writing instruments."

Although hitchhiking on established brands isn't a new idea, Mr. Diefenbach maintains it's an underappreciated one. "We anticipate a world of 100 to 200 superbrands that have found ways to capitalize on their existing reputations," he says.

General Foods is following that approach for its Jell-O Pudding Pops, a frozen dessert on a stick. It borrows the name from the General Foods pudding mix and uses entertainer Bill Cosby, who stars in Jell-O Pudding commercials, for its ads. Another sign that General Foods is paying more attention to its existing names: the company began test-marketing Maxwell House freeze-dried coffee after its Maxim freeze-dried coffee fizzled.

A stroll down any supermarket aisle reveals many names that may have untapped value. Among them, marketers cite R. T. French, Kraft, Fleischmann's, Planter's, Popsicle, Best Foods, Lipton, Hunt, Wesson, Green Giant, and Weight Watchers. Even American Telephone & Telegraph is studying products that could carry the Bell name.

Many companies already have tried to leapfrog into new categories without success. Among products that have been flops: Arm & Hammer antiperspirant, Certs gum, Life Savers gum, Sara Lee Chicken & Noodles Au Gratin and Listerol, a household cleaner from the maker of Listerine.

Many of these have been "me-too" products, those without any significant benefit different from their competitors'; a familiar name alone rarely is enough to ensure prosperity. Welch Foods, known for grape-flavored products, found that out when it tried to sell prune juice.

Marketers need to do some homework before applying their names to new product areas. The first step is "looking at the strengths, weaknesses, and image of the brand," says Richard Tongberg, marketing research manager at Miles Laboratories, the maker of Alka-Seltzer, One-A-Day vitamins, S.O.S. scouring pads and other consumer products. "Most companies haven't even done that."

Next, "assess the boundaries of the brand's franchise," Mr. Tongberg says. "What is its ability to be stretched to different product categories?"

The third step, he says, is to "identify creative ways of communicating the parent brand's image in a new category but in a way that is relevant."

Several obstacles await marketers who try to extend franchises. One is the risk of unexpected problems harming other related brands. The association of Rely tampons with toxic shock syndrome last year might have harmed Procter & Gamble's image even more if the company hadn't followed its tradition of making each of its brands stand alone.

"If you're going to have your name on all your products," says Bic's Mr. Bich, "you should never produce a bad product. If you make a mistake, you'll hurt your whole company."

Spinoffs can hurt parent brands in other ways. Mr. Tauber criticizes Coca-Cola's decision to bring out a line of diet soda flavors, such as root beer and ginger ale, under its Tab name, which has become nearly synonymous with diet cola. "To the extent the line of flavors is a success," he says, "you can't go in and ask for a Tab anymore."

Brands stretched too far could lose their individuality. "The housewife could write 'Charmin, Kleenex, Bounty, and Pampers' on her shopping list and we'd know exactly what she was going to get," ad executives Al Ries and Jack Trout note in *Positioning: The Battle for Your Mind,* their recent book. " 'Scott' on a shopping list has no meaning."

The key to finding new places for old names is to find product categories that are compatible with their parents. Welch Foods frequently has been advised to enter the wine business; the company says it won't. "You can't be the No. 1 name in peanut butter and jelly sandwiches," says Theodore Wolfe, executive vice president, "and the number one name in wine. You have to decide which horse you're going to ride."

Fisher-Price Branches from Toys to Playwear

Dressing toddlers can be a frazzling experience. Executives at Fisher-Price Toys had that point hammered home well to them in 1983. For four hours, they peered through a one-way mirror and eavesdropped as a dozen women in Cleveland complained about their battles with the zippers, buckles, buttons, and snaps on kids' clothing.

"These were combat veterans who had five years' experience with two children," says Stephen Muirhead, a manager in Fisher-Price's diversified-products division. "They were talking about things that touch their daily lives very deeply."

Grumpy mothers were just what Fisher-Price hoped to find. The market research convinced the company that with its famous name and a unique design it could find a niche in the lucrative but increasingly cutthroat children's wear market. So the Quaker Oats Co. subsidiary is rolling out its first line of preschool playwear, and there isn't a button, zipper, or frill to be found. Nearly all the fasteners are Velcro. "Osh-kosh overalls are beautifully designed," says Mr. Muirhead, "but kids being toilet-trained need to be Houdini to get out of them."

The Fisher-Price playwear has other features: padded knees and elbows, extra-long shirttails, cuffs that can be unfurled as children grow and big neck openings to accommodate kids' disproportionately large heads. "Fisher-Price is attacking clothing the way it does everything else," says

Ken Wilcox, director of marketing administration at Tonka Corp. "The company identifies an area where kids aren't being served well and then comes up with a nearly indestructible product that's easy to use."

But it won't be an easy jump from toys to playwear. Fisher-Price is trying to break into a splintered industry where style often matters more than durability. "It's very difficult to position yourself on the basis of functionality and performance," says Peter Brown of Kurt Salmon & Associates, a management consulting firm. "Children's wear, blue jeans, and men's underwear are all advertised for their performance characteristics, but it's hard for consumers to see much difference."

And the business is becoming more crowded as other big companies are tempted by what demographers call the "baby-boom echo"—the rising number of births to women of the baby-boom generation. In 1983 and 1984 alone, Gerber Products Co. acquired three children's clothing companies, including the Buster Brown line. "Incursion of more adult brands into the kids' market is also intensifying the battle on the retail floor," says Terry Jacobs, of Walter K. Levy Associates Inc., retail marketing consultants.

Troubled by sagging sales of jeans to adults, Levi Strauss & Co. introduced baby Levis in 1985. The company offered for sale blue denim pants and diaper covers for infants, as well as tiny knit shirts proclaiming, "My First Levis." Says Bill Oldenburg, general manager of the youthwear division: "We were trying to develop brand loyalty at an earlier age." (But just in case mothers can't picture their newborns clad in Levis, the company will bring out infantwear under both the new Petite Bijou and Little Levis brand names.)

Levi predicts that by 1990, more than 8 million babies will be crawling about, an increase of 11 percent from 1983. Already, the United States has more moppets under five years—17.8 million—than in any year since 1968. What interests marketers most, though, is the growing percentage of births that are first births. That's when parents and

Introducing Fisher-Price Playwear.

The children's clothing that mothers helped design.

55 years of watching children at play have taught Fisher-Price a lot about how children move and think and grow.

But because parents have the most intensive day-to-day experience of all, we asked hundreds of you what you wanted play clothes to be.

And we listened. For example, you told us your children love to do things "all by myself." So we put in snaps and Velcro® closings (always in front, to be absolutely reachable.) And no buttons, no zippers.

We also learned that small knees and elbows spend most of their time on the floor. So we stitched quilted reinforcement in all the right places.

And because children grow right before your eyes, our sleeves have extra-long Gro-Cuffs, our shoulder straps have growing room, and our shirttails are longer to stay tucked in.

We've added an inside label for your child's name and phone number. And of course, everything is foolproof to wash and dry.

The result is a lively, livable collection called Fisher-Price Playwear. Tell us what you think of it. We'll listen.

© 1984 Fisher-Price, East Aurora, New York 14052
Division of The Quaker Oats Company

Courtesy Fisher-Price

doting grandparents tend to make their largest purchases. Kurt Salmon & Associates currently estimates the pre-school clothing market at more than $6 billion a year.

"The outlook is tremendous," says Leo Goulet, president of Gerber. "There are more working mothers who have the money to spend and who are going for better quality merchandise." The baby-food company expects sales of clothing, furniture, and other nonfood products for kids to double to $450 million in five years.

Working mothers in particular are changing the way children's wear companies design and market products. William Carter Co., for instance, is now selling Swifty Change suits that contain more snaps to make diapering babies simpler. Fisher-Price found mothers especially interested in clothing that will enable children to dress themselves at an earlier age.

To make its playwear stand out, Fisher-Price is advertising it as "the children's clothing that mothers helped design." The company is also banking heavily on the strong pull of its brand name and its toys, which it says are in 99 percent of the homes where a child under the age of six lives. Fliers announcing the apparel line will be inserted into toy packages this Christmas season, and from now on, all kids featured in toy ads will be dressed in the playwear.

It became apparent rather quickly to Fisher-Price that fashioning playwear is a world apart from building plastic and wooden toys. So, the company farmed out manufacturing and distribution to a girls' dressmaker. Fisher-Price retains close control over design and marketing, however, and refuses to license its trademark as Tonka and the Playskool division of Milton Bradley Co. have done. Research showed that consumers are fed up with paying a premium for a logo stamped on an otherwise ordinary T-shirt.

Fisher-Price may try to parlay its reputation for durability into kids' underwear and shoes, too. "I doubt if we'll ever try to sell party dresses, though," Mr. Muirhead says. "We're not seen as very stylish or avant-garde."

Update

Fisher-Price's entry into the clothing market shows how even the best-laid marketing plans can go awry. In fact, the company's first season in 1984 nearly turned out to be its last. Because of a strike and other production snags at a Jamaican plant, clothing arrived in department stores late, or in some cases, not at all. Some retailers got stuck with shirts and no pants.

But the company rebounded in 1985, selecting new companies to manufacture the playwear and expanding its line to include swimsuits, hosiery, and outerwear. Fisher-Price skipped the summer 1985 fashion season to regroup, lowered prices, and switched distribution from department stores—some of which were still smarting from the disastrous first season—to mass merchandisers such as J. C. Penney.

Barclay Breaks the Rules

Brown & Williamson broke many of the rules of cigarette marketing when it introduced Barclay in September 1980. Other cigarette ads are set outdoors; Barclay's take place inside cars and homes. Other tobacco companies distribute free packs of new brands; Brown & Williamson is giving away entire cartons. Its rivals typically spend $50 million to $100 million pushing a new product; Brown & Williamson is spending an unprecedented amount for Barclay— $150 million, estimates a competitor.

This unconventional approach appears to be paying off. In the 33 weeks since Barclay went into test markets and the 15 weeks since distribution expanded to the remaining 89 percent of the United States, says Brown & Williamson, the cigarette's market share "very quickly passed 1 percent and is well on the way to 2 percent."

That's no small feat in an industry where 0.5 percent share marks success and each 1 percent of the market is worth about $125 million in revenue to the manufacturer. "We're sure we have substantial success with Barclay," says John Alar, president of Brown & Williamson, a unit of B.A.T. Industries Ltd.

Is the company's exuberance a bit premature? "That's a good beginning, but these things don't work overnight," says John C. Maxwell, an analyst at Lehman Brothers Kuhn Loeb. Added a Brown & Williamson competitor: "The moment of truth will come when they can no longer afford that promotional spending."

The Louisville cigarette maker certainly needs a winner. Its market share—13.7 percent, less than half that of Philip Morris or R. J. Reynolds—has declined steadily from 17.9 percent in 1974, says Mr. Maxwell. Arctic Lights and Fact, its two new-product attempts in the late 1970s, have been duds.

Brown & Williamson went outside the tobacco industry when it hired Mr. Alar in 1979; he'd spent 10 years at Warner-Lambert and 17 at General Foods. Scott Wallace, senior vice president-marketing, came from food processor Swift & Co. in early 1980.

"In the not-too-distant future," says Mr. Alar, Barclay will become one of the top 10 cigarettes, an achievement that would require market share of at least 3 percent. And Barclay's share could reach 4 percent if it reaches its goal of one-fourth of the ultra-low-tar (six or fewer milligrams of tar) category. Now about 10 percent of the cigarette market, that segment could grow to 16 percent within three years, Mr. Alar predicts.

Fifteen entries compete in that category; the leader is American Brands' Carlton with 2.6 percent share. Philip Morris' Cambridge and Reynolds' Now, both supported by lavish marketing budgets, haven't attracted many smokers, nor have most other brands. The weakness of most ultra-low-tars, their manufacturers readily concede, is that they don't have much flavor and are difficult to inhale.

A filter developed by Brown & Williamson in late 1979 gives Barclay what is said to be better flavor and easier draw. The company's problem was to convince smokers—many of them disenchanted with ultra-low-tars, especially those that bragged about taste—to try yet another brand.

"The liars had been there before us," maintains Mr. Wallace, who says Brown & Williamson wants smokers to regard Barclay as a fit competitor for all cigarettes. "We don't want to fight an internecine squabble in this little segment of the market." He says that goal has been met: only about one fifth of Barclay's sales come at the expense of other ultra-low-tars.

Barclay advertising mentions tar content only obliquely with the slogan, "99 percent tar free." Other ultra-low-tar ads frequently use numbers or such bold claims as "Carlton is lowest." Mr. Wallace says these "clinical" ads seem to be "almost antithetical to smoking enjoyment." (Barclay comes in one milligram and three milligram versions, compared with 0.01 milligram or one milligram in Carlton.)

Most of the Barclay ad is given over to a city-cousin version of the Marlboro cowboy: a suave, elegantly dressed man glancing at the woman next to him, her presence shown only by her hand resting on his shoulder. Explains Mr. Wallace: "The ad says this is something for people with great confidence and savoir-faire." The headline of the ad: "The pleasure is back."

It's hard to pick up a major magazine these days without seeing the Barclay man or, in another version of the ad, an equally sophisticated woman. Some issues carry both ads. Based on the amount spent in test markets, the bill for Barclay's first three months of advertising could top $24 million—about the amount Reynolds spent on Now in 1980.

But Brown & Williamson isn't relying on advertising alone. The company has paid retailers to put up checkout-counter displays in more than 75,000 stores and briefly sold two packs for the price of one. The biggest promotional salvo was the offer, to smokers who dialed a toll-free number, of a coupon good for a free carton.

Some competitors contend that Barclay's share is a result of all those freebies. But Brown & Williamson says its goal is to persuade smokers to finish a carton of Barclay; more than half of those who do become regular customers.

Spending for Barclay slowed in the second half of 1981 but, says Mr. Alar, the tobacco maker will back it aggressively "as long as we see we can drive this product up." The only major change in the advertising was the addition of the line "deeply rewarding flavor."

In addition to its apparent hit with Barclay, Brown & Williamson says it has arrested the decline of Kool and its other brands. The result will be improved sales and market

share for the company, its executives say, and a clean-up of its image as an industry also-ran.

Update

Barclay's share of the cigarette market passed the 0.5 percent that is the industry's minimum for a successful new product, but it failed to become a major brand. Mr. Maxwell, the tobacco analyst, says Barclay sales rose as high as 0.8 percent of the total United States cigarette market in 1984, but volume fell 20 percent in 1985 and the brand's market share declined to 0.6 percent. Despite the limited success of Barclay in the United States, a Brown & Williamson spokesman says the cigarette has sold well overseas and that the company is pleased with results worldwide.

Alliance: Overcoming AMC's Dowdy Image

Most of the people now running American Motors Corp. weren't old enough to drive when the company last brought out a big winner. That was the Rambler, introduced in 1950, four years before Nash-Kelvinator Corp. and Hudson Motor Car Co. merged to form AMC.

Finally, AMC has come up with another hit, the Alliance. An American version of a subcompact designed by Renault, the French auto maker that owns 46 percent of AMC, the Alliance is selling faster than AMC can manufacture it. In the six months following the sedan's introduction in September 1982, nearly 70,000 were bought; the Alliance is outselling all but 12 of the 76 domestically made automobiles. AMC has announced plans to increase daily production by 30 percent.

More impressive, though, is Alliance's ability to overcome widespread apathy and occasional hostility toward AMC and Renault. Before the car was marketed, an AMC survey of 605 potential customers found that 55 percent wouldn't consider a model with an AMC nameplate; 69 percent said no to Renault.

Nevertheless, 90 percent of Alliance buyers are first-time AMC owners, the company says. Their decision to switch is a reminder of a basic—and often forgotten—rule: The product itself is far more important than advertising, promotion, or other marketing flourishes.

Drivers and auto experts regard the Alliance as a well-designed, well-built, and fuel-efficient car that, at $5,695 for an unadorned two-door model, is attractively priced. Early in its research, AMC learned that those factors alone would be enough to sell the Alliance.

"The car itself overwhelms what we say about it. It is inherently very appealing," Oxtoby-Smith Inc., AMC's market-research firm, told the automaker in March 1982. Still, AMC—which lost a total of $337 million in 1980 and 1981 and had only 2 percent of U.S. auto sales last year—was unusually careful in testing all the facets of its plan to market the Alliance. "We knew we couldn't afford a mistake with this car," says David Van Peursem, AMC's general manager for marketing. "There was no room for error."

The testing began in 1979, when AMC and Renault decided to bring Renault's popular R-9 model to the United States from Europe. Several hundred drivers were shown the vehicle and asked what they liked and disliked about it. The basic design was received well but changes were made in the suspension, steering, air conditioning, and other features to cater to American tastes; fuel injection was added to make the car peppier.

Then came the issue of marketing. Should the car carry a French-sounding name like Liberte or Lafayette or an American label like Echo or Commander? AMC even considered Kenosha, after the Wisconsin city where the car would be manufactured, before playing it down the middle and choosing Alliance.

The company also wondered which "genealogy"—AMC, Renault, or a combination of the two—the car should stress. Oxtoby-Smith's finding: Consumers preferred Renault, but not strongly. Thus the model was christened the Renault Alliance, with the AMC name relegated to the nameplate and to the tail end of the advertising.

The research firm then considered whether the Alliance should be "positioned" on the basis of its quality, technology, and durability. Again, drivers expressed no strong preference. "While we ought to be smart about choosing a genealogy and a position," Oxtoby-Smith recommended to AMC, "we need not be as concerned with the subtleties of those directions as with getting the car exposed."

The budget for the company's advertising, in other words, was more important than the theme. Still, AMC was cautious. Although Grey Advertising—the agency for AMC passenger cars—was to handle the account, AMC also asked Compton Advertising—the agency for AMC's Jeep—to propose campaigns for Alliance. The two best suggestions from each agency were tested by showing cartoon-like versions to 500 consumers.

Best-rated was a Grey ad that used special visual effects to dramatize the theme that the Alliance represented "European technology, now built in America to be affordable." The commercial opened on a deep chasm in the earth, European cars on one side and a crowd of people on the other. As the announcer talked about closing "the gap between European technology and affordability," the earth closed and the crowd rushed toward an Alliance.

Oddly, though, the rough cartoon version outscored the finished commercial in further tests. After additional research, Grey substituted an announcer with a more authoritative voice and added more distinctive music, Handel's "Water Music."

Once the "chasm" spot began running, AMC found that viewers still weren't recalling all the points it wanted them to remember. To emphasize the car's handling ability, another commercial was made. Instead of visual tricks, it relied on winding roads, drivers in black racing gloves and other clichés of auto "performance" ads.

Recent Alliance commercials have returned to special effects. When Motor Trend magazine named the Alliance its 1983 Car of the Year, the agency rushed out another commercial to brag about that. AMC spent a hefty $14 million to advertise the car in its introductory quarter and has budgeted about $16 million more for the first nine months of 1983.

The popularity of the Alliance, however, has yet to make Renault a household word. A just-completed study finds that, while a majority of car buyers now know of the Alliance, Renault remains relatively anonymous. The French manufacturer's brand name, says an Oxtoby-Smith researcher, "still has a long way to go."

Update

Alliance and Encore, a sportier hatchback companion model that was introduced later in 1983, got off to a solid start but then were caught by a switch in consumer preference toward larger autos. Sales of the two AMC models rose to a peak of 169,601 cars in 1984 from 146,190 in 1983 and then declined to 110,673 cars in 1985. AMC says it plans to continue manufacturing Alliance and Encore for several more years and intends to import other French autos to the United States.

New Coke Shows Risks of Research

When Coca-Cola Co. uncorked its new formula in April 1985, executives boasted that it was the surest move they had ever made. They described as "overwhelming" the results of taste tests with 190,000 consumers, the majority of whom preferred the new recipe over old Coke.

By now, of course, everyone is well aware that it wasn't such a sure thing. Coke has decided to bring back its old flagship product as Coca-Cola Classic to please loyal fans who haven't taken to the new formula. The company's move underscores the dangers of reading too much into taste tests of food and beverages. While important, taste testing is an inexact science, and it is just one element, along with price, packaging, distribution, and advertising, in the whole marketing mix.

What Coke failed to measure was the psychological impact of tampering with a 99-year-old soft drink. "When you have a product with a strong heritage that people could always count on being there, the mind becomes more important than physiological responses," says Penelope Queen, research director at Dancer Fitzgerald Sample, the ad agency for Royal Crown Cola.

Few products could stir as much emotion as all-American Coke, but other factors can also dilute the significance of taste tests. Certainly the image created by advertising affects people's perceptions of taste. That's why researchers often do both blind taste tests and tests in which brand names are revealed. "We did blind tests in the Pepsi Challenge commercials to eliminate brand influences," says Allen Rosenshine, president of BBDO International Inc., an advertising firm. "But then we had to be very careful to say that people preferred the taste of Pepsi, not that they preferred Pepsi."

The color of a product also may make it seem tastier. When light-colored beer gets a shot of food coloring, consumers tend to describe it as heartier. Market researchers also say that 7-Up often beats colas in taste tests partly because people like its clear, light color. Yet, when the same people are asked what they take along on picnics or order at fast-food restaurants, they usually say a cola.

Sandy Swan, manager of consumer research at Dr Pepper Co., is delighted with the outcome of taste tests pitting his brand against new Cherry Coke. About 88 percent of Dr Pepper drinkers described their fruit-flavored soda as good or excellent; only 59 percent were as high on Cherry Coke. Even more encouraging: A scant 4 percent of consumers mistakenly identified Cherry Coke as Dr Pepper. But Mr. Swan still worries. "We could get hurt if Dr Pepper gets knocked out of vending machines and fast-food restaurants by Cherry Coke," he says. "If the product isn't widely available, then taste tests don't mean anything at all."

The sense of taste itself is a complex process that scientists don't fully understand. Researchers say that flavor involves not only one's taste buds but also the sense of smell and the trigeminal nerve, which responds to hot and cold and pain and irritation. "People's responses vary by time of day and what type of food they've eaten most recently," says Beverly Cowart, of the Monell Chemical Senses Center, a research institute in Philadelphia. Generally, people prefer a sweeter taste because it creates a more pleasant sensation in their mouth. But, Ms. Cowart warns, "they may not like the sweeter product in large quantities, and volume is what companies are interested in."

Measuring taste preferences is further confounded because the ability to discriminate between flavors varies greatly from one person to the next. Roy Stout, director of Coca-Cola's market research, says only about half the population has taste buds sensitive enough to distinguish between Coke and Pepsi. "If you remove the caramel color from Coke, a lot of people won't be able to tell it from one of the clear drinks like Sprite," he says.

Testing conditions and procedures can also distort the results of taste studies. Researchers note that responses may be influenced by how hungry or thirsty a subject is, how questions are phrased, and even how the test samples of competing brands are numbered. Typically, companies choose numbers like 697 and 483 to label products because 1 and 2 and A and B carry definite connotations.

Marketing consultant Gordon Wade criticizes taste tests as unrealistic because they often compare only two products, when in reality consumers have many more choices in supermarkets. The tests "also aren't sensitive enough to detect the intensity of taste preferences," he adds. "In many cases, you're doing brain surgery with a meat ax."

Taste tests often are conducted in the unnatural setting of a shopping mall, but research firms try to screen out as many other distorting influences as possible. They make sure test samples are kept at precisely the same temperature, and they serve only one sample from a can or bottle. To neutralize interviewees' palates, they usually feed people a cup of water and an unsalted cracker.

Some companies also do in-home testing to obtain more meaningful data. Campbell Soup Co. researchers say they sometimes get quite different results when people are eating full bowls of soup or drinking glasses of juice at home as opposed to taking a "teaspoon or sip test" at a shopping center. "You have to be careful of the cumulative effect of a product," says Marvin Schoenwald, senior vice president of McCollum/Spielman Associates, which does market research. "After extended use, a product may suddenly seem too sweet or not very thirst quenching."

Senchal: Selling Sex, Selling Perfume

It has taken Charles of the Ritz Group Ltd. 2½ years and $750,000 to develop Senchal, its new women's fragrance. The company and its ad agency have sorted through 250 scents, analyzed competitors' products, studied various bottle shapes and even programmed a computer to name the perfume.

Mostly, though, Charles of the Ritz and the agency have talked to women—not about what they want from a fragrance, but about what they want from life. Their answer: adventure, luxury and sex, especially sex.

That might not sound like much of a revelation, but to perfume marketers, it's a distinct change from industry trends. Charlie, introduced in 1973, was intended for independent, carefree women. In 1975 there were Jontue for the romantic and Aviance for the housewife. Enjoli, for working mothers, came two years later. Now, says Charles of the Ritz, there's yet another sort of female.

"She's looking for some danger. She wants the passionate adventurous life. She's a connoisseur of luxury," says Lois Geraci Ernst, president and creative director of Advertising to Women Inc., the agency for Senchal. "Men are part of her life, but she'll have a meaningful relationship with whom she wants, when she wants. The world is her toy. She's the queen of the jungle." Or, as Senchal ads say: "She's not going to marry the boy next door."

Because it's difficult for consumers to differentiate perfume scents, fragrance makers rely heavily on their ability to create an image that will attract prospective customers. What's in the bottle isn't as important as the bottle itself, the carton, the name and the advertising.

Throughout most of the 1950s and 1960s, fragrance marketers focused on the product. Ads described the scent or simply featured a photo of the bottle; some brands depended on the cachet of a designer's name. "We used to be able to say, 'Wear this perfume and you'll catch a man,'" says Brenda Harburger, a marketing vice president at Charles of the Ritz, a Squibb Corp. unit. "People would believe it."

Since then, however, fragrance manufacturers have paid more attention to the perfume-wearer, trying to make her believe that a brand matches her attitudes and life style. "We have to communicate her ideal self and fantasies back to her," says Mrs. Ernst, who has developed ad campaigns for six fragrances since 1965. "We're talking about a stupid little perfume, but we're dealing with the whole texture of life and relationships."

She says women use perfume for two reasons: sex ("to attract a man") and narcissism ("to glorify their existence"). The trick in marketing a fragrance is balancing those elements while keeping an accurate watch on women's desires. Says Mrs. Harburger: "You're diving into a cauldron of what's going on sociologically." The method: using nearly two dozen "focus groups," free-flowing discussions with groups of single women, 20 years to 30 years old, who were likely Senchal customers.

They were asked: If you could remove just one frustration from your life, what would it be? Do you feel any conflicts about being feminine? Describe your ideal man. What do you like and hate most about yourself?

Meanwhile, Charles of the Ritz and the agency also were testing the other elements of the product's appearance. A computer churned out possible names; none worked, so 10 professional writers were hired. A bottle design was selected, but the marketing executives fretted for weeks before deciding to top it with a ball. Scents from five suppliers were studied.

In the earliest focus groups, conducted in mid-1979, the most striking feature was the absence of talk about men. Women who did speak about them viewed men "as best friends," says Mrs. Ernst. "These women looked so glum about being friends."

Still believing that women really hadn't lost interest in the opposite sex, the agency then showed the groups pictures of men and asked the women to rate them on a scale of one to 10. The discussions perked up. "They were interested in men," says Mrs. Ernst, "but men they hadn't met yet."

The result of the research is a highly stylized, symbol-packed television commercial. Charles of the Ritz will spend $5 million running the ad between September and Christmas. The central character of the commercial, a sort of three-act drama in 30 seconds, is an elegant-looking "Senchal Woman."

Act I: Senchal Woman travels the world, posing in front of Egyptian pyramids, the Leaning Tower of Pisa and six other exotic settings. Photographed from a low camera angle, she appears to be a powerful woman. Her solo travels show her to be independent and adventurous.

Act II: Still pictures of Senchal Woman are juxtaposed with photos of attractive, youthful men. An announcer says: "Take your pick." She is bored. The Senchal bottle appears. Suddenly a more seasoned, dashing fellow drives by in a sports car. He looks her over. Nervously fingering her pearls, she studies him.

Act III: Senchal Woman and her new mate caress on a beach. Scenes of a boy eating ice cream and a girl on a merry-go-round flash by. ("If you have a really great love experience," explains Mrs. Ernst, "you're like a child.") The commercial concludes with a male voice: "I'm so glad you didn't marry the boy next door."

Preliminary tests indicate that viewers understand the commercial's intended message; more than $8 million in orders from drug and department stores have been received. Still, as with any new product, Senchal's success isn't guaranteed. "Perfume is the easiest product to make," says Mrs. Ernst, "but it's the hardest to sell."

Update

All of Charles of the Ritz's detailed planning for Senchal didn't pay off. It failed to become a major perfume brand and advertising for it eventually was discontinued, although Senchal remains on the market. "Senchal didn't fly as high as we had anticipated," says a spokeswoman for Charles of the Ritz.

Jell-O Tries Not to Show Its Age

Jell-O was born in 1897 and held on for 71 years before showing its age. Then the General Foods' dessert entered what looked like its sunset years. Sales volume began falling 2 percent to 4 percent yearly. Jell-O still could be found in nearly every home, but consumers were eating it less often. In 1970 the typical household bought 15.6 packages; in 1979, only 11.4.

But General Foods decided against letting its octogenarian slip quietly away. Like a growing number of marketers, the company learned that brands once given up for dead can be revived with changes in advertising, packaging, pricing, formulation, and even names. The frequent result, as in the case of Jell-O, has been sizable gains in sales and even larger profit advances.

Interest in born-again products has been stimulated by the depressed economy and the increasingly risky and expensive process of introducing products. And many elderly brands simply have grown too large to be ignored.

General Foods, for example, sold 576 million boxes of Jell-O in the fiscal year ended in March 1980; their retail value was $144 million. "No matter how successful we are in new products," says Peter Rosow, general manager of the $5.96 billion concern's desserts division, "when you've got a company as big as ours, you've got to keep your base businesses growing."

Ovaltine, Pet Evaporated Milk, Miss Breck Hair Spray, Bon Ami Cleanser, and Arm & Hammer baking soda are among brands recently saved from the graveyard. Marlboro cigarettes was 30 years old when Philip Morris scrapped its advertising directed at women (Marlboros had been offered with either white filters or red "beauty tips" that hid lipstick stains) and switched to cowboy ads. Sales soon outraced production capacity; today Marlboro is the top-selling United States cigarette.

Even without such success, many old products are worth restoring. Consumers remember them, a sales force doesn't have to win space on store shelves and manufacturing facilities are likely to be fully depreciated. "Nothing is more profitable than adding a few share points to an existing product," says William Tragos, chairman of TBWA Advertising, the agency for Ovaltine.

Jell-O had those assets but it also had problems. Increases in the number of working women, household income and interest in convenience foods didn't bode well for a dessert that required four hours to set in the refrigerator. Ready-to-eat desserts, especially frozen ones, became Jell-O's nemesis.

In early 1979, General Foods decided to look at Jell-O as if it were a new product. Young & Rubicam, which had handled Jell-O advertising for 51 years, interviewed hundreds of consumers and found that Jell-O reminded them of pleasant family gatherings. Says Alexander Kroll, president of the agency, "There's an emotion about Jell-O."

The previous Jell-O campaign, in contrast, was commonplace. Recipes were featured for concoctions such as Jell-O blended with chocolate ice cream. The campaign's economy-minded theme: "To make exciting desserts on a budget, start with Jell-O gelatin." Concedes Mr. Rosow: "In the past we may have been too intellectual. We were too focused on product attributes, not on experience."

Young & Rubicam's new campaign, which began in October 1979, doesn't mention recipes or Jell-O's low cost. The spots resemble soft-drink ads. Fast-paced shots show Jell-O fans of all ages shaking and eating their dessert as a chorus sings a snappy jingle: "Watch that wobble, see that wiggle, taste that jiggle. . . ."

In addition, General Foods increased its TV outlay about 25 percent to $10 million. The added funds went for prime-time commercials as a way to influence Jell-O eaters. Previously, General Foods bought daytime TV to reach Jell-O's buyers, but not necessarily its ultimate consumers.

Since the campaign began, Jell-O sales have risen 1 percent, and its share of the flavored gelatin market has improved to 71.4 percent from 70 percent. "To build volume, even if it's a half-percent, is a tremendous accomplishment," says Mr. Rosow.

Fixing a sick brand often means finding the right ad message and the right audience. Ovaltine dropped former football star Joe Namath from its ads and returned to a pitch about nutrition. Because 17 percent of its customers accounted for 87 percent of its sales, Pet Evaporated Milk focused on "heavy users": blacks, Mexican-Americans, and rural whites.

The repair job may require more than advertising changes. Miss Breck Hair Spray raised its price, changed packaging, and offered coupons and other consumer promotions in addition to new ads. Arm & Hammer pushed new uses. After Revlon acquired Pretty Feet, a lotion for rough skin, it changed the name to Pretty Feet & Hands to cash in on the growing hand-care market.

Sometimes rejuvenation doesn't work. Revlon's Norcliff-Thayer unit, which healed Pretty Feet & Hands, couldn't make a new package and advertising restore Ice Band, a cold-pack for sprains.

For those who'd find the task a challenge, there are plenty of candidates for reincarnation. Franchellie Cadwell and Herman Davis, founding partners of Cadwell Davis Savage, the agency that rekindled Pretty Feet, suggest a list of products they'd restage "if it were our money": Bisquick, Carnation milk, Dickinson's Witch Hazel, Johnson's Baby Cream, Pond's Cold Cream, and Smith Brothers Cough Drops.

Those products Miss Cadwell and Mr. Davis say are hopeless: Barbasol, Burma Shave, Carter's Little Pills, Doan's Pills, 5 Day deodorant pads, Lucky Strikes, and Phillips' Milk of Magnesia.

Update

Jell-O has been a difficult product for General Foods to rejuvenate. Sales of the product declined to 330 million boxes with a total retail value of $150 million in the fiscal year ended March 1986. One third of the volume was a sugar-free version of Jell-O gelatin that was introduced amid growing consumer concerns about sugar. The Jell-O brand has proved to be a durable base for a sizable new business, though. General Foods successfully grafted the Jell-O name onto a line of frozen Pudding Pops, Gelatin Pops, and Fruit Bars.

How to Revive
Worn-Out Products

"Marketers spend an unbelievable amount of money on new products with a very low success ratio," says Neve Savage, the director of account services at Cadwell Davis Savage, an ad agency that claims expertise in reviving "dog-eared" products. "Companies have much too little interest in products under their noses that offer enormous potential if someone looks at them as a new opportunity."

To help companies identify such opportunities, Cadwell Davis Savage has put together a 10-point "Life Signs" quiz that the agency describes as "a vitality test for older products." Here are the questions and examples of products that have been rejuvenated, some of them by Cadwell or its parent, Compton Advertising.

1. Does the product have new or extended uses? Arm & Hammer Baking Soda sales increased markedly after the product was promoted for freshening refrigerators, cat litter boxes, and swimming pools.

2. Is the product a generic item that can be branded? Frank Perdue put his name on chickens; Sunkist did likewise with oranges and lemons.

3. Is the product category "underadvertised"? Tampons were until International Playtex and Johnson & Johnson came in with big ad budgets, particularly for television.

4. Is there a broader target market? Procter & Gamble reversed declining Ivory soap sales in 1971 after promoting it for adults, instead of just for babies.

5. Can you turn disadvantages into advantages? J. M. Smucker used its funny-sounding name for a slogan for its jams and jellies: "With a name like Smucker's, it has to be good."

6. Can you cut price and build volume and profit? Johnson & Johnson's Tylenol analgesic became a success after the company reduced its price to match Bristol-Myers' Datril.

7. Can you market unused byproducts? Several lumber companies also are in the kitty litter business.

8. Can you sell it in a more compelling way? Procter & Gamble's Pampers disposable diapers were only a middling success when marketed as a convenience item for mothers. Sales took off after ads were changed to say that Pampers kept babies dry and happy.

9. Is there a marketplace or social trend to exploit? Dannon yogurt sales skyrocketed after the product was linked to consumer interest in health foods.

10. Can you expand distribution channels? Consolidated Foods' Hanes unit did when it marketed L'eggs panty hose in supermarkets.

3

Advertising Styles

Giving Products Brand Personality

The latest buzzword echoing along Madison Avenue is "brand personality." The phrase is defined by the research director of Young & Rubicam, a major U.S. ad agency, as "how people feel about a brand rather than what the brand does."

Brand personality is being embraced by some agencies and their clients as the elusive quality that separates exceptional advertising from the ordinary. Marlboro has it, for example, but Pall Mall doesn't. Charmin toilet paper does, too, but ScotTissue doesn't. Kool-Aid has it; Wyler's powdered beverages don't.

"You want the consumer to say, 'That's my kind of product,' which is different from 'I need that product,'" explains Kenneth Olshan, chairman of the domestic unit of Wells, Rich, Greene. The ad agency says the personality it created for Bic lighters helped them outsell Gillette's Cricket. Using the theme "Why light up when you can flick your Bic?," Wells Rich wanted to make lighting a cigarette an important part of the ritual of smoking; Cricket ads simply stressed the lighter's durability.

When properly developed, adds Grey Advertising, brand personality results "not just in 'purchase motivation' but in a friendship between the product and the consumer." Grey, which calls its version of the concept "brand character" and even has trademarked the term, also thinks it could lead to some new clients. Advises an internal Grey manual:

"Brand character can be a great door-opener if used in systematic and aggressive manner."

Several top advertisers agree that better-developed personalities can improve advertising. Frito-Lay recently asked its three ad agencies for more research on the subject. Revlon, whose Charlie perfume ads are considered a model of a good brand personality, depends heavily on it when writing ads for its cosmetics. "You can't have a 100 percent success rate," says Sanford Buchsbaum, advertising vice president, "but it gives you a better chance of success."

But skeptics wonder whether brand personality is only a catchy phrase for a trait that always has been part of successful selling. "Advertising people need something to talk about," says David Furman, advertising manager for Bic. "This year's fashion is brand personality. Several years ago it was 'positioning.'"

Defenders of the concept don't disagree entirely. "Great advertising has always had brand character," says Edward Meyer, Grey chairman, "but they stumbled upon it."

A personality has to be defined before it can be shaped. Some agencies are doing that by trying to describe the product as a person. Jell-O, for example, "is that very nice lady who lives next door," says Joseph Plummer, research director at Young & Rubicam, the product's agency. "She's not too old-fashioned, loves children and dogs and has a little streak of creativity, but isn't avant-garde."

Because consumers often have difficulty articulating personality characteristics, researchers are using off-beat methods to find out how products are viewed. Young & Rubicam asked interview subjects to pretend they were Chee-Tos or Fritos, two snack chips made by Frito-Lay, and then discuss various situations in which they might be served. Other consumers were asked to associate headache remedies with famous people; Excedrin was linked most often with Richard Nixon.

Once a personality is defined, it can be used to determine such features as the tone, spokesman, and locales for ads. In keeping with Oil of Olay's character—described as "ageless, sophisticated, foreign, mysterious, and slightly exotic"—Young & Rubicam designs exotic settings; most skincare products focus on a model.

To graft Jell-O Pudding's personality onto Jell-O Pudding Pops, a new frozen dessert, the agency chose Bill Cosby as its spokesman; he'd already starred in Jell-O Pudding ads. Personality also helps select TV programs to sponsor: Grey says it won't advertise Cycle dog food on comedies because it's a "serious" product.

Stepping out of character can lead to advertising flops. Grey learned that when it used the Eiffel Tower as the site for a No-Nonsense panty hose commercial. In previous ads, the commercial's plain-Jane model had been placed in less glamorous settings.

An effective personality, Grey concludes, is distinctive, appealing, and lasts a long time, even though ad campaigns may change. "The litmus test is," says Richard O'Brien, an executive vice president, " 'If I took the name out of the commercial, could you tell me the product?' "

The exception is a product with unsatisfactory sales. Timex, which hasn't kept up with trends in watch styles and technology, is trying to change its personality by abandoning spokesman John Cameron Swayze and its familiar timepiece torture tests. New ads show tennis players and fashionable young couples and emphasize technology instead of durability and price.

Some ad executives fear, though, that formal testing and application of brand personality could restrain creativity. Says Wells Rich's Mr. Olshan: "Bureaucracy is the enemy of this."

Still, the emphasis on personality is likely to grow. "In today's marketplace, product categories are packed with competitive entries that seem, for all practical purposes, to be very much alike," says Frazier Purdy, a Young & Rubicam creative director. And, because there's often little difference between ads for competing products, he says, "the most distinctive thing about a brand may well be its personality."

Linking Corporate and Product Names

If they didn't know it a year ago, chances are many TV viewers are well aware by now that Nabisco Brands Inc. is the company behind the brand name on Oreo cookies, Planters nuts, Life Savers candy and Fleischmann's margarine. Nabisco has tried hard to forge the link, tacking a three-note corporate jingle onto the end of all its commercials.

The reasoning: If you like Oreos, you will also feel warmly about Planters once you learn they're both part of the same corporate family. "We believe the rub-off effect will be especially beneficial in getting people to try new Nabisco products," says W. Lee Abbott, vice president, marketing services.

Although some marketing consultants dispute that logic, more companies are attempting to connect their corporate names with well-known consumer-product brands. ITT Corp., for example, is running print ads with the tag line, "All in the family," to tell investors and consumers it owns such businesses as Sheraton hotels, Burpee seeds, and Scotts lawn-care products.

Beatrice Cos., meantime, is spending $23 million to spread the word that it sells everything from Stiffel lamps to Martha White grits. Using the slogan, "You've known us all along," a typical commercial breezes through a litany of 14 products and drops the Beatrice name 18 times. The rationale is similar to Nabisco's, but Beatrice started cold

"Beatrice."

Samsonite® Luggage

Heard of Samsonite? Then you know Beatrice. We've been standing behind lots of your favorite products for years. Isn't that a good reason to remember our name?

Beatrice
You've known us all along.

Courtesy Beatrice Companies, Inc.

with virtually no name recognition and a much greater hodgepodge of products than Nabisco. Says Nabisco's Mr. Abbott: "There's a significant question as to whether consumers who like Samsonite luggage will find that reason enough to also buy Beatrice food products."

Big industrial companies, brokerage houses, and con- glomerates have long used corporate advertising to make a flattering impression with customers and investors. But corporate advertising by packaged-goods companies raises a basic question: Do consumers really care to know who makes the multitude of mouthwashes, detergents, and snack foods they buy?

Some advertisers say "yes," claiming that people nowadays are more quality conscious than ever, even when buying food and toiletries. "Corporate advertising gives a product an edge," says Keith Reinhard, chairman of the ad agency Needham Harper & Steers USA. "Consumers often can't see much difference between products when confronted by a lot of labels at the grocery store. Knowing something about a company's philosophy and reputation can help to decide the brand they choose."

Many marketers, however, still believe it's more sensible to put all their money into brand advertising. Procter & Gamble Co. takes the view that its brands must make it on their own without corporate advertising support. Chesebrough-Pond's Inc. experimented a few years ago with corporate ads but has stopped running laundry lists of such brands as Vaseline, Q-Tips, and Health-Tex. Says Ron Ziemba, corporate communication director, "Corporate advertising could be a negative if one product gets a shaky reputation and has a harmful rub-off effect on the others."

Corporate promotions can be important in building consumer confidence for marketing big ticket items like cars and appliances. But Thomas Garbett, a Waterford, Connecticut, corporate advertising consultant, contends that the parent company's image is usually inconsequential for low-cost impulse items. "If you invest in a pack of chewing gum and don't like it," he says, "it's no great loss."

Mona Doyle, a market researcher in Philadelphia, agrees, noting that consumers have made it clear "they don't care who owns what." She criticizes the Beatrice ads as being irrelevant to most people, but says corporate advertising can succeed if there is a specific message that people will find useful or interesting.

Richardson-Vicks Inc., for example, found it helpful to catalog such brands as Oil of Olay and Clearasil when introducing itself as a new company in 1981. The ads followed the spinoff of the consumer businesses from Richardson's prescription drug operations. To rebut its junk-food image, Frito-Lay, a subsidiary of PepsiCo Inc., has placed corporate ads in women's magazines, showing all its snack foods and arguing that potato chips are a good source of vitamins. And currently, Campbell Soup Co. is trying to create an aura of a company concerned about people's physical well-being by running eight-page booklets on stress and fitness in *Reader's Digest.*

Tony Adams, research director for marketing at Campbell, maintains that corporate advertising by packaged-goods companies can be merely an ego trip. "Some of our friends in the food business are doing ads that look like a patchwork quilt," he says. "They're talking to themselves."

But Nabisco and Beatrice say they are pleased with results so far from their promotions. Nabisco's consumer research found 85 percent recall of the three-note melody.

Beatrice is still assessing the effects of its commercials, which appeared frequently during the 1984 summer Olympics. It believes the ads "quite satisfactorily" increased awareness of the company name. Whether that translates into increased sales remains an open question. "This year, we're positioning Beatrice as warm and caring because that's what consumers say they are looking for and not getting from companies," says Greg Carrott, a management supervisor at Marsteller Inc., Beatrice's ad agency. "Next year, when a new Beatrice logo is plastered all over packages in the supermarket, it will mean something special to shoppers."

Celebrity Advertising: Proceed with Caution

In the winter of 1985, TV viewers could catch Tony Randall demonstrating Easy Off oven cleaner, Larry Hagman lending his J. R. Ewing endorsement to BVD underwear, Susan Anton gobbling a slice of Pizza Hut pizza, Barbara Mandrell gushing about clothing made of Visa fabric, and George Burns talking up Anheuser-Busch's new LA beer. Whew! And all those commercials might appear in the space of an hour or so.

In their struggle to keep viewers from tuning them out, advertisers are hiring a slew of celebrities to try to make their commercials look special. Hollywood talent agents claim they've never been busier filling advertising jobs. "Nowadays, we have a new star a week, so there are always celebrities around willing to do commercials," says Marty Ingels, a former TV actor who runs a "celebrity brokering" firm in Los Angeles. His company arranges about eight celebrity ads a week, compared with two a week in the late 1970s.

But recent consumer research suggests that advertisers are turning to big-name entertainers and athletes too often and that people are growing more cynical about such endorsements. Some ad agency executives are advising clients to be more wary about investing hundreds of thousands of dollars in a famous face. "We look at the celebrity thing very, very carefully," says Steve Bowen, manager of J. Walter Thompson Co.'s New York office. "Personalities don't have the same impact they did a few years ago when people

BVD

"LARRY HAGMAN TELLS EVEN MORE" :30

(MUSIC UNDER)
ANNCR: Larry Hagman tells even more...

WOMAN INTERVIEWER: Larry, women would love to get their hands on you - what's your secret?

LARRY: Secret?

LARRY: Legendary quality darlin'.

LARRY: Quality— top to bottom!
WOMAN: C'mon now-

WOMAN: don't women see right thru' you?

LARRY: Noooo...that's a hidden strength my dear.

LARRY: To be strong, soft-

LARRY: and verrry rich...

WOMAN: But - how does it really feel to be a living legend?

LARRY: It's a quality feeling.

LARRY: It fits me to a Tee!

ANNCR: With BVD you get legendary quality.

LARRY: You know, there are some things—I just can't get enough of!

Courtesy Saatchi & Saatchi Compton

would say, 'Golly, look, there's Lorne Greene doing a dog food commercial.'"

Only a very few celebrities, such as Robert Redford, still refuse to appear in ads. According to the Screen Actors Guild, its members rely on advertising jobs for about 48 percent of their income.

In a new study, however, Video Storyboard Tests Inc. found that just 19 percent of the 1,000 consumers surveyed feel that celebrities and athletes increase their interest in products. About half said celebrities do commercials only for the money, while 27 percent believe entertainers don't actually use the products they tout. (Ad agencies generally require celebrities to sign sworn statements that they use the products they're promoting.)

The study also showed how quickly celebrities fall from favor. Only half of the 10 "most convincing" Hollywood celebrities picked in a 1982 survey also turned up on the new list, and three of those five slipped in the rankings. Such stars as Linda Evans, Cliff Robertson, and Dom De-Luise are newcomers to the list. Among the casualties: George Burns, John Houseman, and Tom Selleck.

Still in first place, though, is Bill Cosby, who defies the rule that overexposure weakens a celebrity endorser's appeal. Over the years, he has promoted Jell-O, Del Monte products, Coca-Cola, Texas Instruments Inc., and Ford Motor Co. Mr. Cosby's success in ads may be due partly to the fact that he varies his style. He plays it for laughs with little kids in the Jell-O spots, while badmouthing Pepsi as too sweet in his Coke commercials.

In contrast, John Houseman used the identical approach—stern and professorial—first in ads for Smith Barney, then for Puritan cooking oil, Plymouth cars, and McDonald's. In the process, he sacrificed credibility. "Such overexposure also may confuse people about which brands the celebrity endorsed," says Barry Day, vice chairman of McCann-Erickson Worldwide, an ad agency. Smith Barney, an investment house, however, finds that Mr. Houseman's connection is strongest with it, and signed him to a new three-year contract.

Consumers not only aren't influenced easily by celebrities these days, but some also feel hostile toward companies that use stars in their ads. Consumer Network Inc. in Philadelphia found that about half the people it surveyed try to avoid buying certain products because they believe celebrities' expensive contracts inflate the price. Another study showed that more than 70 percent of the consumers, mostly women, resent advice on household products from "cutesy starlets."

When choosing celebrities, advertisers often depend heavily on Performer Q ratings compiled by Marketing Evaluations Inc. They measure how well-liked celebrities are but don't necessarily predict salesmanship potential. Atari signed a multimillion-dollar contract with Alan Alda in 1983 when he sat at the top of the Performer Q ratings. But Mr. Alda didn't make Video Storyboard Tests' list of the most convincing celebrity endorsers, and many ad agency executives believe Atari's choice was way off the mark.

Despite the glut, celebrity ads still may work if the product match is right and the star is believable. Grey Advertising says it is pleased with Dinah Shore's recurring role as spokeswoman for Holly Farms chicken because she is known as a good cook. The agency also finds comedienne Martha Raye, who wears dentures and goes by the nickname "the big mouth," perfect for Polident ads.

Another way to produce celebrity ads without offending viewers is simply to leave out the hype. Commercials for Pizza Hut, for example, show Rita Moreno, Martin Mull, Herbie Hancock, and other performers ad libbing about the joys of pizza. The entertainers themselves never mention Pizza Hut; only the logo flashes on the screen. Mr. Mull, instead, gives etiquette lessons on eating pizza, and Miss Moreno explains how she orders toppings according to her moods.

"We never say these celebrities eat at Pizza Hut restaurants," notes Jay Chiat, chairman of Chiat/Day Inc., the pizza-chain's ad agency. "But I think people will believe they're eating real Pizza Hut pizza in the ad and that they're having fun."

Using the Consumer as Pitchman

Standing amid flowering dogwood trees in a Maplewood, New Jersey, park, Betty Staples is singing the praises of her local Oldsmobile dealer. "They treated me fantastic, just like a brother," she says, as a camera rolls and a microphone dangles above her. Nearby, a Little League baseball team warms up, and honking cars threaten to drown her out.

Ms. Staples has been told the interview is strictly for research purposes, but she probably will be asked to allow her testimonial to appear in a TV commercial for the National Oldsmobile Marketing Association. "We can't change the negative image of car salesmen," says Albert Maysles, who filmed the commercial. "But showing satisfied customers up close, instead of actors, may make the commercial more convincing."

Although such testimonial ads are often criticized for being boring and ineffective, they are alive and well even in this era of glitzy special effects and multimillion-dollar celebrity endorsements. Procter & Gamble Co., which first included "real people" in a 1958 commercial for Cheer detergent, still employs the technique in campaigns for such brands as Folgers coffee and Ivory soap. Johnson & Johnson is in its 10th year of real-people advertising for Tylenol. While plain folks turn up most often in ads for soaps, food, beverages, and medicine, they also have appeared in recent spots for banks, airlines, spark plugs, and magazines.

"Consumers see real people as their peers and surrogates in the ad," says Richard Earle, creative director for Saatchi & Saatchi Compton Inc., which does hidden-camera interviews for Tylenol showing people in the throes of a migraine.

For all the fans of real-people ads, though, there are at least as many critics. Some ad agency executives are skeptical because TV viewers have watched so many testimonials through the years, and they tend to zap repetitive commercials with their remote-control channel selectors. Indeed, in real-people ads women still are sprinkling two brands of cleanser on their sinks and smearing different brands of soap on their arms. Identical lines also keep popping up. Two favorites: "I'm amazed" and "I'm going to buy your brand from now on."

"Testimonials are kind of a cop-out for want of a better idea," declares Roy Grace, executive creative director at Doyle Dane Bernbach. His agency used the technique just once in recent times, for a Polaroid commercial that was filmed at a Texas barbecue and was done only at the client's insistence.

Ciba-Geigy Corp. deliberately shunned testimonials to keep viewers tuned to its ad for a weight-control pill called Acutrim. Instead of featuring a bunch of former fatties as competitors typically do, Ciba-Geigy's commercial shows an actress flying through the air as her refrigerator sucks her toward a luscious cheesecake. Similarly, SmithKline Beckman Corp., searching for a way to revive sales of its Contac cold medicine, adopted a bouncy jingle to replace its real-people campaign.

Credibility is a growing concern in real-people ads. Many TV viewers believe the people are told exactly what to say and know they will be paid well for their spiel. Although directors generally interview consumers under the guise of research, even they concede that some people probably play to the camera, realizing they could earn as much as $10,000 in residuals. "People sense a hidden camera is in the room and start saying what they think the advertiser wants to hear," says Alvin Hampel, executive vice president at D'Arcy MacManus Masius, an ad agency.

Although he considers it a "tired technique," Mr. Hampel acknowledges that sometimes directors do strike gold with real people. He fondly recalls, for example, a Grape Nuts commercial in which a San Diego schoolteacher described with gusto how the crunchy cereal created "stereophonic effects" in her head as she chewed.

Companies that continue to believe in the power of real-people endorsements are trying to liven up their ads. Rather than include only talking heads, recent Tylenol commercials show an airline reservations clerk under stress at her computer terminal. In new Budweiser ads, cameramen descended into a coal mine.

Casting is what makes all the difference. "But finding the right person is like the needle-in-the-haystack trick," says Laura Slutsky, who runs a company called PeopleFinders. She roamed Dallas construction sites for days looking for a young man who loved Milky Way candy bars and also happened to bowl.

Some directors pick subjects at random off the street, but many pre-screen hundreds of people to find articulate spokesmen. People don't have to look like fashion models, although those with blemishes, weird hairdos, and other "distracting" features usually are rejected. As one ad agency executive put it: "The people should be ones you'd like sitting next to on an airplane."

The Maysles brothers, who have produced such documentaries as "Gimme Shelter" with the Rolling Stones, are considered by many advertisers to be the masters at making real people appear real on film. "We're looking to be surprised by what comes out of people's mouths," says David Maysles, who along with his brother Albert, worked on the Oldsmobile commercial in New Jersey. "We keep all the gestures, hesitations, and errors in pronunciation in our films." One of the pair's favorites was a Ragu commercial in which a woman tastes the sauce, pauses several seconds, then exclaims, "It's gorgeous." Says David Maysles: "No copywriter would ever have attributed that word to spaghetti sauce."

Comparative Advertising Takes Off the Gloves

Madison Avenue used to think it ungentlemanly to knock a competitor in public. Advertisers referred to rivals only as "other leading brands" or, more often, ignored them. Advertising practitioners believed what they'd learned in Sunday school: If you can't say something nice about someone, don't say anything.

No longer. In its ad campaign, struggling Seven-Up Co. brags that its lemon-lime soda doesn't contain caffeine. The company doesn't explain what, if anything, is wrong with caffeine but notes that most other soft drinks have it. Drackett Co. has told homemakers to use its Vanish toilet-bowl cleaner because, the company claims, other brands could wreck plumbing. Pillsbury Co.'s Totino's pizza contends that the crust on other frozen pizzas "tastes like cardboard," while another pizza marketer once ran TV commercials saying its rivals made their cheese from a substance that is "the main ingredient in some glues."

This is what might be called the Don Rickles school of advertising, where nothing scores as well as a put-down. The guiding principle: Don't tell consumers why they should buy your product. Try to persuade them *not* to buy your competitors'.

"Comparative advertising is becoming more hard hitting," says Jeffery Edelstein, a director of broadcast standards and practices at American Broadcasting Cos. "Competitors are taking each other by the throat."

Comparative advertising is a relatively recent development. Only a decade ago it was prohibited by two of the three television networks and frowned on by advertising and broadcast-industry self-regulatory codes.

One of the first companies to try comparative ads was Avis Rent A Car System in the mid-1960s. Its "We try harder" campaign helped the floundering concern become a strong competitor of Hertz Corp. The most important breakthrough for comparative ads came in 1971 and 1972, when the Federal Trade Commission began pressuring the TV networks to allow ads that named competitors.

Savin Business Machines compared its copiers with Xerox Corp.'s and prospered. Helene Curtis Industries showed its shampoo against five others and said in ads, "We do what theirs does for less than half the price." Without naming Warner-Lambert Co.'s Listerine, Procter & Gamble Co.'s Scope mouthwash referred to it as the brand that gave users "medicine breath."

Then, in 1979, the FTC formally endorsed comparative advertising and said that ads disparaging other products weren't necessarily illegal. "Comparative advertising, where truthful and nondeceptive," the FTC said, "is a source of important information to consumers and assists them in making rational purchase decisions."

Even the sharpest critics of comparative advertising have softened their views. Ogilvy & Mather, a leading ad agency, strongly opposed it for many years but changed its position in late 1980, after acknowledging that comparative advertising had been effective in some instances. Coca-Cola Co. criticized such advertising when rival PepsiCo Inc. used it but then employed taste comparisons to introduce a new wine.

Comparative advertising now is a widely accepted marketing device, particularly for brands that don't lead their categories. Mr. Edelstein of ABC says 23 percent of the 29,000 radio and television commercials it screened in 1981 were comparative ads. Two years earlier, 14 percent had been.

Most are relatively mild, with claims that a particular product works or tastes better or is otherwise more effective than another. Put-down ads, in contrast, suggest that rival brands are unwholesome or even dangerous.

Norcliff-Thayer Inc., a Revlon Inc. subsidiary, took the put-down approach to market its Nature's Remedy laxative with advertising that described rival Ex-Lax as containing "an artificial chemical." Coca-Cola, in ads for Minute Maid lemonade, blasted General Foods Corp.'s Country Time as the "no-lemon lemonade." Raisin growers advised mothers: "There are a lot of 'extras' in most manufactured snacks . . . things you may not want your kids to eat."

Many ads of this type "make specific claims about a competitor's product having negative attributes that the consumer might not be aware of," says Richard Kurnit, a New York advertising lawyer. Some marketers believe such tactics make consumers skeptical about an entire product category; beverage sources say powdered lemonade sales went flat after Minute Maid's attack on Country Time.

Another risk: legal or regulatory challenges from the targets of comparative ads. Most companies protest first to the broadcasting networks in the hope that they'll drop the ads. In 1981, ABC received 131 such challenges and upheld 30 percent of the protests.

Complaints also are heard by the advertising industry's self-regulatory body, the National Advertising Division of the Council of Better Business Bureaus. Among the ads modified or dropped after it began to investigate them were ones from Minute Maid, Nature's Remedy laxative, and the California Raisin Advisory Board.

Increasingly, companies are taking their gripes directly to federal courts. The Drackett attack on toilet-bowl cleaners was blunted by competitors' lawsuits, and Pillsbury went to court to defend its pizza advertising. Plaintiffs sometimes want more than a halt of the ads in question. Gillette Co. and its ad agency, J. Walter Thompson, once paid $4.3 million to Alberto-Culver Co. after running ads saying its shampoos left hair too oily.

Jingles Sell through Nostalgia

Feel like listening to some golden oldies? Just turn on the TV. In a commercial for Campbell's chunky soup, a teenager gyrates around the kitchen, lip-syncing the Sam and Dave hit, "Soul Man." Then there's the Downy fabric softener ad in which a little boy misses mom's towels and croons a take-off of the comical '60s song, "Hello Mudduh, Hello Fadduh." And to get "anything you want," the place to visit nowadays is a Ponderosa steakhouse, not "Alice's Restaurant."

This recent proliferation of classic pop songs is just one sign of the growing importance advertisers are attaching to music. While soft drink and beer marketers have long relied on jingles to help sell products, makers of cereals, detergents, and automobiles now are jazzing up many of their ads by acquiring the rights to hit songs or composing original music, usually with a rock beat.

Quality differences between many consumer-product brands have become less and less perceptible in recent years. So companies need more emotional hooks in their ads, such as music, to make their products stand out in people's minds. They also realize that many consumers are bored with traditional slice-of-life and product-demonstration ads.

"It's an entirely different ball game for advertisers because music has become a bigger part of people's lives," says Stephen Novick, an executive vice president at Grey Advertising Inc. He notes the large following that music-video programs have attracted and the legions of people plugged into radio earphones.

Even packaged-goods giants are more receptive to music. For example, John Loeffler, composer of the theme song for the TV series "Kate & Allie," wrote a ballad for General Foods' new Grape Nuts cereal commercials. "These big companies are in transition in their use of music," Mr. Novick says. "It wasn't a musical milestone when Procter & Gamble used a song from the '70s called 'Let Your Love Flow' for Joy detergent, but it sure beat two ladies talking about shiny dishes."

Much of the new music is slicker than the jingles of years past. Companies are investing heavily to buy rights to popular songs and to hire top producers, composers, and singers. The rights to songs can cost from $30,000 to more than $200,000, music producers say, while the price of an original composition usually runs from $10,000 to $50,000. Although expensive, popular singers are less squeamish these days about performing for commercials. PepsiCo got all the headlines for snaring Michael Jackson and Lionel Richie, but Roberta Flack also performs for Oil of Olay, Aretha Franklin sings a Coke jingle, and Chuck Berry adapted his rock and roll tune, "No Particular Place to Go," for a Volkswagen commercial.

"Music can be one of the best buys, but a brand name and product message should be tied into the tune," says Lee Weinblatt, chief executive officer of an advertising research firm called Pretesting Co. "It's not enough to have everyone humming the tune."

Ads aimed at children are even becoming more musically hip. No bunnies or nursery rhymes in a Chef Boy-Ar-Dee spot. Instead, a group of kids belt out Donna Summer's old disco hit, "Hot Stuff." Because of the strong influence of TV and earlier socialization at day-care centers, kids are more precocious, says Elizabeth Nickles, a senior vice president for D'Arcy MacManus Masius, an ad agency. "If you try to give children over four a message from the mouth of a bumblebee, they'll laugh at you." She created a commercial encouraging milk consumption that is based on the Adam

Ant rock song, "Goody Two Shoes." "We didn't want kids to think of milk as baby stuff that they would be embarrassed to drink around their friends," she says.

Advertisers still take music most seriously in trying to reach teenagers, a fickle group easily turned off by bland ads. Young & Rubicam was quick to develop new music for Dr Pepper when the 1984 campaign turned out to be too "anthemlike." Says Hunter Murtaugh, the ad agency's music director: "We needed a driving dance beat that would get everybody's juices flowing."

Coca-Cola studies the lyrics of the top 20 singles each week for clues on what young people like in music. "Because there are fewer teenagers than in the 1970s, competition for their attention is fiercer, and targeting them demands greater precision than ever before," says Sergio Zyman, senior vice president, marketing. Teenagers are important targets, he adds, because they form brand loyalties that last into adulthood.

Rock songs from the 1950s and 1960s are being commercialized primarily for products aimed at the 25-to-40-year-old baby-boom generation. Even Beatles songs are beginning to be heard in ads in both the United States and Europe. Advertisers hope such pop songs will make their commercials more memorable and that people's warm, nostalgic feelings about the tunes will rub off on their products.

Some companies, including Ford Motor's Lincoln-Mercury division, have been careful to preserve the original lyrics of such songs as "Proud Mary" in commercials. But the use of classics can backfire if people resent the way advertisers mess with their favorite songs. "In exploiting 1960s nostalgia, there are certain symbols and values you don't touch," says Mr. Zyman of Coke. "You shouldn't touch John Lennon, Kent State, and flower kids."

Tugging on the Consumer's Heartstrings

As the young mother gently nestles her newborn child into a crib, her worried five-year-old son asks: "Who do you like better?" Mom replies: "I love you both." Says an off-camera announcer: "He's got a new baby brother. Now he has to share your attention. You try to reassure him. . . . You give him lots of love."

This is how Coca-Cola Co. advertises Minute Maid orange juice these days. No more Bing Crosby touting it as "the best there is," no comparison with other brands, not even much talk about taste, freshness, or ingredients. Just an unabashed yank of the heartstrings—what Marschalk Co., Minute Maid's ad agency, calls "emotional hard sell."

Or, say others, old-fashioned schmaltz. Whatever the name, sentimentality—a device usually associated with such advertisers as Hallmark and Eastman Kodak—is being put to work on a growing list of products that most folks would find decidedly unemotional.

Procter & Gamble uses it to sell White Cloud toilet paper, Sterling Drug for Lysol disinfectant, General Foods for Maxwell House coffee and Jell-O, Cannon Mills for towels and sheets, and General Electric for light bulbs and toasters.

"We want the people we're talking to to relate our product to their lives," says Malcolm MacDougall, president of SSC&B Inc., the agency for Lysol. "Emotion is one of the best ways of doing that."

Frisky puppies, cute children, and doting parents populate many of these ads. Uplifting music is commonplace, and what's shown on the screen frequently is more important than what's being said. Slogans often talk about feeling (Maxwell House), touching (Cannon Mills, American Telephone & Telegraph), and sharing (Hershey, E.&J. Gallo Winery). Soft sell is the rule, and a product's purported emotional benefits are stressed over its functional ones.

Cannon manages to shoehorn all of that into its new ad campaign. Its commercials are a fast-paced montage of happy people—a father reading a story to his two daughters, a mother cuddling an infant, kids and a puppy frolicking under a garden hose. The slogan, as sung four times in the commercial: "Cannon touches your life." The products themselves—sheets, towels, and blankets—are mentioned only once.

"A towel is an insignificant thing until you relate it to a person's involvement with it," says Jerry Siano, creative director at N. W. Ayer, Cannon's agency. "It's what you get out of it, the way it makes you feel."

Ayer's "Reach out and touch someone" campaign, which AT&T began running in 1979, is one reason for the growth of sentimentality as a selling ploy; few agencies are above borrowing ideas from successful campaigns.

Many advertisers have turned to sentiment because they've run out of compelling appeals to logic. Their own sales pitches have lost their punch and, for the increasing number of products that don't differ markedly from their competitors, new arguments are hard to find.

That was partly behind General Foods' decision to sack Cora, its middle-aged spokeswoman who explained how to make tasty coffee. Maxwell House commercials instead consist of such vignettes as a harried commuter pausing for coffee after missing his train and kids waking their parents with a bugle blast on the morning of a scout outing. Through both, Ray Charles sings about "that good-to-the-last-drop feeling."

Changing regulations also have narrowed the scope of claims that advertisers can make. Coca-Cola, for example, says it couldn't make its "the best there is" claim for Minute Maid now without developing extensive documentation.

Other agencies say they're making more emotion-filled ads because consumers are weary of the hard sell. "Irritating people to get their attention," maintains Ayer's Mr. Siano, "is the wrong way of developing a relationship with your customer." Adds Mr. MacDougall of SSC&B, "Love and motherhood are back in style."

But sentiment won't sell every product, as SSC&B found out when it made a Bayer aspirin commercial with a family-run Italian restaurant where "Mama" had a headache. The ad bombed, and Bayer switched to a stone-faced announcer and this unemotional pitch: "Nothing works better than Bayer. Nothing."

Some unemotional products can be sold with emotional advertising, though, says ad agency Foote, Cone & Belding. It tested "thinking" and "feeling" commercials for common food, drug, and household products and found them equal in memorability.

Other agencies say they've found emotional ads score well on memorability tests but only after viewers have seen the commercials several times; the ads don't do as well on single-exposure tests, the type most often used to evaluate new commercials. Indeed, many agencies have avoided emotional commercials out of concern that they wouldn't pass so-called day-after-recall tests.

Like most commercials, sentimental ones present an unreal picture of life, suggesting that many of its most difficult moments can be eliminated by the right products. Sibling rivalry or a child's anxiety about school are cured with Minute Maid orange juice. A young girl, frightened awake by a thunderstorm, calms down after talking to her mother about White Cloud toilet paper.

"You're playing with something that can be absolute garbage, sentimental slop," says John Bergin, president of McCann-Erickson, the agency that doles out emotion for Coca-Cola soft drinks. "Everyone will start throwing up if it's overdone."

Finding the Best
Advertising Climate

Next time the weatherman forecasts gusty winds, soft-drink companies might want to step up their advertising. Soda pop consumption curiously increases with wind velocity. And when storm clouds form, the climate may be just right for a barrage of hot cereal ads. Research indicates that's when cereal eaters are most likely to treat themselves to an extra bowl.

Struggling to get the most for their advertising dollar, some marketers have started paying close attention to such meteorological trivia. "Weather can change people's habits and taste preferences enough to boost consumption of a product by 50 percent to 100 percent," declares Fred Ward, a former TV weatherman and one of the founders of Advertiming, a service in New York that uses computer models to match product usage with weather conditions.

It's just common sense to advertise beer and suntan oil more heavily in the summer and cold medicine and ear muffs more in the winter. But now some companies are monitoring the daily weather outlook to help them select the best times to run their commercials. Vitt Media International Inc., New York, one of the partners in Advertiming, claims it can buy local TV and radio time with just 24 hours notice.

Connecticut Radio Network Inc. in Hamden, Connecticut, also provides weather guidance, placing ads for Campbell soup before snowstorms strike and devising a chapped lips index for Blistex based on temperature, wind, and humidity. The company's Mediarology service plans to alert Quaker Oats Co. to impending cold snaps in some of its cereal markets.

With media costs rising rapidly, "we're looking for every bit of leverage we can get," says George Mahrlig, director of media services at Campbell Soup Co. "Based on reaction from the supermarket trade and consumers, we believe the winter storm ads have given us an edge." This winter, Campbell will boost its storm ad budget 50 percent to about $750,000.

Whenever a storm is forecast, radio ads are aired urging listeners to stock up on soup before the weather worsens. After the storm hits, the ad copy is changed to tell people to relax indoors and warm themselves with soup. Connecticut Radio Network monitors the weather in more than 30 cities, 24 hours a day, for Campbell. Barry Berman, the network's president, says he sometimes has to roust radio salesmen from bed to schedule the ads.

Consumers' perception of the weather often is more important than meteorological readings alone. Mr. Ward of Advertiming notes that people eat soup and hot cereal when it's cloudy because they "feel colder." Likewise, Mr. Berman might not urge Quaker Oats to run more ads when the thermometer reads 16 degrees in Chicago, but he probably would if the temperature dipped to 25 in Atlanta. Says Mr. Berman: "We have to measure the misery index."

Connecticut Radio Network has turned down some companies. An aspirin manufacturer wanted to time its ads to run when a cold spell was about to begin. But research revealed that people buy more aspirin whenever they run out, regardless of the weather.

Giving Food Ads a Mouthwatering Look

Loretta Swit, Mr. T, and other celebrities ham it up in some recent Burger King commercials. But the real star of the ads is the Whopper, which was recently beefed up to provide stiffer competition for Wendy's and the Big Mac.

Using a special lens, director Elbert Budin filmed the burger from less than an inch away to make it look gargantuan. To create an ideal bun, extra sesame seeds were pasted on with tweezers and egg white. Water was squirted on the tomatoes to give them a "dewy, fresh look," and the condiments were dabbed on meticulously with Q-tips. Says Mr. Budin: "We tried to get the Whopper as perfect as possible without making it appear pristine. Food must always remain earthy and approachable."

Although shooting pictures of food and beverages may seem rudimentary, advertisers fuss as much over corn flakes and TV dinners as they do over stunning fashion models. The lighting in a recent Wendy's commercial was done by John Alcott, winner of an Academy Award for his cinematography for the movie, "Barry Lyndon." On the Duncan Hines account at Saatchi & Saatchi Compton Inc., employees are required to bake brownies and blueberry muffins themselves to get to know the products intimately. Even Vice Chairman Philip Voss spent an afternoon flipping hamburgers for Krystal's, the agency's fast-food restaurant client.

"It's much more interesting to work all day with Christie Brinkley than with a tomato," says Charles Piccirillo, executive creative director at Leber Katz Partners, an ad agency. "But food can really look bland on a big TV screen if you don't pay attention to the tiniest of details."

The aim of food advertising, of course, is to make people lick their chops and rush out to a restaurant or supermarket. Seldom are actors in commercials shown eating food, because that might turn consumers off. "People shoving food in their mouths isn't the greatest thing to look at," Mr. Voss says. "What you want to do is move the camera in close and make love to the product." But increasingly the food in commercials does more than just sit there and look succulent. Recently, there have been flying potato chips and pickles, talking sandwiches, and a bacon cheeseburger cruising along an expressway.

"That stuff is as expensive as blazes," says Paul Mulcahy, president of Campbell Soup Co.'s in-house advertising agency. "You have to wonder if a nicely decorated plate isn't as effective as food hurtling through the air."

But even simple advertisements can be painstaking ordeals, because food products seldom behave the way directors want. For one thing, food is very temperamental under hot lights. Directors say they must be careful that the tops of hamburger buns don't dry out and cave in or that raw meat doesn't turn a sickly brown. They also must be sure that beer gushes into a mug at just the right speed and with just the right amount of head.

No one knows more about such challenges than Ralcie Ceass, supervisor of food photography at General Mills Inc. For a typical Bisquick TV commercial, she may cook 1,000 pancakes to come up with enough that have a smooth contour and golden-brown color. "It's especially important that food looks gorgeous on package labels," she says, "because the box sits on the grocery shelf for days surrounded by competing brands."

Indeed, Victor Scocozza, who does package shots, says some finicky ad agency people insist that he photograph a piece of cake on a plate first with four crumbs, then eight crumbs, then 12 crumbs. He once spent 7½ hours on a single chocolate-chip cookie.

In trying to glorify food, companies may go too far. In 1984, the Council of Better Business Bureaus concluded that ads for Old El Paso sauce misrepresented the thickness of the product. The council also objected to a Mauna Loa commercial that seemed to show only whole macadamia nuts. A consumer had complained that jars typically contain many broken nuts.

"But by and large, advertisements are far more honest today than they were 10 years ago," says Marianne Langan, a so-called food stylist who gussies up food for photo sessions. "Years ago, we would have used milk of magnesia in a picture for cream of mushroom soup."

Campbell Soup was cited in 1969 by the Federal Trade Commission for adding marbles to bowls of vegetable soup so it would look chunkier. Now, the company says, it polices its advertising scrupulously. To ensure that the soup shown in ads is representative, the company purchases it at random in grocery stores. Vegetables and meat are evenly split between the two bowls that come from each can. And top marketing and legal executives scrutinize proofs of each ad to make sure that during the printing process a pale yellow broth doesn't magically turn golden.

While fewer ads are downright misleading these days, companies still fudge a lot. For example, maraschino-cherry syrup is painted on ham for appetite appeal. Some products are sprayed with glycerin to make them glisten. Cigarette smoke and humidifiers are used to simulate steam for baked goods. And plastic sometimes substitutes for ice. Director Lee Howard even vacuums individual corn flakes and applies a chemical fixative so that when they are poured from a box and collide in mid-air, little pieces don't break off. "We never actually cheat," Mr. Howard says. "We merely handle the food in a different way than a housewife would."

4

Advertising Campaigns

J&B I: Getting Scotch off the Rocks

A bottle of booze, accompanied by a full glass and brief copy, has been the staple of liquor advertising since Prohibition's end. Few spirits brands have followed that style more faithfully than J&B Scotch.

Now (1980), in a big-budget ad campaign, J&B is dropping its bottle to enliven its stagnant sales, the victim of declining interest in Scotch and other "brown" liquors. The ads also are the first new campaign from Backer & Spielvogel, the ad agency started last year by several former McCann-Erickson executives.

In place of the J&B bottle and glass will be a view of a Scottish castle, surrounded by a moor and a quiet blue lake. Superimposed on the water is J&B's label. The ad copy: "J&B. It whispers."

As the top-selling Scotch in the United States, J&B hasn't had a problem with anonymity. The trouble has been "inertia," says Alvin Ferro, president of Paddington Corp., which imports J&B. Although its previous ads helped give J&B what he says is "the highest brand-awareness of any liquor in the United States," they provided little motivation for consumers. "We didn't give any conclusive reasons why people should drink it."

The new ads don't give any explicit reasons, either. Instead, the liquor marketer and its agency hope the inviting scene and "whispers" copy will suggest lightness. J&B owes much of its popularity to its lighter color and taste, but

Courtesy The Paddington Corp.

Paddington advertising never highlighted that difference from other Scotches. "We're taking advantage of a product attribute that's been there all the time," Mr. Ferro says.

Despite all the Scottish effects, the scene in the new ads "could be a bayou in Louisiana," he says. "The idea isn't to lend the character of Scotland to this, but to set a scene in which people can be relaxed and comfortable." Adds Carl Spielvogel, chairman of the agency, "You should want to jump into this page."

Paddington will spend $12 million over the next 12 months on the "whispers" campaign, compared with $8 million for J&B advertising in the prior year. At least 80 percent of the budget will go for magazine ads.

Because sales of indulgence products respond to greater ad spending, that budget—possibly the largest ever for a single spirits brand—could be decisive. Based on current sales volumes, J&B has budgeted roughly double the amount its rival Scotches spend on advertising.

Like most liquor ads, J&B's are aimed at typical Scotch drinkers: college-educated people, most often male, aged 25 to 44, who earn at least $22,000 yearly. Southerners, who appear to be losing their preference for bourbon, are a special target. Generally, says Mr. Ferro, the J&B ads should appeal to "the hard-working guy who has earned his reward."

If that customer sounds like a richer version of the Miller beer drinker, it's no coincidence. Several Backer & Spielvogel executives, while at McCann-Erickson, helped create the Miller campaign, built on the notion that beer is a reward for a hard day's work. Miller was Backer & Spielvogel's first client.

And if the scene in the J&B ad resembles the calm lake and snowy mountains in magazine ads for Canadian Mist, a Canadian whiskey sold by Brown-Forman Distillers, that mightn't be a coincidence, either. When those ads were created in 1968 at McCann-Erickson, the account manager was Mr. Spielvogel and the creative boss was William Backer.

J&B II: No One Heard the Whispers

Searching for a distinctive selling point for J&B Scotch, Paddington Corp. hit upon the slogan, "It whispers," back in 1980. That bit of ad copy alongside dreamy pictures of Scottish castles and lakes was meant to suggest the smooth taste of America's best-selling Scotch. Five years later, however, it seems that the Whispers campaign was too soft-spoken.

J&B's sales have steadily eroded, knocking the brand into second place behind Dewar's and prompting Paddington to create a new marketing campaign that is longer on words and shorter on romance. "We feel Whispers was too subtle and too myopic," says Chuck Nardizzi, vice president, marketing. "We need to tell our story more forcefully."

So Paddington, the U.S. importer of J&B, will abandon the bucolic Scottish scenery that is fast becoming a cliché in Scotch advertising. New ads instead will feature toy soldiers in red coats toting a J&B bottle as they troop off to battle. The ads gush about pride and conviction and boast that, "the heart of this blend is married in oak casks longer than any other Scotch whisky." The new slogan: "Scotch of rare character."

"People know the care that goes into making a great wine," Mr. Nardizzi says. "But we have to educate the public to the heritage and craftsmanship of our Scotch, which was created for British aristocrats who didn't like coarser whiskies."

Pride.

Taking pride in what you do makes a real difference in the way you do it.

Justerini and Brooks understood this when they custom blended a Scotch whisky for their aristocratic clients nearly a century ago.

That's why J&B is a complex blend of some forty whiskies, including several of the world's finest single malts.

That's why the heart of this blend is "married" in oak casks longer than any other Scotch whisky.

And that's why J&B tastes the way it does —uniquely smooth and refined.

J&B. It's a Scotch of rare character, blended with pride.

Scotch of Rare Character.

Courtesy The Paddington Corp.

While J&B's heritage may be unique, it isn't unusual these days for marketers of alcoholic beverages to hype tradition. Miller Brewing Co., for example, has been running ads that tell how German immigrant Frederic Miller insisted on pure ingredients when he started making beer here more than 100 years ago. For some time, Brown-Forman Inc.'s ads have played up the 19th century Tennessee roots of Jack Daniel's whiskey.

What is unusual about the new J&B ads is the toy-soldier theme. Why military imagery for a product associated with good cheer? "It's evocative of the British spirit," says Dean Scaros, senior vice president of Backer & Spielvogel, J&B's advertising agency. "What better symbol of heritage, pride, and consistency than a soldier."

Perhaps. But soldiers seem apt for yet another reason: The $2 billion Scotch market is one of the most savagely competitive in the distilled spirits industry today. Since 1980, Scotch shipments in the United States have plunged to 17.5 million cases from 19.6 million, according to the newsletter *Impact*. J&B's 1984 sales totaled 2.2 million cases, down from 2.6 million in 1980. In contrast, Schenley Imports Co.'s Dewar's brand has grown slightly in popularity with case sales of 2,650,000 last year, compared with 2,595,000 in 1980. Schenley ascribes its success in a down market partly to the long-running Dewar's Profile ads. They feature sketches about interesting young achievers like a dog-sled racer and a harpsichord builder.

"Paddington hasn't been working J&B hard enough," says Steve Boone, operations manager at Safeway Stores Inc.'s Liquor Barn division. "People selling Dewar's, Cutty Sark, and Chivas Regal call on us regularly and are aggressive about getting their brands promoted in our stores. I don't remember the last time I saw someone representing J&B." (Paddington should be making more calls soon; it says it recently fattened its sales force by 50 percent.)

Some liquor industry experts also believe J&B is losing customers who have decided to trade up to more expensive brands. Reflecting that trend is a Chivas Regal ad that says, "Drinking less? Then drink better."

Despite the gloomy first half of the 1980s, Paddington executives remain confident about the Scotch business. "We totally reject the notion that Scotch is on the rocks," says President Peter Thompson. His goal is a 15 percent share of the Scotch market by 1990; J&B now stands at 12.5 percent. To that end, Paddington will spend more than $10 million on its new ad campaign in the next 12 months, a 25 percent increase from the year before.

For extra punch, the company is designing some ads specifically for certain newspapers and magazines. In *The Wall Street Journal,* Paddington is publishing the newspaper's first crossword puzzle in an ad that will appear every Friday for the next year. And in *Inc.* magazine, J&B ads will promote free gifts of cheese and smoked turkey to small businessmen who order cases of Scotch for their customers at Christmas.

Paddington also has set its sights on minority groups. It will spend about $1 million advertising to blacks and Hispanics, four times more than in past years. "Blacks and Hispanics tend to be quality-oriented consumers," says Mr. Thompson, "so, they're ideal targets for Scotch."

The company plans to hire an ad agency specializing in the Hispanic market, and recently, with the help of a black consultant, it began offering free posters profiling significant but lesser-known blacks, such as Jim Beckwourth, a scout and Indian fighter. Schenley Imports took a somewhat similar tack in a recent Dewar's ad that paid tribute to Harlem's Apollo theater.

Paddington also will spend more money on promotions, including a large sampling program patterned after wine tastings. A Scotch connoisseur from Scotland will address retailers and wholesalers at some tastings, and Paddington will continue a consumer tasting program that already has reached about 100,000 New Yorkers at off-Broadway plays. According to Paddington's research, the New York area accounts for about 25 percent of U.S. Scotch sales. "We went off-Broadway," Mr. Nardizzi, the Paddington marketing executive, says, "because we wanted upscale New York trendsetters to try J&B, not tourists."

Revlon Keeps Charlie Contemporary

The equal rights amendment has failed. Author Betty Friedan, whose "The Feminine Mystique" helped spawn the women's movement, today says that feminism and the family aren't incompatible. Now Revlon Inc., no slouch at figuring out what women will buy, has decided to let the woman in its Charlie fragrance commercials have a serious romance. She may even get married.

That's a big switch for an advertising character who was introduced in 1973 as the quintessential liberated woman. Charlie, as Revlon calls her, was single, had a job, and wore pants to the office before it was fashionable. She went into bars unescorted, signed the check in restaurants, and dressed in tuxedos at night. Her walk—a long stride, with arms swinging—bespoke independence, confidence, and a touch of insouciance.

Most of all, she didn't need a man. Men were bit players in Charlie ads. Charlie wore cologne not as part of some husband-hunting scheme but because she liked the stuff.

Suddenly, in the latest Charlie commercial, there's a wholesome-looking fellow proposing marriage and hinting that Charlie should put their relationship before her career. Revlon spent nearly a year preparing this commercial, carefully analyzing public-opinion research. What is the perfume maker trying to tell us?

Advertising is a meter of social and cultural change. Unlike the ERA or Betty Friedan, though, advertising is

112

rarely controversial. Only when a new idea no longer is threatening do marketers move in to exploit it through advertising. They oversimplify and stylize the idea in order to sell products and make profits.

In the late 1960s, for example, love, peace, and brotherhood among nations were in vogue. By 1971 Coca-Cola Co. was advertising soft drinks by showing youths from several countries gathered on a hillside singing: "I'd like to buy the world a Coke."

The women's movement led Madison Avenue to populate its commercials with female cops, reporters, and executives. But such images were too clumsy for Revlon and other manufacturers of fragrances and cosmetics. Those companies sold fantasy. As Charles Revson, Revlon's late founder, is said to have put it: "In the factory, we make cosmetics; in the store, we sell hope."

In the new Charlie ad, Revlon has replaced actress Shelley Hack, who has starred in the campaign since 1975 (and later joined "Charlie's Angels," the TV series). In her place is actress Tamara Norman, a woman with a more rounded figure. She is wearing a strapless evening gown, not pants.

The 30-second commercial opens with Charlie and her date leaving a party. "Nice party," she says. An announcer sets the scene: "The best part of the party's when the party's over."

Standing under the orange neon sign of a late-night restaurant, he nuzzles her ear lobe. "Mmm, Charlie?" he inquires. She answers: "Uh huh." They then approach two huge stone lions. He pops the question: "Would you cancel your trip to the coast if I proposed?" She ignores him: "I wonder how much this lion weighs?"

As dawn approaches they stop to buy rolls at an Italian bakery. He is persistent: "Listen, I'm serious about what I said before." She continues to fend him off: "Eat your breakfast."

They stand outside her brownstone. A jogger passes by and milk bottles—an anachronism—wait on the stoop. "Even my mother thinks it's time for you to settle down," he argues. Grinning, she replies: "Your mother's right."

Did she agree to marry him? Or does "settle down" mean live together? And what about her trip, presumably for business? Will she skip it and risk ruining her career? Has she had enough of liberation and decided to trade her job for marriage and family?

"Charlie hasn't changed," says Sanford Buchsbaum, Revlon executive vice president for advertising. "The world has changed." He insists that the ad character won't give up her career, but "has proven her independence" and is ready for "another dimension to her life." Everything else about the commercial is purposely ambiguous, designed to make viewers pay closer attention and perhaps debate possible endings with friends. "I hate to call it a commercial," says Mr. Buchsbaum. "This is really a minimovie."

Revlon has been modifying the campaign subtly over the years, he explains, to stay on "the leading edge of where people's emotions, psyches, and intellects have been going." In 1979, for example, Charlie got a boyfriend who appeared briefly in the ad as she playfully kissed him on the nose.

Now Revlon's research indicates that it's safe to advance Charlie's romantic interests further. Yankelovich, Skelly & White Inc., a market-research concern that Revlon and many other big advertisers rely on for advice about social trends, says there's more interest in traditional relationships, marriage, and families.

More than ever, Revlon needs to keep up with the times. In 1982, U.S. sales of Charlie showed their first decline ever—to between $35 and $40 million from a 1980 peak of more than $50 million, Revlon estimates. Although Charlie sales continue to grow worldwide, the domestic fragrance market has declined generally this year. Charlie also faces competition from numerous new brands.

Without waiting to see if Charlie's romance catches on, Revlon is at work on a new ad. Charlie heads down the aisle? Charlie and her beau break up? Charlie has a baby? All Revlon's Mr. Buchsbaum will say is that "we've got some ideas."

Ring around the Collar: Irritating but Effective

The most obnoxious ad on television, in the view of some Madison Avenue professionals, is the "ring around the collar" commercial for Wisk detergent. Critics say it is irritating, insults women—especially the housewives who are Wisk's most important customers—and even damages the credibility of advertising in general.

"Ring around the collar," it also can be argued, is one of the greatest advertising campaigns ever. It reversed the fortunes of a troubled brand and has kept it growing ever since. Ranking third in U.S. detergent sales, Wisk accounts for about 8 percent of the market and brings Lever Brothers Co., its manufacturer, revenue of more than $200 million a year.

The campaign has lasted 15 years—far longer than most—and has outscored dozens of alternatives tested by Lever and its agency, Batten, Barton, Durstine & Osborn. Procter & Gamble Co. and Colgate-Palmolive Co. have brought out their own liquid detergents to compete with Wisk but never have come close to its success.

"It would be fair to call that commercial a screeching commercial, an abrasive commercial, an intrusive commercial," says James Jordan, author of the slogan and now chairman of his own agency. "But the one thing you can't call it is a bad commercial because the purpose of a commercial is to do a commercial job."

Nevertheless, campaigns such as "ring" and the 18-year-old "Mr. Whipple" series for P&G's Charmin toilet paper are favorite targets for criticism. A group of advertising writers once gave the Wisk ads one of its "Lemmy" (as in "Lemon") awards for bad campaigns. A Boston women's group threatened Lever with a boycott over "ring."

"I hate 'ring around the collar,'" says Shepard Kurnit, a New York ad agency chairman who recently completed two years of interviews with 5,000 consumers about their views of advertising. "I think it's insulting to the intelligence of the American people."

Wisk advertising "sells merchandise to people and makes them hate it at the same time," writes John O'Toole, chairman of Foote, Cone & Belding, in "The Trouble With Advertising," his recent book. "They feel, with some justification, that they're being talked down to."

Marschalk Co., a New York ad agency, says its surveys show that a disliked commercial may prompt 33 percent of its viewers to consider buying a competing brand. Notes Rena Bartos, a J. Walter Thompson senior vice president, "Many people buy a product in spite of its advertising, not because of it." Her studies of irritating commercials show that they generate negative attitudes toward the entire advertising industry.

Defenders of "ring" say that critics are the sort of folks who, unlike most consumers, rarely are troubled by dirty collars. "The people who are critical work in air-conditioned offices and send their shirts to the laundry," says Sam Thurm, an official of the Association of National Advertisers and Lever's advertising chief when "ring" was born in 1967.

Before that, Wisk had been in trouble. Introduced in 1956 as the first liquid detergent, it was unfamiliar to consumers and cost twice as much per washload as powders. Wisk advertising talked about the "liquid miracle for family wash" but said nothing about its ability to remove many stains when poured directly on them.

That message became part of the next Wisk campaign, whose slogan was "Wisk puts its strength where the dirt is."

It did little to help, though, as Wisk's share of the detergent market fell to 2.8 percent in 1967 from its peak of 4.2 percent.

Then came "ring," blurted out by Mr. Jordan after another B.B.D.O. executive mentioned Lever research that identified dirty shirt collars as a laundry problem frequently cited by women. As a takeoff on a familiar schoolyard chant, "ring around the collar" was easy to remember. And unlike the "strength" campaign, which explained Wisk in a straightforward way, "ring" employed a bit of imagery to relate it to a specific consumer problem.

Embarrassment is critical to the commercial's effectiveness. A typical 30-second "ring" ad of the early 1970s shows a couple arriving for a Hawaiian vacation. As a grass-skirted native places a lei around the husband's neck, she loudly discovers his dirty collar. He looks at his wife as if she'd just murdered their firstborn. She is horrified and ashamed.

"Those dirty stains," intones an off-camera voice, which explains why she should use Wisk. She does, and the commercial closes with the husband placing a lei around her neck as they smile together. The problem is gone, the tension resolved. The tension was gone at Lever, too; Wisk sales tripled between 1967 and 1974.

Still, Lever and B.B.D.O. decided the campaign wasn't quite right. In 1979, blame for dirty collars was shifted to competitors' detergents; the wife's moment of shame was cut. "We wanted to tone down the pain a little bit," explains Kenneth Rogers of B.B.D.O.

Little else has changed. Not every version uses husband and wife, and new spots scheduled for next year will feature new scenarios but the same format. When Lever recently experimented with a "hidden camera" ad in which ordinary consumers talked about ring-around-the collar ("I got crazy and ran out of the room," a wife confesses after her husband's collar became a topic of conversation at a party), Wisk sales fell in test cities.

Lever says the "ring" campaign's work isn't finished.

There are new liquid detergents to fight and powdered-detergent buyers to convert. And even after 15 years and more than $100 million worth of "ring" on TV, some people haven't gotten the message. Although the slogan is almost universally known, Lever research shows that one of every three viewers still doesn't associate it with Wisk.

Alka-Seltzer Goes Back to Laughs

Ever feel like your stomach was literally on fire? Some new Alka-Seltzer commercials bring that sensation vividly to life. In one spot, a man settles back in his easy chair after a chili dinner when suddenly fire bells and sirens start blaring. His bulging tummy lights up like a torch, igniting his newspaper and sending him off to the medicine chest. Playing off a Wild West theme, another ad shows a man who emits smoke signals and hears tom-toms and war whoops in his head after devouring a barbecue buffalo burger.

The two commercials mark Alka-Seltzer's return to heartburn and humor, the advertising approach the brand became so famous for in the 1960s and early 1970s. "We're going back to basics," says Edward Gustafson, president of the Miles Laboratories, Inc., division that markets Alka-Seltzer. "Overindulgence and speed of relief are what the brand was built on."

To try to halt a steady drop in unit sales, Miles had strayed from that strategy. Last year, the company promoted its flagship product—with annual sales of about $100 million—as a remedy for stress in the executive suite. Miles believed that because many people were cutting back on rich food and liquor, the old "hangover medicine" image was passé.

But the "symptoms of stress" strategy didn't propel Alka-Seltzer out of its decade-long sales slump. Regular customers consumed less of the fizzy antacid and analgesic,

Consumer Products Division

MILES LABORATORIES, INC.

P.O. Box 340
Elkhart, IN 46515
Phone (219) 264-8988
TWX 810/294-2259

CLIENT: MILES LABORATORY
PRODUCT: ALKA-SELTZER
TITLE: "BUFFALO BILL'S"

COMM'L. NO.: MIAS 5263
LENGTH: 30 SECONDS

(SFX Indian Tom-Toms, chants and yells)

That spicey barbecue Buffalo burger has started to send you smoke signals.

ALKA-SELTZER TO THE RESCUE (SFX Bugle Charge)
Alka-Seltzer relieves the acid indigestion that's hot on your trail. And also quiets the tom-toms in your head.
(SFX END, MUSIC STARTS) So when your stomach and head go on the warpath (SINGERS: "HELP")

Send Alka-Seltzer to the rescue

And bring peace to your body fast.

(SINGERS AND MUSIC)
ALKA-SELTZER TO THE RESCUE

Courtesy Miles Laboratories, Inc.

claiming they couldn't relate as well to stress as to spicy food. "We did pick up some new upscale users," says Mel Philpott, account director at the McCann-Erickson ad agency. "I gather a lot of yuppies identified with the ads, thinking they have more stress than other people."

The new commercials will raise again the question of whether belly laughs really sell Alka-Seltzer. Advertising executives frequently cite classic Alka-Seltzer commercials as examples of funny, award-winning spots that didn't move the product. But Miles officials disagree. "Humor has sold the brand," asserts Stephen Reim, a marketing vice president. "People saw Ralph sitting on the bed groaning, 'I can't believe I ate the whole thing,' and said to themselves, 'Yeah, I've had nights like that.'"

While the latest commercials are amusing, they lack the daffy charm of the vintage Alka-Seltzer ads. They don't rival, for instance, the 1970 commercial, in which a young bride chortled over recipes for "marshmallowed meatballs" and "poached oysters," while her gagging husband furtively downed Alka-Seltzer. And the new slogan—"Alka-Seltzer to the rescue"—establishes the idea of fast relief, but it doesn't seem destined to catch the public's fancy the way "Try it, you'll like it" did.

Miles, a subsidiary of Bayer AG of West Germany, won't disclose its advertising budget, but it says it will spend about as much as it did in 1984 when, it is estimated, Alka-Seltzer advertising totaled more than $17 million. In addition to commercials, Miles will hammer home its "To the rescue" slogan with a Super Bowl coupon tie-in, toy fire-truck promotion, free T-shirts showing a blazing stomach, and a heavy sampling program at chili festivals.

Miles is particularly concerned about replacing Alka-Seltzer's loyal, but aging customer base. Many young people find Alka-Seltzer's taste bitter and salty, and choose Tums or Rolaids instead. So, this month, Miles will try to tempt consumers with new lemon-lime Alka-Seltzer. The company experimented with such flavors as root beer, grape, and ginger, but lemon-lime won handily in taste tests.

However, even before it mails out 10 million free samples

of the lemon-lime formula to consumers, Miles will face new competition from several other antacids also being billed as tastier. Warner-Lambert Co. just began marketing a chewy antacid called Remegel that the company claims is almost like eating candy.

"Remegel is going into a very competitive market," says John Carroll, president of Warner-Lambert's American Chicle Group. "It used to be nice and sleepy, but since 1982, there have been a lot of new products." Rolaids, Maalox, and Alka-Seltzer dominate the flat antacid market, which amounts to $700 million to $800 million a year in retail sales.

Because of the market's sluggish growth, antacid manufacturers have started promoting attributes unrelated to indigestion. Schering-Plough Corp. is making a calcium-rich claim for Di-Gel to appeal to women worried about osteoporosis, and a new Rolaids formula is being advertised as both calcium-rich and sodium-free.

Miles believes it has a much more compelling new selling point for 55-year-old Alka-Seltzer. The company plans to capitalize on the Food and Drug Administration's recent endorsement of an aspirin-a-day regimen to reduce the risk of heart attacks. Alka-Seltzer, which contains sodium bicarbonate and aspirin, was prescribed in a major heart-disease study, a point Miles plans to trumpet at medical conventions and in cardiology journal ads.

"We need to bring some good news to the brand," says Mr. Gustafson. "We haven't had much but bad publicity to deal with for a number of years." He refers to charges in the 1970s that Alka-Seltzer should not be recommended for upset stomachs because the aspirin in it could cause gastric bleeding. Miles successfully rebutted the claim, but the attack nevertheless raised doubts in consumers' minds and hurt sales for many years.

Dr Pepper Shuns
the Ordinary

For four years actor David Naughton pranced his way through Dr Pepper commercials coaxing people to join the parade and "be a Pepper, too." The snappy ads seemed to be a hit: Consumer surveys consistently rated them among the most memorable campaigns on the air.

These days, however, executives at Young & Rubicam Inc., Dr Pepper Co.'s ad agency, would just as soon people forget those ads. "We unfortunately tried to become a drink for the masses," says William Thompson, executive vice president at Y&R. "That made our advertising a lot like Coke's and Pepsi's, except they had a much better-accepted flavor and much more money to spend." "Be a Pepper" backfired and contributed to the brand's market-share slide in the early 1980s.

Finally in 1984, Dr Pepper returned to the advertising strategy that fueled its growth in the 1970s. In 1975, the company had found success with the slogan, "the most original soft drink ever in the whole wide world." Now, the current jingle—"hold out for the out-of-the-ordinary"—again tries to position 100-year-old Dr Pepper as the choice of independent thinkers looking for an alternative to colas.

That and other marketing changes are putting fizz back in Dr Pepper's sales. Through August 1985 sales were up 10 percent from the year before. Dr Pepper says it has passed 7-Up to become America's fourth most popular soft drink, behind diet Coke. (Seven-Up Co. calls the claim "wishful thinking.")

Dr Pepper won't disclose sales or market-share data, but beverage analyst John Maxwell estimates that the company sold nearly 350 million 192-ounce cases of regular Dr Pepper in 1984, thus claiming about 5 percent of the soft-drink market. Sales of Sugar-Free Dr Pepper totaled about 68 million cases in 1984, but 1985 volume is off slightly.

Some devotees of Coca-Cola switched to Dr Pepper in all the commotion in 1985 over the new flavor of Coke and the rebirth of old Coke as Coke Classic. But Coke's blunders don't deserve too much of the credit; Dr Pepper believes its brand has rebounded primarily because it is being marketed more intelligently.

Around 1982, researchers at Young & Rubicam began realizing that a mass appeal like "Be a Pepper" contradicted psychographic studies showing fans of Dr Pepper's unusual fruity taste to be "inner-directed" people. "The Dr Pepper prospect believes he should live life in accordance with his own personal values and not try to meet other people's expectations," says William McCaffrey, a research supervisor at Y&R. "He views himself as original, even a little crazy, and looks for interesting experiences." In contrast, the typical Coke or Pepsi drinker tends to be an "outer-directed belonger" who follows the latest trends and seeks peer approval.

Commercials for 1985 fit the psychographic profile well by focusing on a couple of mavericks who will stop at nothing to get their Dr Pepper. In one spot, a cranky Godzilla demolishes entire city blocks after guzzling the contents of a cola tanker truck. He is appeased only after tasting the Dr Pepper inside a water tower. Another ad shows a space cowboy at an extraterrestrial bar who demands "the unusual" but rejects a concoction with an eyeball floating in it in favor of Dr Pepper.

Back on track, Dr Pepper planned to stick with its "out-of-the-ordinary" theme in 1986 with sequels to the Godzilla and space cowboy ads. The company plans radio spots featuring celebrity sex therapist Ruth Westheimer, and Young & Rubicam promises to capitalize on the similarity of new Coke and Pepsi. "But we can't trash Coke and Pepsi because it might alienate Dr Pepper bottlers," most of whom also distribute a cola, says Louis DiJoseph, a Y&R executive.

To reach its youthful target audience more effectively, Dr Pepper is advertising every week on MTV and even has licensed its name and flavor for a new bubble gum.

Dr Pepper also is concentrating more on single-drink distribution channels, such as vending machines and fountain dispensers. For example, the company has been offering discounts of as much as $350 on vending machines and expects to sell a record number in 1985. Dr Pepper derives about 55 percent of its sales from single-drink purchases, whereas they account for only 45 percent of total U.S. soft-drink volume. Says company president John Albers: "Because our customers are young and mobile, they buy a lot of Dr Pepper in fast-food restaurants, movie theaters, and convenience stores."

Previously, when some ex-Procter & Gamble marketers were running the show, Dr Pepper put more effort behind food stores, the main battleground in the cola war. What Dr Pepper quickly found was that the expense of discounts and other supermarket promotions cut deeply into profits. "Fountains and vending machines are much more attractive because all the drinks are the same price," says Mr. Albers. "That puts us on more equal footing with Coke and Pepsi."

Dr Pepper will have to defend its single-drink turf more vigorously as Coca-Cola presses hard to get new Cherry Coke into fountain outlets. There's a slight taste similarity between the two beverages to start with, but the real problem is the limited number of spigots in a fountain. Robert Hamlin, vice president of marketing, says the company has lost its spot to Cherry Coke in only a few places thus far, but "it definitely is a concern, and we're devoting a lot of time to telling the Dr Pepper story."

Prudential I: Insurance with Humor

Death sells. Life insurance marketers are starting to accept that advertising philosophy after years of tiptoeing around the reason that people buy their product. The latest insurer to face death head-on is Prudential, which has begun ads patterned after "Heaven Can Wait," a 1978 movie starring Warren Beatty.

In a typical Prudential commercial, two angels in white three-piece suits fetch their customer, a healthy-looking man far from his sunset years, at his weekly bowling match. As they escort him up an escalator to heaven, he protests, "I thought I'd have more time." Replies one of the angels: "Doesn't everybody?"

Prudential is the nation's largest life insurer, and its whimsical approach contrasts markedly with the industry's delicate treatment of death. Even the name of their product, insurance marketers say, is a euphemism; "death insurance" would be more accurate.

"Many life insurance companies have been reluctant to back the hearse up to the door," says Ernest Rockey, president of Gallup & Robinson, a research concern that has tested advertising for Prudential and other major insurers. "They'd talk about anything but what they really were selling."

Less reticent about dealing with the subject of death is Independent Life Insurance of Jacksonville, Florida. In a TV commercial showing in seven Southeastern states, a married couple sit on a lawn watching three fountains spout water. Suddenly a lightning bolt strikes the husband, leaving behind only his smoking tennis shoes. Calmly, the wife opens her purse to find her insurance policy.

Such ads were pioneered by New England Mutual Life Insurance, whose 14-year-old print campaign is based on cartoons showing an unsuspecting person about to face calamity, such as a falling piano. The caption: "My insurance company? New England Life, of course. Why?"

Mutual of New York tried a serious approach to death in 1975. One of its TV commercials featured a young man (portrayed by John Travolta before he became a star) sweeping the floor in a diner and explaining that his college plans were ruined when his father died. That campaign went off the air in 1978, a victim of high TV costs, but continues in print. In New York, ads for Savings Bank Life Insurance show a family snapshot with the caption: "What if your wife dies first?"

Death ads, serious or comic, tend to perform better in audience tests than traditional life insurance ads. Barry Kaye Associates, a Los Angeles insurance agency, says recognition of its name "went through the roof" last year after it began a campaign featuring angels.

But some critics wonder whether death ads, although attention-getting, are too morbid. Says an ad executive for an insurer, "We seriously wonder whether they haven't gone too far for their own good."

Agencies that have used such ads say that negative reaction is minimal. An executive at Ted Bates, the agency for Prudential, says humor makes its commercials "more palatable." Tests of Independent's commercials resulted in complaints from only four of 200 viewers. Independent's ad agency, Cecil West & Associates, says its commercials "really don't present death in a way that would be fearsome."

Prudential II: Death Is No Joke

Enough jokes. After three years of whimsical commercials for life insurance, Prudential Insurance Co. of America is turning joltingly serious. It believes people have overcome their squeamishness about the subject of death.

"I remember hearing somebody say I was . . . dead," whispers a man's voice as one of Prudential's new 30-second TV spots begins. Unseen, the man is lying on an operating table as doctors look down on him. The wavy green line of an oscilloscope monitoring his pulse goes flat. "I thought about Janice and Bobby," he says. "Who'd take care of them now?"

The doctors pump on his chest. As the patient responds, they are heard saying, "He's coming back. He's all right now."

This scene is the latest step in the evolution of life-insurance advertising. Once so genteel that it never mentioned the word "death," it has slowly stopped skirting the reason that people buy the product. As Prudential did in its three-year campaign that ended in 1983, some insurers have used humor to overcome viewers' anxiety about death.

The Prudential campaign was inspired by "Heaven Can Wait," a 1978 movie comedy starring Warren Beatty. In the commercials, angels dressed in white three-piece suits came to collect the deceased, generally young men who had died unexpectedly.

Those ads didn't stop working, says Connie Sartain, Prudential's advertising vice president. Instead, the straight-

forward portrayal of death simply out-scored humor in consumer tests. "You just keep trying to beat what you have on
the air," she says.

Prudential has four commercials in the new campaign. In
addition to the surgery patient, they feature a woman
drowning, a volunteer fireman overcome by smoke in a
burning building, and a man being rushed to a hospital in
an ambulance. Each recovers from the close call.

After that moment of "resurrection," as Prudential's ad
agency calls it, the scene shifts to the protagonist, fully
revived and back in safer surroundings. The drowning
woman, for example, is walking on a beach with her two
young daughters. "I got a second chance to do all those
things I meant to do," she says.

An off-camera announcer concludes the pitch: "At Prudential we know that most of us don't get a second chance."
He recommends a chat with a Prudential agent.

The switch in campaigns comes amid increased media
attention to death, "near-death experiences," and what one
news magazine calls a "gloom boom." "If we've timed it
right, this campaign should exploit the trend," says Lee
Hines, executive vice president at Ted Bates Advertising,
Prudential's agency.

Tests of viewers' reactions to Prudential's treatment of
death in the "angels" campaign showed that about 15 percent of the audience objected to it. Preliminary tests of the
new ads show that a slightly smaller number dislikes the
serious approach.

Both campaigns have the same purpose, says Mr. Hines.
"The idea is to get people to stop procrastinating, to put a
sharp stick in their eye," he explains. "It's human nature
not to face up to your own mortality."

ITT Fixes Its Image

A hairdresser combs actress Alix Elias's pile of curls as a technician fiddles with sound equipment. A makeup man sits nearby, working on a crossword puzzle. Crew members and hangers-on munch brownies, Brie, and bagels.

The director calls out: "Let's try one more time before we commit this to film history."

The crew's purpose, something short of making film history, is to help gussie up the corporate face of International Telephone & Telegraph Corp. This commercial, part of an eight-year-old "image" ad campaign, is designed to counteract a poll's finding that 60 percent of the public confuses ITT with American Telephone & Telegraph Co.

So-called image advertising has become a burgeoning business for Madison Avenue. Nearly half of the 800 largest U.S. companies use advertising to sell ideas as well as their products, the Association of National Advertisers says. It estimates that $1 billion was spent on such nonproduct advertising last year, with ITT and 16 other companies budgeting at least $10 million each.

The advertisers aim to make the companies more memorable, raise employee morale, and attract investors and customers. Corporate ads can also help divert attention from information the companies would like the public to forget.

That ITT's biggest image problem these days is only the public's confusion between it and Ma Bell is quite a change for a company whose name a few years ago was linked with Watergate and the downfall of Chilean President Salvador Allende.

Although the company says it was planning its campaign even before those setbacks, the advertising is credited with helping to restore ITT's reputation. And the company isn't planning to quit while it's ahead.

To sort out the current problem involving the public's confusing of ITT with AT&T, the company has come up with a commercial in which Miss Elias portrays an ITT telephone operator showing the ropes to a befuddled trainee.

The phone rings. "No, dear, you want AT&T, not ITT," Miss Elias tells a caller. "We are two totally different companies."

In a bubbly, adenoidal voice, she then instructs the trainee: "Sometimes, Cheryl, you have to explain what ITT really does. I mean, we make telecommunications equipment all over the world. But we also make Wonder bread." Her tone is reverent. "And we're Sheraton."

She clutches her heart. "And Hartford Insurance. And Scott's lawn products. And lots of other companies. . . . "

The 60-second commercial was first aired, along with 11 minutes of other ITT ads, during a two-hour presentation of Charles Dickens's "Oliver Twist" on CBS-TV. The evening's tab: $2.5 million, out of a 1982 budget of $10 million.

The overall purpose of the broadcast and print ads? "We don't want people to think of ITT as a monolithic, contentious, rather hard-nosed corporation," says John Lowden, the vice president for corporate relations and advertising.

Image advertising in general remains a controversial form of salesmanship. Critics contend that it is often trite, stuffy, and irrelevant. "At least half the dollars invested in it are wasted," says Ronald Hoff, an executive vice president of the ad agency of Foote, Cone & Belding Inc. "Companies are talking to themselves, staring into their own navels."

But ITT's image advertising is viewed as highly effective. "They've done themselves proud in creating a new image for themselves," says J. Douglas Johnson, an Indiana University marketing professor who has studied the campaign.

"They're saying something, not just blowing their horn."

They aren't telling *everything* about the company, however. Image advertisers are carefully selective about the subject matter they present to the public. ITT scrapped a commercial about dietary matters and its Fresh Horizons bread in 1977, for instance, after Sen. George McGovern publicly attacked the high-fiber bread as being made from "sawdust" and "wood pulp."

Also not mentioned, of course, was the 1979 sacking of Lyman Hamilton as ITT chief executive after only 18 months on the job, or the company's recent troubles in finding a buyer for its Rayonier forest-products business.

Mr. Lowden, the ITT vice president, says he depends on the media to deliver those messages. "Too many corporations protest their innocence through advertising," he says. "We just tell people what we're doing and let them draw their own conclusions."

People seem to be drawing the conclusions that ITT wants. A January 1982 survey by Roper Organization Inc. shows that, among six large companies, ITT ranked eighth in the number of people who viewed it favorably. Almost as well regarded as Xerox Corp. and U.S. Steel Corp., ITT was even with AT&T and ahead of such firms as Chrysler Corp., Exxon Corp., and Toyota Motor Co.

It wasn't always so. In the 1960s, ITT's problem was anonymity. The company's surveys showed that two thirds of the public knew it vaguely or not at all. Even its own executives, hard-pressed to keep up with the rapidly diversifying conglomerate, jokingly referred to ITT as "International This & That."

Then, in the early 1970s, ITT's involvement in United States and international politics made the company a lightning rod for growing anti-big-business sentiment. In 1972 a published memo allegedly written by ITT lobbyist Dita Beard linked settlement of Justice Department antitrust charges against the company with a purported ITT pledge of $400,000 to finance the 1972 Republican convention in San Diego (the convention subsequently was switched to Miami Beach). A year later came revelations that ITT had offered advice and money to the Nixon administration and the Central Intelligence Agency to help unseat Chilean President Allende.

Although ITT vigorously denied any wrongdoing, the company's reputation was blotted. ITT's name appeared regularly in front-page headlines, its offices in the United States and abroad were bombed and its campus recruiters often were assailed by protesters. Even some copywriters at Needham, Harper & Steers Inc., ITT's ad agency, refused to work on its accounts.

"We were running uphill. No matter what you explained, nobody wanted to accept it," says Edward Gerrity, an ITT senior vice president. "Perception is the reality. You had to deal with the perceptions."

After the controversies erupted, ITT advertising executives decided to shelve the company's preachy magazine ads ("Creating jobs is our most important social responsibility") and vague slogan ("Serving people and nations everywhere"). They increased the advertising budget to $7 million in 1974 from $1.3 million the previous year and designed flashy new TV commercials to portray ITT as a technologically sophisticated company that cares about people and uses its profits, says Mr. Lowden, "to help improve the quality of life." The new slogan: "The best ideas are the ideas that help people."

The first commercial, introduced in January 1974, featured a woman staring at viewers as she soberly announced, "I'm going blind." Explaining that she suffered from night blindness, she told how a binocular-like device made by "the people at ITT" enabled her to see.

Yankelovich, Skelly & White Inc., a market-research concern, conducted polls before and after the campaign's start to monitor the company's reputation. Improvement was rapid. Within a year, awareness of ITT rose 65 percent and it became known by nearly three out of every four people (compared with half before the campaign) as a "leader in technology." Also growing was the number of people who told pollsters that ITT was "very profitable," "makes quality products," and "cares about the general public."

In other respects, though, many remained skeptical. Yankelovich found that less than a third of those polled believed that ITT struck a good balance between profits and public interest—29 percent before the campaign and 31 percent a year later. Some people tore the ads from ITT image ads from magazines and mailed them to ITT with angry messages. Today, views on the question of profit and public interest still aren't much higher: 35 percent say ITT balances both well.

The targets of the ads continue to be people ITT calls "movers and shakers." They are 30 to 55 years old, have family incomes of $35,000 (up from $25,000 when the campaign began), work in managerial or professional jobs, and have traded stock and written a letter to a government representative within the past year. ITT estimates their number at 11 million, and its TV campaign is intended to reach them an average of 15 times a year.

ITT and Needham continue to churn out about four commercials and six print ads a year. Featured recently have been a mannequin used to train medical students, a monitoring device to prevent pollution from ships, shock absorbers for high-speed trains, and compressors that pump pure air into infant incubators.

Many of the company's more prosaic products are avoided for image ads (Hostess Twinkies lack "inherent drama" says Mr. Lowden), with many of the ads working hard to tug on viewers' heartstrings. "To try to convince people of something on a logical basis in 60 seconds is impossible," says Barron Biederman, the president of Needham's Issues & Images division, which was established a year ago to handle corporate advertising. "People respond more to situations with emotion."

Last December, though, the annual Yankelovich survey turned up the problem of confusion between ITT and AT&T. ITT executives became worried, particularly because AT&T's controversial agreement with antitrust regulators to break up its empire was likely to keep Ma Bell in the spotlight for several months. So Mr. Biederman came up with the skit involving two telephone operators.

The commercial, which cost $40,000 to produce, was re-shot 22 times to yield the finished ad. Last year, to film ITT shock absorbers mounted underneath a moving train, a camera was buried under railroad tracks. That ad cost $175,000.

ITT also painstakingly promotes its commercials. To publicize the Dickens special, ITT advertised it widely in magazines and newspapers; mailed 100,000 program guides to schools, libraries, and scout troops; and distributed posters to Sheraton hotels and 10,000 agents of its Hartford Insurance Group.

Would all this effort come in handy if ITT ever became embroiled in another scandal? Other companies' experience suggests that it might. Union Carbide Corp., for example, ran image ads during the late 1960s. When chemical companies were under attack for producing material for use in the Vietnam war, Union Carbide didn't drop in opinion polls conducted by Opinion Research Corp. Du Pont Co. and Dow Chemical Co., however, didn't advertise, and lost favor with the public. And when Union Carbide later reduced its ad spending, favorable attitudes toward the company also declined, according to the Opinion Research study.

"You can never sit back, rest on your oars, and say the job is done," says ITT's Mr. Lowden. "It is absolutely never done."

135

5

Packaging and Promotion

Getting an Edge with Better Packages

The toothpaste cap that drops on the bathroom floor or, worse, down the sink. The little aspirin tin that refuses to open when, as instructed, you "press red dots with both thumbs." The breakfast cereal that goes stale because the inner bag tears or won't reseal securely. The last bit of skin lotion or shampoo that's retrievable only by balancing the plastic bottle upside-down for a while.

These are only a few examples of packages that don't always do what you want them to do. They're annoying, result in costly waste and often lead shoppers to switch to another brand. A familiar packaging problem even inspired light-verse writer Richard Armour to this lament: "Shake and shake the ketchup bottle, none'll come and then a lot'll."

Companies routinely redesign package graphics, change ad campaigns or agencies and distribute millions of coupons to sell their products, but changes in "physical packaging" come much slower. As a result, marketers may be overlooking ways to satisfy customers and stay ahead of competitors.

"When you have products that are almost identical, physical packaging could make the difference," says Roy Parcels of Dixon & Parcels, a New York designer. "You don't have to be a major company to get a marketing edge by changing your packaging."

Because few consumers go so far as to complain to manufacturers about packaging and because a container design isn't tested as extensively as a TV commercial, dissatisfaction isn't readily apparent.

It is, however, surprisingly common. When A. C. Nielsen Co. polled 985 consumers to see if they had discarded or returned a product because of defective packaging within the previous 12 months, 46 percent said they had. The market research concern said the greatest number came from those with the largest families, highest incomes, and biggest grocery bills.

And fewer consumers are suffering silently. In 1979, Nielsen found that 54 percent of the people with packaging problems took no immediate action; three years later, only 39 percent did nothing. Of the rest, half discarded the product and one-third returned it to the retailer.

There often are longer-term effects, too. Although 50 percent of the packaging problems didn't affect brand loyalty, a significant number—19 percent—resulted in shoppers refusing to buy the same brand again. In another 24 percent of the cases, consumers said they'd "shop more cautiously" or "buy a different type of package."

Another survey conducted by the Package Designers Council, a trade group, asked consumers to list the package characteristics most important to them. Their responses, in order: storage life of the unused portion, the ability to recognize the contents by looking at the package graphics, resealability, and ease of storage.

What packages irk people the most? Consumer Network Inc., a Philadelphia research concern and packaging consultant, asked that question of its shoppers panel. Following are some of their choices, along with the percentage of the 145 respondents who indicated dissatisfaction:

Lunch meat	77%	Snack chips	53%
Bacon	76	Cookies	51
Flour	65	Detergents	50
Sugar	63	Fresh meat	50
Ice cream	57	Noodles	49

Lipstick	47%	Frozen seafood	40%
Nail polish	46	Nuts	39
Honey	44	Cooking oil	37
Crackers	44	Ketchup	34

Change is likely to be slow, though. The main reason is cost: A major package modification may require new molds, dies, and handling equipment. "A physical change is much more difficult to achieve than a graphic change," says Richard Gerstman, president of Gerstman & Meyers, a New York design firm. "It involves much more than changing a printing plate."

Improved materials also may be costlier. A cardboard canister with a plastic cap—the type used for Procter & Gamble's Pringles potato chips and Nabisco Brands' Planter's snack chips—keeps products fresh, prevents breakage of fragile chips and is easily resealed. Its cost, estimates Mr. Parcels: 15 cents for an eight-ounce container, compared with nine cents for a foil bag, seven cents for a metal-coated plastic bag and even less for a plain plastic bag.

Another obstacle is the long wait for new packaging machinery and supplies. "No fast-track brand manager is going to opt for the relatively slower payoff of innovative packaging changes," says Mona Doyle, president of Consumer Network.

Sometimes, though, what seems to be a bright idea turns out to be a dud, as Procter & Gamble apparently learned with its Wondra skin lotion. By putting a spigot cap on the bottom of the bottle, P&G had solved the problem of getting every drop of lotion out.

Consumers were unimpressed. Its package may not be wholly to blame, but Wondra's market share fell to about 6 percent from 8 percent within a year. When a competitor tested skin lotion in a conventional bottle against the Wondra design, it found that consumers just weren't comfortable modifying their lotioning motion: grab the lotion, flip open the cap and turn the bottle upside-down.

Putting Color
into Marketing

The Ritz cracker box celebrated a milestone in 1984: It turned 50. And like many fading beauties of that vintage, the box got a face lift. The new package is redder and trimmed with a thin gold band.

"We tried to make Ritz look ritzier," says John Lister, whose firm did the redesign for Nabisco Brands Inc. "We want it to speak to young, affluent consumers."

The colors of packages, logos, and signs have always been important in marketing consumer goods, but companies like Nabisco are taking color more seriously than ever. In the past, colors were chosen quite subjectively. The famous Campbell soup can, for example, was the inspiration of a company executive who liked the Cornell University football team's red and white uniforms.

But in this era of market segmentation with menthol, caffeine-free, sugar-free, and low-salt versions of many products, companies are paying consultants thousands of dollars for advice on which colors will stand out most on cluttered shelves and in advertising. Perception researchers flash slides of package displays, while a camera and computer track consumers' eye movements to detect what they see first.

"Color isn't the most important thing; it's the only thing," declares Alvin Schechter, a New York package designer. "Color goes immediately to the psyche and can be a direct sales stimulus."

Some new industries are just starting to use color strategically. Microsoft Corp., for example, is counting on zippy new crimson red and royal blue packages to help it compete in the crowded computer software market. The company's old forest green packages weren't very eye catching. What's more, color consultants note, green connotes frozen vegetables and chewing gum, not high tech. Says Patricia McGinnis, Microsoft's design director: "Packaging is where the software war may be won or lost."

But color affects food marketing even more because people taste with their eyes. When designers at Berni Corp. changed the background hue on Barrelhead Sugar-Free Root Beer cans to beige from blue, people swore it tasted more like old-fashioned root beer served in frosty mugs. No matter that the beverage itself remained exactly the same. Similarly, consumers ascribe a sweeter taste to orange drinks the darker the orange shade of the can or bottle.

It's difficult to correlate color with product sales. But Berni claims that when it changed Canada Dry's sugar-free ginger ale can to green and white from red, sales shot up more than 25 percent. The red can had sent a misleading cola message to consumers.

Changing package colors is harder than it looks. Consultant Thomas Paul says Campbell Soup Co. executives agonized before dumping the turquoise triangle on Swanson frozen dinners in 1984. "Turquoise is a dated '50's color," says Mr. Paul, "but the company felt it was too important to the brand identity to lose it. I reminded them that consumers no longer liked the old identity."

The diet Coke can seems like a simple enough color design: It has red lettering on a white backdrop, just the reverse of the regular Coke can. But Mr. Schechter, the package designer, spent six months and created more than 150 different cans before finding a winner. At first, he says, red on white looked too sterile and lacked taste appeal. Ultimately, the red letters were fattened and "a gray pinstripe" was added, resulting in what Mr. Schechter calls "an active, richer can." Coca-Cola Co. executives thought Mr. Schechter was a heretic when he suggested at one point a blue can, the trademark of arch-enemy PepsiCo Inc.

Courtesy The Schechter Group

Consumer-product companies often try originality to get attention. The successful Mrs. Fields cookie-store chain chose red for its stores, even though brown and tan suggest cookies and chocolate better. "It was a risky gamble not looking like grandma's kitchen," says Michael Purvis, senior vice president of S&O Consultants Inc. "But most cookie purchases are made on impulse by young women, and we felt they would respond to a more stylish look."

Sometimes, though, marketers are bound by a traditional color vocabulary that cues consumers to the product being sold. It's unwise to sell whole milk in anything but a red carton or to stray from blue labels for club soda. And thanks to McDonald's, many consumers don't believe a restaurant serves fast food if its signs don't have at least a smidgen of red and yellow.

Although not as faddish as fashion colors, package colors can be fickle, too. White is losing popularity even though it's a symbol of purity. That's partly because companies don't want brand-name goods to be confused with the generic products that come in plain white wrappers. Black, in contrast, is coming on strong after years of being taboo because of its funereal symbolism. Minute Maid orange juice was a pioneer; now black is turning up on cigarette packs, Heinz vinegar bottles, and frozen Armour Dinner Classics to suggest quality and elegance.

Legally, companies can't claim exclusive rights to a color, but sometimes they can stop competitors from mimicking a certain combination of colors or a color used along with a specific design. Eastman Kodak Co. has successfully prevented companies from copying its yellow, black and red "trade dress," but courts have refused to extend such protection to the striped Life Savers wrapper and Campbell soup can. Says trademark attorney Jerome Gilson: "The courts' view is that there are only so many colors in the rainbow. They tend to limit the use of color only when the public might be confused about what brand they're buying."

'800' Numbers: Staying Close to Customers

When gizzards and livers were dropped from the Kentucky Fried Chicken menu, disappointed customers in Louisville didn't have to stew in silence. They could air their gripes on a toll-free telephone hot line the chicken chain is testing there.

Likewise, Avis patrons with complaints about rental cars now have a number to call for help. Dishwasher on the fritz? Phone General Electric, whose customer-service staff also can answer questions about GE jet engines or the composers of music in GE television commercials.

Those three companies are among the latest to join a growing list of marketers with "800" phone lines for their customers. Pioneered several years ago by Whirlpool, Polaroid, Clairol, and Procter & Gamble, the toll-free services have spread rapidly in the past year.

Among those that have introduced or are testing them: Drackett, Pillsbury, General Mills, Buick, Sony, Burroughs, Coleco, Atari, Kraft, and General Foods.

"Major companies, including GE, have become somewhat faceless," says Powell Taylor, manager of GE's Answer Center, which expected 1.5 million calls in 1983. "We're trying to put a face on the company and make a large company like a small one."

Answering a complaint or inquiry costs roughly $3 for a three-minute phone conversation. Often that's more than the cost of the product itself and several times the profit the manufacturer makes from the sale. The payoff comes in happier customers.

"Companies no longer are looking at complaints as just a nuisance," says John Goodman, president of Technical Assistance Research Programs Inc., a customer-service consultant. "By aggressively soliciting them, you can improve brand loyalty."

Many companies have overlooked the cost of alienating consumers, says Mr. Goodman. His company's studies show that only about 4 percent of dissatisfied customers complain to a manufacturer. Instead they usually stop buying the product and also bad-mouth it to 9 or 10 other people.

In contrast, complaints that are resolved quickly lead to repeat purchases in 95 percent of the cases involving inexpensive items and 82 percent of those involving products that cost at least $100. General Electric says its typical satisfied caller passes the word to five other people within 10 days.

In addition to keeping buyers loyal, the toll-free lines help producers stay closer to consumers. Procter & Gamble learned of faulty bottle caps through telephone complaints, and Polaroid has picked up several ideas for improvements to its cameras and film. Johnson & Johnson found its 800 number useful when news of toxic-shock syndrome (the company makes O.B. tampons) hit. In 1982 J&J answered more than 425,000 calls about Tylenol poisonings.

For such companies as Whirlpool, GE, and Polaroid, hot lines also reduce warranty costs as routine problems are handled by phone. Answering a telephone call also costs one half to one third as much as responding to a letter.

Companies that have started hot lines say their volume of mail doesn't drop, though. The net result is a sharp increase in the number of contacts companies have with consumers. In 1977, before it started printing 800 numbers on all its packages, P&G heard from about 160,000 people a year. In 1982 the company received 300,000 letters and the same number of calls (including 54,000 calls asking about rumors that devil worshippers ran P&G).

In the future, customer-service specialists say, consumers

may come to expect toll-free complaint lines; marketers that don't offer them may be at a competitive disadvantage. Already 1 adult in 11 has used a toll-free number to register a complaint, says R. H. Bruskin Associates, a market-survey company. Its recent poll of 1,007 adults also found that 28 percent had used an 800 number to ask for information about a product.

Indeed, when some people can't find an 800 number on a package, they call directory assistance for one. Drackett, which makes Windex, Drano, and other household products, says it began receiving calls on its three-month-old line before the number was included on the company's products.

Not all 800 lines have been successful. American Motors scrapped its in 1977 after five years, instead telling customers to call dealers or regional offices. ITT Continental Baking gave up on a hot-line experiment because there were too few calls. Kellogg stopped testing a toll-free number on Sugar Frosted Flakes after receiving hundreds of calls from children asking to speak to Tony the Tiger.

A hot line also can backfire if poorly planned. Callers quickly become irritated with busy signals, long waits on hold, or operators who can't answer routine questions. To avoid such problems, many companies are testing lines carefully and phasing them in slowly.

Training also is important. Clairol gives its telephone representatives 50 hours of classroom instruction. GE uses techniques borrowed from Disney World to teach employees to deal with the public; answers to questions about GE's 8,500 products come from computer terminals stocked with 500,000 pieces of data.

Surprisingly, only a minority of calls are actual complaints. P&G classifies one third of its calls as such; Clairol, 15 percent, and GE, 8 percent. Even irate customers frequently compliment the companies for providing human contact. As one complainer told Pillsbury: "Although I'm mad at the packaging, I think a company really cares about its customers if it puts an 800 number on the can."

Making Coupons Count

Clorox Co. is getting pickier about who receives cents-off coupons for its Hidden Valley Ranch salad dressing. If you happen to be a Californian who buys lettuce and tomatoes, then you might just be eligible for one next time you pass through a supermarket checkout line. You also might be a coupon candidate if you purchase Kraft or Seven Seas dressings.

Like a growing number of packaged-goods marketers and retailers, Clorox wants to make smarter use of its coupons. Rather than simply distribute them haphazardly through newspaper inserts, Clorox is targeting coupons to prime sales prospects, thanks to some new technology. Several Los Angeles area stores are installing computerized printers that automatically spit out coupons at the cash register when certain products pass over the scanner.

"Companies are wasting a lot of money distributing coupons for diapers and cat food to homes without any babies or pets," says Michael O'Brien, president of Catalina Marketing Corp., which developed the checkout coupon system. Catalina has matched buyers of baby food with coupons for Huggies diapers and buyers of kitty litter with coupons for Tender Vittles.

Companies are particularly concerned about effectiveness these days because the volume of coupons is surging wildly. A. C. Nielsen estimated that the number of coupons distributed rose 14 percent to 163.2 billion in 1984, while the redemption rate merely held steady at about 4 percent. Some experts predict a flood of 375 billion coupons by 1989. "Coupon clutter is a monster that can terrorize a promotion budget," says Ed Meyer, director of promotion services at Dancer Fitzgerald Sample, an ad agency.

The popular free-standing inserts in Sunday newspapers best exemplify the clutter problem. At one time, a company could be guaranteed that it would be the only advertiser of, say, cereal or soft drinks, on a particular Sunday. But later it became common for three or four of the inserts to tumble out when a consumer opened the Sunday paper.

"This lack of exclusivity raises many questions in manufacturers' minds," says James Pyles, a manager of sales promotion at Miles Laboratories. "I lose my edge if my vitamin coupon appears along with two or three others." Miles is considering several alternatives to newspapers; already it is attaching more "instant coupons" to packages.

To prevent defections from their Sunday inserts, coupon companies are trying to make a bigger splash. Product Movers advertised a forthcoming insert on TV in Chicago, for example, and lined up San Francisco 49ers' quarterback Joe Montana to plug a summer-barbecue coupon promotion.

But such ploys aren't stopping companies from experimenting. In several regions of the country, electronic coupon dispensers are being tested near supermarket entrances. Some companies believe their coupons have greater impact if they are handed out when people have shopping lists in hand. They figure that many people don't want to waste time clipping coupons from newspapers, and that others forget to bring them from home.

For instance, at yellow kiosks in some New England stores, consumers punch in an ID number they have received in the mail and get a packet of eight or so coupons each week. Promoters of that system claim a redemption rate of about 12 percent, triple that of many newspaper coupons. Other in-store machines allow people to choose only the coupons they really want. "But with those systems, you may end up rewarding too many people who would have bought your product anyway," says Tom McClure, promotions director for Beatrice Cos.' U.S. food operations.

Indeed, companies are especially hungry for techniques to steal more business from competitors. Marketers believe 65 percent to 85 percent of their coupons are redeemed by current customers. So, to make sure coupons land in the mailboxes of competitive brand users, several specialized market research firms have sprung up. They survey households by phone or printed questionnaires to determine favorite brands, then send out coupons for other brands. Computerized Marketing Technologies Inc. tailors the value of its coupons to how often a household buys certain products and even asks consumers about their hobbies. "We might send out a coupon saying that this brand of coffee would be great for your next camping trip," says Gary Blau, a partner in the firm. "We want to create a personalized dialogue with each household."

Of course, precise targeting is expensive. CSI Tele-Marketing Inc. says the average cost per coupon redeemed in its program is about $1, compared with 62 cents for a Sunday newspaper insert. But it adds that its cost per new user of a brand is also $1, versus $4.77 for Sunday papers.

One drawback has been CSI's limited reach. "It's a costly program that has been confined to the Northeast and Florida," says Robert Hall, promotion operations manager at Lever Brothers. "When you're a national company, you have trouble justifying such a service." CSI plans to expand to Southern California, Detroit, and Pittsburgh.

Despite geographical constraints, though, Mr. Hall remains high on target marketing of coupons. He notes that CSI helped his detergents make inroads against such archrivals as Procter & Gamble Co. "That," he says, "is the joy of the program."

Warranties: Guaranteeing Satisfaction

Warranties don't attract customers. That, at least, is the conventional wisdom among marketers and a reason why product guarantees have often been ignored as a potential sales tool. Ask any marketing executive when was the last time his company reviewed its warranty policies; more often than not, the answer will be a shrug. Warranties, the official will probably add, don't generate that much excitement in the market.

There's plenty of evidence to support that view. In survey after survey, consumers almost always rank warranties near the bottom of their list of purchase considerations. A recent study by a major appliance manufacturer found that fewer than 7 percent of its customers bought a product because of the guarantee that accompanied it.

Still, for a variety of reasons, many companies in recent years have taken a second look at their warranties—some because they were searching for an alternative to price competition, others because they wanted to find ways to satisfy increasingly critical customers. In the process, many of them have discovered hidden advantages in aggressively using warranties as part of their marketing strategies.

Holiday Inns Inc. found that offering a money-back guarantee on accommodations not only helped gain it a second chance with unhappy customers but also helped improve its service. "Before we started offering the guarantee there was a good chance someone might leave one of our hotels mad without ever telling us what was wrong," says Douglas Bell, vice president of system marketing. "That probably meant we'd lose them forever as customers."

Now, he says, guests seem more willing to express unhappiness if something is amiss. "That at least gives us a chance to do something about it." Mr. Bell adds that since Holiday Inns began advertising the guarantee program nationwide early last year, the evaluation forms it distributes to its guests have grown increasingly positive. At the same time, he says, the hotel chain has had to pay refunds to only a tiny fraction of its customers. "It's been a good success for us," Mr. Bell concludes.

An attractive or unusual warranty can also give a company an advantage in the market without having to resort to lowering its prices, an action that is both expensive and often easily matched by competitors. Mainly for that reason, Republic Airlines earlier this year offered travelers to Florida and Southern California a free round-trip ticket if they traveled on the airline only to have it rain during most of their vacation. "The last thing we wanted to do was get into another price war," says a Republic official. "The guarantee program gave us a relatively inexpensive alternative."

Some marketing experts believe the expanded and more creative use of warranties may eventually play an important role in a trend toward emphasizing customer satisfaction and service in marketing. "It's no longer good enough for companies to tell customers they make the perfect product," says John Goodman, president of a Washington, D.C., marketing consulting firm. "Customers don't want to hear that anymore. What they want to know is that the company is prepared to stand by its product."

One sign that customers may be more interested in warranties than some surveys show is the booming business in extended warranties sold separately by retailers. At Highland Appliance, a Detroit chain, officials say 30 percent of all customers now purchase long-term service contracts. Demand for the extended warranties tends to be much higher on more fragile appliances such as television sets and dishwashers, and lower on sturdier goods such as refrigerators and gas ranges, Highland officials say.

Nevertheless, some companies shy away from warranties because they find it difficult to measure the precise advantages against the projected expense. The Cadillac division of General Motors Corp. decided to offer a longer-than-usual warranty on its new full-size cars, but only after spending more than three years researching customer interest in such guarantees. "It was still a seat-of-the-pants decision," says William Lewellen, Cadillac's assistant general sales manager. "The research gets so complicated it's hard to draw conclusions."

Another drawback is the potential for a warranty to backfire if something goes wrong with the product that either specifically isn't covered under the guarantee or is due to customer negligence. In either case the buyer can feel cheated if the company refuses to fix it.

To avoid that, Cadillac gives customers a cassette tape that explains the warranty and maintenance schedule to buyers of its cars. Similarly, Armstrong World Industries prints an "800" toll-free telephone number on the surface of its linoleum floor coverings. When consumers call the number to find out how to get the marking off their new floor, a company representative explains how and also how the floor should be cleaned in the future to keep it under warranty.

A final reason for offering a warranty is to promote obligations to the consumer that are required anyway under contract law. Automakers, for instance, presumably could be required to make repairs on defective cars under "implied" warranties even if they didn't offer their own formal warranty. And it may sound nice when a direct-mail marketer offers guaranteed delivery within six weeks, but the fact is that, even if the company didn't make the offer, it could be held to the delivery time under the law.

Taking Broadway
on the Road

Never mind that "The Real Thing" swept the 1984 Tony awards for excellence in the theater. When the play hits San Antonio, Dallas, and New Orleans, the major promotion will have little to say about the quality of the writing and acting.

The producers of the road version will try to spark interest in the play through a diamond-ring sweepstakes in which people go to jewelry stores and try to pick the real gem over a fake. "The contest will say that people can tell their love they're 'the real thing' with a real diamond," says Scott Zeiger, marketing director of the theatrical subsidiary of Pace Management Corp., a promoter of rock concerts, tractor pulls, and more recently, plays.

Even Pace concedes that the diamond ploy seems hokey and undignified for a critically acclaimed drama, but such gimmicks are helping hawk tickets to more and more Broadway plays when they go on tour. Consider: "Pump Boys and Dinettes" was plugged on waiters' aprons in a Nashville, Tenn., restaurant; discount ticket offers on sugar-free Dr Pepper cans helped make "Sophisticated Ladies" a hit in Houston; "Torch Song Trilogy" was targeted to Kansas City gays through a San Francisco vacation promotion; and "My One and Only" was advertised on grocery bags in Texas. "We'll go on the side of a milk carton," Mr. Zeiger says. "We're not proud."

In East Coast cities, producers typically need only advertise in newspapers and on radio and TV. But promoters say more inventive marketing is called for to cultivate some up-and-coming theater cities in the Sun Belt.

Road shows are becoming more expensive to do. Producers estimate the cost of assembling a musical to go on the road at $1.5 million to $3 million. That doesn't include salaries and transportation costs between cities.

Such expenses make it more critical that producers pack the house, and to do that in some cities they say they must overcome naiveté about the theater. "The extra exposure from promotional tie-ins with the local media and other businesses can mean the difference between the life or death of a show," says Zev Buffman, a Broadway producer and operator of theaters. "It helps draw first-time playgoers who don't even know how to go about buying a ticket. I hear some people in Southern cities say they're afraid to sit too close to the stage because all they can relate to is the movies."

Pace Management also contends with theater patrons who would rather see "South Pacific" for the tenth time than a new production of, say, "Hurlyburly." But, says Allen Becker, president of Pace, "we figure if we can force them into the theater by hyping a play, they might like it enough to become a subscriber."

What Pace attempts to do is involve newspapers, radio and TV stations, hotels, banks, airlines, and retailers so the play gets maximum publicity, whether in sweepstakes ads or inserts in bank statements and department store bills. Sponsors in return are listed in the playbill, in advertisements for the show, and occasionally even on the marquee. Allied Bank in Houston credits its sponsorship of a whole series of plays with attracting hundreds of thousands of dollars in deposits. "But mostly it just got our name out to an upscale audience," says chairman Wayne Lapham.

Pace figures it may spend only $35,000 of its money to advertise a show but will end up with more than $150,000 of media exposure through cross-promotions. For example, "Jerry's Girls" played Houston the summer of 1984 and was marketed with a contest that included tickets donated by

Courtesy of Pace Management Corp.

Eastern Airlines, rooms courtesy of Hyatt Regency hotels, gifts from Foley's department store, and free ads in the local media. The total value of the prizes and free advertising was about $70,000.

In Nashville, it took a real dream coat to make "Joseph and the Amazing Technicolor Dreamcoat" a success. Pace teamed up with the Cain-Sloan department store and a local TV station and offered a $7,500 fur coat. " 'Joseph' was a tough sell because it didn't have a name star," says Terry McDonald, a vice president at Cain-Sloan. "We had to transform the show into a media event." The hostess of the local "PM Magazine" program modeled the coat in ads, and actors from the play chose the winner on the evening news show. As it turned out, Pace says, it grossed about $300,000 on "Joseph." The break-even figure was only about $200,000.

Some purists find such promotions distasteful. In some of the ads, they note, it's hard to pick out the play's name for all the commercial logos surrounding it. "That's not our style," says Arthur Rubin, vice president and general manager of the Nederlander Organization, which promotes plays merely by advertising subscriptions and individual shows in newspapers and on TV. But, he adds, "I wouldn't frown too much on a gimmick that helps sell tickets, as long as it's not a fraud."

While honest, not all of Pace's promotions are winners. In Dallas, the company had trouble finding anyone to affiliate with. The problem: the play, "Night Mother," concerns a woman planning to commit suicide. So, instead of a razzle-dazzle giveaway, Pace persuaded two local TV stations to use some of their unsold inventory of commercial time to push the play. In return, they were to receive a cut of the profits.

The only snag was that "Night Mother" still failed to break even. Says Mr. Zeiger of Pace: "We blamed the bad weather in Dallas. We'd never say our promotions didn't work."

No Rest for
the Ad-Weary

Supermarkets may already seem like zoos with all their promotional displays, but consumers haven't seen anything yet. For a preview of what your friendly neighborhood store might be like soon, picture this: advertisements plastered on all the shopping carts and aisle directories, giant clocks covered with ads and promotional messages rolling by on video monitors mounted throughout the store.

When you glance down at the "electronic handle" of the shopping cart, an ad will flash. And every few minutes, you will be jolted to attention by a booming commercial on the store's public-address system.

Those are just the varieties of in-store advertising already being tested. Some store managers claim that an entrepreneur also has been trying to peddle floor tiles carrying advertising. For a "Star Trek" effect, the Point-of-Purchase Advertising Institute predicts that laser images of famous personalities will "beam down" from store ceilings to greet customers and pitch products.

Clearly, consumer-product companies are hustling more than ever to snare customers at the point of sale, where research indicates two thirds of buying decisions are made. Marketers are buying more advertising space within stores partly because of their disillusionment with the high cost and debatable impact of traditional television and print ads. It isn't as easy, for example, to communicate with female shoppers now that fewer sit at home watching daytime programs. But "in-store ads constantly remind people of our products as they wheel their carts down the aisles," says Jay Sloofman, a marketing manager for Pepsi-Cola.

In-store ads also appeal to companies that can't negotiate as much promotional display space from store managers as marketing heavyweights like General Foods Corp. can. "The retail trade is reluctant to let us put a lot of our own point-of-sale materials on shelves," says William Johnson, a marketing vice president at H. J. Heinz Co. So, it hypes its ketchup and Weight Watchers products on shopping carts.

Carts are probably the most entrenched vehicle for in-store advertising. Actmedia Inc. claims it is affixing ads to nearly two million carts in 7,700 stores, giving it broader reach than even commercials during Super Bowl telecasts. Van Wagner Communications Inc., meantime, says it expects to have nearly 6,000 of its so-called superclocks with ads hanging in stores by year-end.

But both companies concede that it isn't easy to convince stores of the merits of their ad programs. Many store managers still remember all too well the TV sets that some promoters persuaded them to place over checkout counters several years ago. The premise: While shoppers wait to pay their bills, they are a captive audience for commercials. But the TV sets flopped because the ads appeared too late, after people had finished shopping. "Consumers also don't want to be distracted," says Sheldon Sosna, publisher of Supermarket Advertising Newsletter. "Buying groceries is a very focused experience. Women are trying hard to get the best values by reading prices and ingredient labels, not ads."

Although they would receive some of the advertising revenue, a few retailers reject ads to keep their stores from looking junky. One purist is Giant Food Inc. in the Washington, D.C., area. Says Terry Gans, a vice president there: "We have worked hard to make shopping pleasurable by keeping aisles wide and stores clean. We don't want to risk losing even a few customers because of intrusive ads."

Consumer-product manufacturers also have some qualms about advertising in stores. The main question nagging them is whether people really notice clocks, shopping-cart ads, and video-display screens. Van Wagner, for example, boasts that its superclock ads increased sales of Campbell Soup Co.'s Le Menu frozen dinners by 25 percent in some Boston-area stores. But Campbell remains unconvinced of the value. "We're very interested in doing something that's affordable and produces sales results," a Campbell executive says, "but it's expensive when you consider the thousands of stores we're in." Van Wagner says it charges $230 per store for a month of exposure on its clocks.

Several companies are pushing in-store broadcast advertising to capitalize on marketers' concerns that customers ignore their printed ads. "People will listen to a voice in the sky, especially if it's telling them what's on sale," says Ike Egan, executive director of In-Store Satellite Network. His company installs satellite dishes at stores and then transmits commercials from Salt Lake City.

Instore Broadcast Advertising Inc., which got its start in Buffalo, New York, in 1972, makes sure people pay attention by raising the volume when ads interrupt the background music. To try to keep the irritation level low, the company peppers its broadcasts with recipes and household hints.

Instore seemed to help Sealtest ice cream sales with commercials trumpeting the product as having "that ice cream parlor taste." The result: Sales rose 7.2 percent in Buffalo stores that carried the broadcast, compared with gains of only 1.5 percent in control stores. In Rochester, New York, though, the commercials couldn't keep Sealtest sales from falling. The drop was 22.4 percent in test stores, slightly less than the 26.1 percent in control stores.

An In-Store Ad
Scheme Flops

For a man watching a $1.6 million investment go sour, Dean Rollings is surprisingly philosophical.

"I've gotten a slice of life that's quite unique," he says, kneading his fingers as he sits in his Madison Avenue office. "How many people get this experience? I'm thankful for it."

Kenneth Moss shares that it's-only-money attitude about the enterprise, which once was worth $18.7 million to him but yielded only $30,000 when he sold out in early 1982. Mr. Moss is no stranger to setbacks, having lost almost $2 million on a charter airline venture and having spent 78 days in jail for involuntary manslaughter.

They both thought they had found a bright idea for a new advertising medium: On-Line Media Inc. To take advantage of supermarket shoppers trapped in checkout lines, the company would mount closed-circuit television monitors over cash registers and play a 6½-minute reel of silent commercials.

That plan—which, Mr. Moss confides, occurred to him late one night in 1977, just after making love—has come to naught. On-Line is flat broke, far from its goal of capturing one third of the nation's 30,000 largest supermarkets. Its shares, which once sold for $6.25 each, now are worth only a few cents. Mr. Rollings, who owns nearly half the company's shares, spends his days hunting for a buyer.

On-Line did have its heyday, however brief. Glowing reports came from *Newsweek*, the *New York Times*, the *Los*

Angeles Times, an NBC-TV station in Chicago, and others. An executive at J. Walter Thompson Co., the big advertising agency, predicted that the company might pull in as much as $380 million a year in revenue. A book titled "How to Cash In on the Coming Stock Market Boom!" listed On-Line as a hot stock for the 1980s.

"It may be just fantasy," says Mr. Moss, "but I believe it could have been done if we had the money." Adds Mr. Rollings: "If it were successful, it would have been bigger than CBS, NBC or ABC."

To understand On-Line's history, it is important to know the two men who ran it at various times.

Mr. Moss, a 39-year-old New Yorker, is the sort of go-getter who often comes up with offbeat ideas. At 21, he was a stockbroker. At 25, he co-founded a company that made paper thermometers. At 27, he sold his stake in it for nearly $2 million.

Mr. Moss's next idea was Freelandia Air Travel Club, a discount travel venture that got a lot of publicity, including an appearance by Mr. Moss on the "Tonight" show. But Freelandia failed in 1975, and Mr. Moss's small fortune was wiped out.

A month later he faced an even bigger problem. A rock musician overdosed on drugs at a party at Mr. Moss's Los Angeles home and later died. Mr. Moss went to prison after pleading guilty to involuntary manslaughter—the drugs were taken at his home but he denied involvement in the drug-taking and noted that the musician died after leaving the house.

Mr. Rollings, in contrast, was the product of the laid-back, introspective cultures of Colorado and California. Now 37, he has been a champion skier, and he spent nine years in a family furniture business. Since 1973, though, his main interest has been the Rolf Institute of Structural Integration, which promotes a painful form of massage known as Rolfing. Mr. Rollings also believes that his investments—and those of his wife, a Texas oil heiress—should serve social purposes.

At first, he says, "I had reservations about bringing more

junk into the environment." Then he mellowed to the notion, agreeing to be one of the five investors who bankrolled Mr. Moss with $10,000 apiece in September 1977.

"I felt it was a great contribution to society," says Mr. Rollings. "This is taking advertising to the marketplace, where it belongs. I don't want to know about toilet paper when I'm home watching TV."

Initially, Mr. Rollings was a silent investor. Mr. Moss spent most of the next two years shaping his idea and working at a New York brokerage firm to make some money and renew his contacts on Wall Street.

In late 1979, the pace picked up as Mr. Moss began working full-time to advance On-Line. He raised $125,000 from private investors and another $750,000 by selling shares to the public. N.W. Ayer Inc., a New York ad agency, signed on to lend its advice and its well-regarded name. A handsome suite of Madison Avenue offices was leased for $52,637 a year.

In May 1980, On-Line put its first monitors in two suburban New Jersey A&P supermarkets. Tests by a research firm found that only 6 percent of the shoppers objected to the ads; 50 percent liked them and the rest were indifferent.

More than 30 big-name advertisers agreed to participate while On-Line wasn't yet charging them to run their plugs. Ira Kuhlik, a New York commodity trader, invested $450,000. John Muir & Co., a now-defunct brokerage house, was retained to prepare a public offering of 1 million On-Line shares.

On-Line expanded to 25 supermarkets in New York, Chicago, and Los Angeles. Another research study showed that advertised brands had sales increases of 15 percent and more.

But funds were running out rapidly. Mr. Moss turned to Mr. Rollings and his wife, Laurie, and they agreed to lend the company $400,000 in November 1980. Plans for the public offering fell through, however, and a pitch to Mr. Kuhlik for another $1 million was unsuccessful. Finally, the Rollings purchased $1 million of On-Line shares, allowing the company to pay its debts to the couple and to stay alive.

In July 1981, full-scale operations began, with advertisers paying $7,000 for a 10-second spot, less for a three-second or five-second ad. Twenty products were advertised in a total of 119 seconds on a 6½-minute loop. The rest of the time was filled with household hints ("Bacon won't curl if you dip the strip in warm water before frying") and trivia ("What was the name of Babe Ruth's baseball bat?" Answer: "Black Betsy"). The number of participating stores grew to 60.

But On-Line only pulled in $189,250 in revenue through August 1981. Mrs. Rollings lent yet another $100,000. She and her husband also left their lakeside cabin in Aspen, Colorado, and moved to Manhattan. "The people and the access to the pulse of business are here," says Mr. Rollings.

So was his investment and, as he took a more active interest in it, tension with Mr. Moss increased. In November, Mr. Moss resigned as chairman and Mr. Rollings took over.

He figured he needed $60 million to install a system that would reach 32 million shoppers a week in 12 major cities. On-Line tried to sell "affiliateships," similar to franchises, in various cities; only one was sold, in Rochester, New York. Mr. Rollings sought money from Wall Street investment firms and major media companies, including Warner Communications Inc.

There were no takers. In January 1982, a $457,000 line of credit from Barclay's Bank was canceled. The Rollings lent On-line $520,000 to keep its doors open.

According to its latest financial statement of May 31, On-Line revenue has totaled only $251,322 in the company's lifetime; its total loss is $3.5 million and its working-capital deficit is $1.5 million. Mr. Rollings continues to hope for a buyer or investor who might be interested in On-Line's concept, its $3.5 million tax loss or its listing as a publicly traded stock.

The Rollings aren't bitter, though. "We've gleaned every bit of the experience and are using it creatively," says Mrs. Rollings. Adds her husband: "This was my price of entry into New York City's world of business." He talks eagerly about other ventures: mobile cancer-detection laboratories, computerized libraries, dosimeters to measure household radiation, and an instrument to warn dolphins about approaching tuna fishermen.

Mr. Moss, who recently returned from a lengthy vacation in California and the Caribbean, also is plotting his next projects. There is a land deal in Jamaica, multi-language magazines for travelers and coat hangers that adjust to fit different-sized men's suits.

Pulling out a newspaper listing of money-market funds, he explains his latest "flash." Unlike many other investments, they aren't insured. Why not offer money-fund insurance? "The numbers are big enough," he says excitedly. "There's a real need. I perceive that it would be easy."

6

Retailing and Distribution

Stores Gain the
Upper Hand

Procter & Gamble Co. considers itself a friend to the retailer. By redesigning the bottle for its Ivory shampoo from a teardrop shape to a tall cylinder, for example, the company estimates that it saves stores 29 cents a case in handling and storage costs. Even better was the move to repackage Pringle's potato chips in a "super-size" can rather than sell two smaller cans wrapped in plastic that hog more shelf space. The cost savings on the chips: 93 cents a case.

But the relationship wasn't always so pleasant. A former P&G manager recalls that for many years the company had a reputation for being arrogant and heavy-handed. "Retailers sometimes felt new products were being jammed down their throats," he says. "But P&G is trying much harder to be diplomatic and improve its relations with the retail trade."

So are other packaged-goods companies as the scrapping for shelf space in supermarkets and drug stores intensifies. Once viewed as funnels for delivering new products to consumers, retailers now act more as filters. They screen out many copycat products, forcing manufacturers to think twice before investing millions of dollars to launch a new item. "Retail buyers are fully aware of the high rate of new-product failure and the appalling oversell that frequently accompanies the biggest dogs," says Joseph Smith, president of Oxtoby-Smith Inc., a market-research firm. "A salesperson's theme today needs to be 'Let me help you' rather than 'Let me sell you.'"

To ingratiate itself with supermarket managers, General Foods Corp. recently developed computer software that measures product turnover and could help boost retail profits. It is also experimenting with "computer-to-computer" placement of orders, which would allow stores to keep less inventory on hand. Some companies are shipping pre-assembled product displays, cutting the setup time in half. And whenever possible, the Jimmy Dean Meat Co. division of Sara Lee Corp. tailors its sausage promotions to fit local retailers' needs. For example, it might use advertising and refund offers rather than cents-off coupons in a city where stores are in the midst of a coupon war.

"Retailers used to be the monkey in the middle," says John Rockwell, a senior vice president at Booz-Allen & Hamilton Inc. "But they are becoming much more informed and sophisticated." Supermarket and drugstore chains are hiring more buyers and managers with college degrees in business and finance. Through computers and the automated scanners at checkout counters, they also can track the sales and profitability of individual products, as well as measure the effectiveness of consumer promotions. Dan Valentine, director of marketing services at Coca-Cola Co.'s food division, notes that stores now can tell him precisely how much a 10 percent price reduction on Hi-C drinks increases their sales.

Buyers today also are more apt to scrutinize test-market data to judge whether a new product will actually increase their sales or merely cannibalize other brands in the store. "Besides telling us sales were terrific in Des Moines, many salesmen weren't offering us any hard data unless we sent them back to their research departments for it," complains Robert Wunderle, an economist at Supermarkets General Corp.

Some retailers are demanding heftier up-front payments to cover the costs and risk of giving a new product a try. Packaged-goods companies say such so-called listing fees are especially common in Canada and some European countries. To introduce a new product nationally in Canada, for example, companies may spend $200,000 to $500,000 simply to get shelf space and a spot in newspaper advertising, according to a survey by Marketing Intelligence Service of Naples, New York.

"Seven chains control about 75 percent of the business in Canada, and they are using their power to extract more money from us," says Robert Hawthorne, senior vice president of marketing at General Mills Inc.'s Canadian subsidiary. "So, we're very careful that we have a good new product that will last a long time." Only after much pre-testing did General Mills roll out Pro-Stars, Canada's first breakfast cereal containing NutraSweet artificial sweetener instead of sugar.

All the muscle-flexing by retailers should result in a wave of new *and* better products, Marketing Intelligence Service predicts. It surveyed large consumer-product companies and found increasing emphasis on new products that are truly innovative and satisfy a consumer craving. Some companies are developing better products by looking to the packaging and delivery system, rather than holding out for a big technological breakthrough. Marketing consultants, for example, cite the new d-Con bug killer in a marking-pen style container, Aqua-fresh toothpaste in a see-through pump, and Warner-Lambert's Mediquell chewy cough squares that are advertised as a dose of cough syrup without the spoon.

Sara Lee is finding strong retail acceptance for its fudge brownies without icing and frozen croissant sandwiches stuffed with ham, chicken, broccoli, and other ingredients. "A new cake flavor would be a much tougher sell," says Thomas MacLeod, president of Kitchens of Sara Lee. "But our lunch and dinner croissants address retailers' need to fight the trend toward eating out in restaurants, and the new brownies meet consumers' desire for a quality snack they can eat on the run."

Retailers Target
Low-Income Shoppers

Dolores Barich is the kind of customer most retailers hate. She lives on a monthly $175 alimony payment, food stamps, and rent from a boarder in her Youngstown, Ohio, home. And when she has enough money to shop, a big purchase is a $10 polyester blouse.

But Cal Turner, Jr., loves customers like Mrs. Barich. As president of Dollar General Corp., he has earned millions by selling most of the chain's merchandise to low-income shoppers for under $10 an item. "As my dad says, 'the retailer who has the lowest prices on the basics will have to beat the customers away with baseball bats,'" says Mr. Turner, quoting the company's founder and chairman.

In recent years, many retailers have abandoned poor shoppers to pursue more affluent ones. The market they have left behind is relatively small in dollar terms. Combined sales of Dollar General, Family Dollar Stores Inc., and Stuarts Department Stores Inc.—chains that primarily target lower-income shoppers—account for only about 4 percent of K mart Corp.'s annual revenue. But for these retailers and the others that continue to sell to low-income customers, the departure of competitors has meant rapid growth.

Primarily located in rural and inner-city areas, the merchants to the poor maintain a tight rein on expenses, sell large amounts of basic products at very low prices and have a keen sense of their customers' shopping habits.

Dollar General, for example, is based in Scottsville, Kentucky, and operates most of its 1,300 stores in tiny Sun Belt communities such as Horse Cave, Kentucky. The stores are small (you could fit about 10 in a 60,000-square-foot K mart), and they are stocked mostly with clothing and household items, including lots of irregulars and factory overruns. To keep labor costs down, each is typically operated by only three employees. (There would be fewer, a store manager contends, but someone has to watch the cash register while the others unload delivery trucks.)

Other chains' formats differ. The Matthews, North Carolina-based Family Dollar, which expects to operate 1,000 stores by the end of the year, eschews irregular garments, though it is like Dollar General in other ways. The store size and product selection at Needham Heights, Massachusetts-based Stuarts Department Stores recall a traditional discount outlet. At Stuarts, for example, shoppers can even buy pricey items like food processors. And secondhand stores, such as those run by the Salvation Army and other not-for-profit groups, offer lower-income shoppers everything from used T-shirts and appliances to month-old issues of Time magazine.

Low-income shoppers are attractive because "there are so many of them," says Leo Shapiro, a Chicago consumer researcher. According to the latest federal government figures, 36 percent of the nation's households earn less than $15,000. "Collectively they have a substantial amount of income," Mr. Shapiro says.

Earnings growth reflects that. Over the past five years, Dollar General's annual profit increase has averaged 37 percent, far out-pacing the discount-industry average of about 18 percent. Family Dollar's profit rose at an annual rate of 30 percent from fiscal 1980 through fiscal 1984, ended Aug. 31, and the chain reported fiscal 1984 sales of $340.9 million. Meanwhile, Stuarts' five-year profit growth averaged 51 percent a year, and sales exceeded $74 million in fiscal 1985, ended Feb. 2.

Having few competitors has helped. Once, the low-income shopper was served gladly by big mass merchants like

K mart and J. C. Penney. But with fewer places to expand, these chains had to increase earnings and sales at existing outlets. Their solution was to remodel their stores and add more expensive merchandise in hopes of attracting affluent shoppers. They also stopped carrying some low-priced products. "I don't want the moderate- and upper-income shoppers," says Paul Cammerano, the chief executive officer of Stuarts. "They have more places to shop than they know what to do with."

At the same time, the economic downturn in the early 1980s led the middle class to try shopping at the low-income chains. "We weren't supposed to do particularly well here, but the middle class has slipped three or four rungs," says Jack Nardella, the manager of Value Village, a secondhand-merchandise store in Riverdale, Maryland, a Washington, D.C., suburb.

Low-income merchants also prosper by knowing their customers' life styles inside out. Some retailers delay buying weather-related clothes, such as summer shorts, because they know that low-income shoppers won't buy seasonal merchandise until the weather breaks. "They buy it when they need it," says Howard Levine, senior vice president at Family Dollar. In fact, it wouldn't be unusual to spot a Family Dollar customer wearing a heavy flannel shirt in a heat wave while he shopped for summer T-shirts. Because low-income consumers shop later in the season, Family Dollar and the others can buy end-of-season closeouts from manufacturers and curb inventory costs.

The chains also know that their customers can afford to spend only small amounts of money at a time. Thus, about 95 percent of Family Dollar's prices are under $17, and 90 percent of Dollar General's goods are under $10. "Because of their limited income, (customers) tend to buy as they need things. They buy sizes and quality that minimize their cash outlay," says Mr. Shapiro, the Chicago researcher.

That is how Patricia Lewis shops. She and her husband are raising three children on about $165 a week and food stamps. It's a day to splurge, though, when Mrs. Lewis gets a $15 refund for the crutches her son used for a broken leg.

She is considering buying two pairs of $5 slacks at a Dollar Bargain Store in Austintown, Ohio. "When you don't have much, you have to economize," Mrs. Lewis says.

But shoppers like Mrs. Lewis also want merchandise that resembles the products available to well-to-do consumers. "These people are constantly being bombarded by the media with 'the good life' role models. They react to it, and they want all those things," says Arthur Stuart, the president of Kingsway Department Stores, a small discount chain in inner-city Detroit. "They may be poor, but they don't want to look poor."

There are a lot of customers like that at Value Village, which is a chain of secondhand-merchandise stores. Value Village sells such products as used, $20 wedding dresses, $8.95 Sears-brand boys' suits, $19.95 sofas, and even discarded underwear.

Jack Nardella, the manager of the Riverdale store, says about four trucks a day deliver goods collected from area homes. This store, one of four in the Washington-Baltimore area, is owned by the National Children's Center, a charitable organization. From the outside, it resembles an abandoned bowling alley. "Psychologically, people don't feel good about shopping here," says Mr. Nardella of the store's bleak exterior. But on the inside, Value Village is a 14,000-square-foot sea of pipe racks and junky displays that attract about 3,500 customers a week.

Kathryn Johnson has been shopping in secondhand-clothing stores for 30 years now. "If I didn't have this store, I don't know what I'd do. I raised my sons in these stores and furnished my house in these stores," says Ms. Johnson, who supports two children on a monthly $800 disability check.

Frances Cofske sees Value Village as a way of keeping up with the Joneses in College Park, Maryland. She shops there as often as three times a week in search of brand-name dresses that she can't afford elsewhere. "I don't mind wearing other people's clothes," she says. "I just take it home, wash it, and I look like anyone out on the street."

Melba Brown sees this every day at the Dollar General store she manages in Russellville, a small farm town in south-central Kentucky. A big item is a pair of 100 percent leather men's deck shoes for $15. The shoes aren't the best-quality leather, but they resemble a pair that costs $52 at Barneys New York, an expensive New York clothing store.

Teen-age girls, meanwhile, buy canvas handbags embroidered with ducks for $2.95. At a department store 30 miles away in Bowling Green, a similar bag costs $7.95. "These kids can carry handbags just like the upper crust," Mrs. Brown says. "A child who comes from a poor family wants to look like anyone else. That peer pressure they feel is so enormous, especially in a small town."

Often the merchandise doesn't last, though. Kingsway's Mr. Stuart says it is usually cheaper to replace inexpensive merchandise than repair it. "For example," he says, "we sell a huge quantity of shoes. Now, it costs $15 to replace heels and soles. It simply costs too much to repair shoes when you can buy a pair for $20." Adds Mr. Nardella of Value Village, "It's something that goes with poverty. These people come in here, and they buy clothes that aren't going to last. So people replace it."

But Mr. Nardella concedes that replacing the merchandise often forces shoppers to spend the little they have. "You know what hurts?" he asks. "You're actually perpetuating it. Everything that happens (here) just keeps them down where they're at."

Buying for low-income customers can also be risky. Merchandise that is priced too high can lead to big inventories and high interest expenses.

Dollar General, for instance, frequently experiments with higher-priced products in order to increase same-store sales, which rose 13 percent in 1984. But sometimes mistakes are made. At the Russellville store, dozens of imported stainless-steel sauce pans are languishing on shelves. "It's a great buy," Mrs. Brown, the manager, says. "But our customers don't expect us to carry a sauce pan for $15." The store's best seller, which comes in flimsy, lightweight aluminum, costs $3.95.

Security costs are another big expense for chains with inner-city stores such as Kingsway. Mr. Stuart, who affectionately refers to one fenced-in outlet as "Fortress Kingsway," spends about $250,000 a year in each store for security employees and equipment.

Nevertheless, analysts say long-term prospects for low-income retailers remain bright. Even if there is a recession, says Thomas H. Tashjian, an analyst with Prudential-Bache Securities Inc., low-income stores will probably be immune. In fact, he adds, these stores often attract more customers when money is tight.

Mr. Turner likes to think such customers are already shopping at Dollar General. "A lady at the beauty parlor told me she has a customer whose son is an Izod snob," he says. "She buys a pair of Izod socks, takes off the alligator and sews it onto a Dollar General polo shirt."

Selling Packaged Goods by Mail

Leafing through the February 1985 issue of Bon Appetit, some readers may have been tempted to order gourmet cheeses, coffees, and pastas from a new mail-order service called Thomas Garraway Ltd. The flowery ad talked about the company's roots as a coffee house and food shop in 17th century London and its mention in some of Charles Dickens's novels.

What few people reading the ad realized, though, is that Thomas Garraway Ltd. is run by General Foods Corp., the same company that sells them Cool Whip and Maxwell House coffee at the supermarket. The U.S. company simply borrowed the British name to add a touch of class to its fancy-food venture.

Like a growing number of other packaged-goods companies, General Foods is breaking from its normal distribution channels to try its hand at direct marketing. For some years, mass marketers have sold low-volume products by mail. Procter & Gamble Co., for example, uses a toll-free 800 number to market Pampers for premature infants, and the Hanes division of Consolidated Foods Corp. sells imperfect nylons and white stockings for nurses by mail.

But now such companies as Nestlé, Thomas J. Lipton, Sunkist, Whitman's Chocolates, and R. J. Reynolds Industries all are using catalogs and 800 numbers to sell premium-quality products directly to consumers without relying on the retailer as middleman. Thomas Garraway, in

THOMAS GARRAWAY STARTED SHOPPING FOR YOU IN 1657.

From the heart of London to the four corners of the earth, Thomas Garraway Ltd. searches the world for its most exquisitely delicious foods and presents them to you.

320 years ago, Garraway's was founded as a London coffee house. It soon became famous for its superb coffees and teas and other fine foods. Sir Richard Steele writes in the *Tatler* of a fine wine auction held at Garraway's featuring "Extra-a-ordinary French claret." Charles Dickens tells us Mr. Pickwick dined frequently at Garraway's. One of his favorite dishes: "pork chops and tomato sauce."

Today, Thomas Garraway Ltd. carries on the tradition, combing the world for its choice foodstuffs and rushing them directly to your home anywhere in the U.S. through the Thomas Garraway Ltd. Fresh Delivery Service. The result is a wide array of foods with a freshness of flavour that can rarely be found.

Now you can taste a Gruyère de Comté made by hand in an isolated mountain village in France. Or a sauce of freshly picked Italian plum tomatoes grown in the lava-rich soil of San Marzano near Mt. Vesuvius. Or a blend of rare, rich coffees from Kenya and Ethiopia, Costa Rica and Java. Or tea leaves from Darjeeling, mustard from Dijon, spices from Madagascar. They're all here for you to choose from. And so much more!

Every one of our glorious cheeses is meticulously selected by a renowned French expert. We've developed a patented freshness pack that allows our rare coffees to be sealed airtight sooner after roasting to lock in their magnificent aroma and ensure impeccable freshness.

Every product that bears the Thomas Garraway label has been made with natural ingredients, contains no artificial flavours or preservatives, and has been handled with the utmost care.

And now we'd like to become your food purveyor — your specialty food store. We invite you to shop with us by strolling through this catalogue and sending for our delicacies. We hope you will have as much pleasure in feasting on these superb offerings as we have had in selecting them for you.

Courtesy General Foods Corporation

179

fact, is General Foods' second stab at direct-marketing, following mail-order sales of Swedish coffee.

Direct-marketing consultants say more big companies are planning to try direct-mail but are moving quietly to avoid tipping off competitors or alienating retailers. "The smartest marketers will learn to sell goods by the dozen, by the case to one person at a time, bypassing the whole distribution chain," says Laurel Cutler, vice chairman of Leber Katz Partners, a New York ad agency. By 1989, she predicts, all major packaged-goods companies will have a direct-marketing profit center.

"Direct-marketing is such a hot button with consumers that we felt we had to get our feet wet," says Demar Moeller, marketing director at Whitman's Chocolates. Since 1842, people have been stopping at the neighborhood store to buy Whitman's. Now, in an experiment in the Southwest, consumers need only dial an 800 number and for $25, a gift tin of candy will be delivered within 48 hours.

In 1983, consumers spent an estimated $45 billion shopping at home. Fueling the demand is the growth of two-income households with plenty of disposable income but not much disposable time.

"We want mail-order in our arsenal of capabilities for any product we may have going to consumers," says Robert Van Camp, president of R. J. Reynolds's Development Corp. subsidiary. In 1984, the marketer of cigarettes and food established a direct-marketing base by acquiring a fruit-of-the-month club and rose-bush business with combined sales of more than $100 million a year.

It seems unlikely that people will start ordering toothpaste and detergent by mail, but some companies aren't ruling out the possibility. Says David Pease, manager of new ventures at Lipton: "It isn't cost-effective now to sell such products directly to consumers, but down the road someone could come up with a way to deliver the 50 percent to 60 percent of a grocery order that doesn't change from week to week." For now, Lipton is mailing out more than one million of its Sir Thomas Lipton Collection catalogs that feature exotic tea blends, tea kettles and shortbread.

With their vast financial resources, packaged-goods companies seemingly could dominate direct marketing and drive smaller catalog houses out of business. But there are many potential pitfalls as these giants try to make that big stretch from mass marketing to direct selling. Accustomed to blanketing the country with flashy TV ads and delivering truckloads of diapers or soda pop to supermarket warehouses, they have no real relationship with their customers.

But in direct marketing, companies must build a data base of prospective customers, learn as much as possible about their tastes and buying habits and then woo them with repeated mailings of catalogs. Consultants advise that direct-mail businesses be managed autonomously, untainted by the packaged-goods mentality.

Mass marketers also can't count on a fast profit from direct selling. "Companies often require a payout in a year or two on a new product sold through stores," says Lipton's Mr. Pease. "But with the cluttered competition now in direct marketing, the investment period may run three to five years."

Ambitious companies such as General Foods and Nestlé aren't deterred. In late 1984, Nestlé mailed the second edition of its Chocolate Collection, expanding it to 24 pages from 16 and adding an espresso machine, pinatas, and teddy-bear molds. "The catalog is designed to make a profit but also to upgrade the company's Nestlé Crunch bar image in the United States," says James Kobs, chairman of Kobs & Brady Advertising Inc. in Chicago.

Whereas mail-order gourmet food has been primarily a holiday gift business, General Foods hopes to make it lucrative year-round. Its Thomas Garraway division encourages gastronomes to sign up as subscribers and receive a food basket each month. But some direct-marketing experts are skeptical about such a strategy. "I'm afraid some subscribers will find themselves up to their eyeballs in cheese and unable to consume it all," says Maxwell Sroge, publisher of a direct-marketing newsletter. "It's not the same as getting records or books in the mail each month and storing them on the shelf."

Update

General Foods Corp.'s foray into direct mail was well received. The company won't disclose figures, but it claims the subscription rate and customer retention rate were higher than it had projected. As a result, the catalog was expanded in 1986 to include vinegars, herbs, spices, and new baked goods. An unexpected twist: The company accepted an invitation to sell some of its gourmet products through a specialty food shop. The shop is located inside a Rich's department store in Atlanta.

Shulman's Keeps It Simple

Only a dozen customers meander through Revco Discount Drugs in the Eastgate Shopping Center in suburban Cleveland. It's 5:15 P.M. on a slushy Wednesday in February. With most of the city commuting or cooking dinner, there are no lines at Revco's two cash registers.

But the hour and weather haven't prevented more than 100 shoppers from filling the aisles at Bernie Shulman's drugstore at the opposite end of the shopping center. Customers wait at 6 of 15 checkout lanes. On a *busy* day, all the lanes will be full and, during an average week, 30,000 people will pass through.

It's estimated that they'll leave behind more than $20 million a year, making Shulman's one of the most successful drugstores in the United States. A typical independent drugstore—or one of Revco's 1,630 outlets—will need about five months to pull in as much as Shulman's sees in a week. Shulman's does it with little advertising, plain linoleum floors, and no computers in its office.

What the store offers is price. A 32-ounce bottle of Fantastik cleaning spray sells there for $1.10, compared with $1.49 at the nearby Revco. Two Eveready batteries are 76 cents, 23 cents less than at Revco. A can of Noxema shaving cream is $1.37 at Shulman's, almost half the manufacturer's suggested retail price of $2.56 and even below the normal wholesale cost of $1.50.

Shulman's formula is simple: The store buys goods only when manufacturers offer discounts. Nothing is sold at a loss—or at a large profit. Every item in the store is marked up 20 percent from its net cost. All that matters is volume.

"It makes no difference to us if the customer fills his basket with toothpaste, greeting cards, or shampoo—as long as he fills his basket," says Theresa Shulman, who has run the store since her husband Bernie died.

Mr. Shulman, who founded Revco in 1956 and left it 10 years later, first designed a store of this type in 1956 for an uncle in Detroit. After several years of retirement in California, he returned to Cleveland and in 1975 opened the low-price drugstore.

Although Mrs. Shulman says she doesn't intend to expand beyond the Cleveland store and another in Florida, other retailers have begun imitating the format. One is Marc Glassman, a 37-year-old Harvard Business School graduate who learned the business while working at Shulman's. He now operates his three-year-old Marc's in a Cleveland suburb and says 1982 sales were $25 million; he plans to expand by franchising.

Other followers include Freddie's in Rochester, New York; Jote's in Cleveland; Drug Palace in Cincinnati; Heartland in New England; Drug Mart in Dayton, Ohio; and Pete 'n' Larry's in Buffalo, New York. Drug Emporium, based in Columbus, Ohio, has 18 U.S. locations.

These stores could become as important as so-called warehouse stores have been in the food industry. The number of these low-price, high-volume supermarkets has grown to 2,200 from 175 in 1976, says Willard Bishop, a retailing consultant. They account for 6 percent of U.S. grocery sales, and 25 percent or more in Milwaukee, Minneapolis, St. Paul, and Kansas City.

Shulman's and others can offer low prices because manufacturers of health and beauty products sell a large proportion of their output—often as much as 75 percent—on a discount, or "deal," basis. Thus, Shulman's can sell Noxema shaving cream at $1.37 by buying it at the deal price of $1.27 a can. Discounts for advertising displays, prompt payment, and a large order further reduce the store's cost to $1.14 before a 20 percent markup is added. Shulman's orders enough Noxema to last 18 weeks. If it runs out before the next discount, customers will just have to buy another brand.

Conventional retailers take advantage of manufacturers' deals, too, but don't necessarily pass all discounts on to shoppers. Traditional drugstores also work on higher markups and, unlike Shulman's, buy regular-price merchandise to ensure a wider, more consistent variety of brands and sizes. Shulman's customers have to look elsewhere for Crest toothpaste or Head & Shoulders shampoo, because Procter & Gamble Co. refuses to sell most of its products to retailers who buy only on a "deal" basis.

Many shoppers at Shulman's, Marc's, or similar stores don't carry their savings home, though. Rose Avery recently went to Shulman's to buy contact lens solution but soon was loading her basket with dishwasher soap, candy, toothpaste, and aspirin. Pulling a package of vacuum cleaner bags off a pegboard, she concedes: "I really don't need these but, at 44 cents, who can pass them up?"

Marc's has increased impulse sales by expanding its wares. Food items include Coca-Cola (Marc's sells more than any other single store in the world) and bread (1,000 loaves a day). From auctions and closeouts come brass hat racks (priced at $14.70), midget chopping blocks with cleavers ($2.41) and small plastic boxes with sayings like "I love San Diego" (25 cents).

Profits don't come easily, though: Mr. Glassman says he didn't make any until his sales reached $4 million. He and Mrs. Shulman say their stores require them to work long hours seven days a week. There's also the risk of slow-moving merchandise. Mr. Glassman is stuck with thousands of imitation Rubik's Cubes bought for 25 cents apiece but duds at 30 cents last Christmas.

Most important, says Mrs. Shulman, is the discipline needed to stick to the purchasing and pricing formula. "The hardest part of this business," she adds, "is not to get greedy."

Book Chains Help Make Best-Sellers

As first novels go, *In Country* by Bobbie Ann Mason seems to have the right stuff to be a hit: an author who has already won an award for her short stories, an enthusiastic publisher, favorable trade reviews, and, by today's standards, a reasonable price of $15.95.

But Michael J. Hejny has doubts.

"I don't think this is a book I can take very far," says Mr. Hejny, who was responsible for most of the 1985 fall selection of hard-cover fiction for the B. Dalton Bookseller chain. His reasoning: The dust jacket isn't interesting enough, the author isn't widely known, and the writing and the story—a young woman's attempt to understand Vietnam and its veterans—are "not at all commercial."

He planned to order about 2,500 copies, a supportive yet moderate number.

That judgment is only one of hundreds made each day during the month of June as the big book chains place their orders for the fall and Christmas seasons. At B. Dalton's headquarters here and at other chains, buyers like Mr. Hejny may consider more than 2,000 new fiction titles a year and buy more than 1,000 of them, often influencing within minutes the fate of a book that may have taken years to write.

The sheer number of offerings, however, means that store buyers can't read more than a fraction of the books they eventually stock—sometimes not more than a few pages. So they judge books mostly by commercial criteria, such as the marketability of the author, whether the publisher has bought space in the chain's catalog, and the drawing power of the dust jacket.

"Merit has a lot to do with certain kinds of books," says Mr. Hejny, who was recently promoted to a distribution manager. But "most of the time, it's not the most important consideration."

For consumers, the results are chain bookstores with a greater proportion of predictable works offering proven formulas. Independent stores, often operated more on the basis of the owner's reading preferences and less with an eye toward profit, tend to support more unusual works.

"People often write novels because they want to tell a story," Mr. Hejny says, "and how a book sells isn't their No. 1 concern."

But how a book sells *is* B. Dalton's top concern. And that's why the chain will be featuring *Lucky,* the Jackie Collins novel, in a special promotional program. Kay Sexton, a B. Dalton vice president, concedes that Miss Collins "is not a literary giant by any stretch of the imagination." But she is a "brand name": an author with a built-in audience because of previous best sellers such as *Chances* and *Hollywood Wives.* What's more, publisher Simon & Schuster Inc. has given *Lucky* an arresting blue and pink cover, a catchy advertising campaign ("Make tomorrow your Lucky Day!") and a $10,000 budget for special displays in B. Dalton stores.

Then there's Anita Brookner. B. Dalton will order just 800 to 1,200 copies of her book *Family and Friends,* a novel described by Random House Inc. as a "portrait of a rich European family transplanted to pre-war London." Miss Brookner is well-regarded, but Mr. Hejny says: "She has an upscale, snobby audience.... We're a middle-class suburban store. Her customer isn't our customer."

Family and Friends, of course, may still sell well. Many books succeed despite a chilly initial reception from the chains. *The Hunt for Red October,* a submarine thriller, was all but shunned by the chains because it was a "double" first novel—the first written by unknown Tom Clancy, and the first work of fiction published by the somewhat academic Naval Institute Press. But favorable reviews helped to make the book a best-seller.

Red October and other surprisingly successful books—such as *The Name of the Rose,* the medieval mystery by Umberto Eco—caught on mostly because of support by independent bookstores. But most publishers agree that the chains' support eventually becomes essential. "To get a book to sell extremely well, you need good display space in the chains," says Joseph Friedman, vice president, sales, for Arbor House Publishing Co.

Despite their clout, the chains rarely attempt to make a promising book into a best-seller on their own. Publishers, alarmed about costly returns of unsold books, sometimes refuse to honor orders that they consider to be too large. And while B. Dalton executives fondly recall obscure books they believe they powered into best-sellers—such as *Zen and the Art of Motorcycle Maintenance*—far more common is the apparently strong book that fizzled. "We're going to sell a certain number of books because we're highlighting them, but you don't fool the public very long," says Miss Sexton.

For the most part, Mr. Hejny relies on the publisher's assessment of a book when placing his orders. But Mr. Hejny balances what he is told against his own book-evaluation criteria. The most important factors:

The author. "Brand-name" authors, such as James Michener or Robert Ludlum, produce sure-fire best-sellers. That's why Mr. Hejny is placing B. Dalton's largest-ever single order for 150,000 copies of *Texas,* Mr. Michener's latest novel. "This is such a big book that we don't need to read it or talk about it," Mr. Hejny says.

All other authors pose a problem. At best, an unknown name won't repel a buyer; at worst, it may hurt a book's chances, especially when a well-known author weighs in with a book on the same subject.

For example, B. Dalton ordered 5,000 copies of *Nutcracker,* Shana Alexander's account of the 1978 murder of Franklin Bradshaw by his grandson. The chain ordered only 2,000 copies of Jonathan Coleman's book on the same subject, *At Mother's Request.* The chain reasoned that Miss Alexander, a well-known reporter, would receive more publicity and be preferred by more customers over Mr. Coleman, a former Simon & Schuster editor and former associate producer for CBS News. Early sales indicate that B. Dalton guessed right," says Brian Baxter, the chain's buyer for biographies, history, current affairs, and academic subjects.

The publisher. Buyers know which publishers tend to overrate their books and which are conservative. For instance, sales presentations at Random House are "almost a sea of calm and reason" in an industry of hyperbole, says Mr. Hejny. "They know how many copies of a book they'd like to advance, and if you want too many books, it makes them nervous."

By contrast, Simon & Schuster "wants to advance as many copies as they can," says Mr. Hejny, and thus is known for a harder sell. Similarly, he says, William Morrow & Co.'s enthusiastic projections of how many copies it will print are often viewed skeptically because the publisher frequently doesn't hit the mark.

Buyers are also wary of publishers who venture into new categories, such as the Naval Institute Press's foray into fiction with *Red October.*

Price. Prices are set by publishers, but if they're too high, buyers complain. Viking Penguin Inc. proposed a $35 price for *Norman Rockwell's Patriotic Times,* but when B. Dalton and Waldenbooks objected, the price dropped to $19.95. On the other hand, Mr. Hejny says one of the best values of the spring season was *Glitz,* by Elmore Leonard. At $14.95, the novel is "about the least-expensive book on the best-seller list," Mr. Hejny says.

Mr. Hejny figures the top price for a mystery should be $14.95 or $15.95. Spy books can fetch a dollar or two more. Brand-name fiction goes for $17.95 or more; *Texas* is priced at $21.95, too high by Mr. Hejny's estimate, but most copies will be sold at a discount.

Page count. "Serious books should be weighty," says Mr. Hejny, and increasingly, so should expensive fiction. Mr.

Hejny objected when Random House proposed a $17.95 price for *World's Fair*, a new E. L. Doctorow novel that is only 220 pages long.

But Simon & Schuster figures that *Lonesome Dove,* a novel by popular author Larry McMurtry and priced at $18.95, will be aided by its 843-page size. And Mr. Hejny rates as an unusual bargain *And Ladies of the Club,* a 1,176-page behemoth that sold for just $19.95.

The cover. Simon & Schuster redesigned the cover for *Lonesome Dove* after Mr. Hejny and others objected that the original was too dull. "The author and title of the book have to tell it all, and it all has to show on the cover," he says.

One especially good recent cover, Mr. Hejny and Mr. Baxter say, was fashioned by Random House for the 1983 book *The Discoverers,* by Daniel Boorstin, the Librarian of Congress. The cover—black with a montage of a man crawling through natural and cosmic symbols—"made it alluring to reach out, pick it up, and see what was inside, which was a tremendous story," Mr. Baxter says.

Mr. Baxter was disappointed with the cover for the autobiography of test-pilot Chuck Yeager. The Bantam Books Inc. cover shows the retired general with an F-20 Tigershark jet in the far background. "I wanted the black jet, something that looked fast and mean, right there in front, something to appeal to younger people," says Mr. Baxter, who nonetheless ordered 37,000 copies of the book.

Advertising money. Bookstores earn cooperative advertising money from publishers based on the number of books they buy. B. Dalton often uses its money, amounting to hundreds of thousands of dollars annually, to pay costs of promotional programs, such as its catalog.

At a booksellers' convention in San Francisco, Mr. Hejny and other buyers sell publishers space in the chain's November catalog at prices ranging from $9,500 for a "regular" spot to $25,000 for a "promotional" slot. The publishers, in effect, are also buying desirable store display space. A "regular" book, for instance, is guaranteed high-visibility display in the stores, while "promotional" books are stacked on the right-front display table.

Fall buying begins as early as March, when B. Dalton strategists begin evaluating book-market trends to determine which categories to feature in the chain's 733 stores. Serious evaluation of thousands of books begins for the buyers in May, when about 20 major publishing houses present their fall lists, describing each book by content, price, size, author, and advertising plans. The buyers collect more information at the book convention in late May and lodge most of their orders in June, for September and October delivery.

When Mr. Hejny is through, he will have ordered books valued at about $27 million at retail for fall, $48 million for the full year. About 20 percent of all books B. Dalton orders will be returned to publishers for refunds, while about 30 percent of Mr. Hejny's novels are returned. Often, no one knows why the books didn't sell as expected.

"A writer can do a dozen books, and they sit on the shelf," says Mr. Baxter. "Then something happens. People respond. You never know when it will happen, or why. It's magic, and it's what makes this business so wonderful."

Electronic Shopping: The Experimenters

Sometime in the 1970s, predicted two marketing professors in a 1967 *Harvard Business Review* article, most consumers wouldn't be going to stores anymore for such everyday items as toothpaste, meat, paper napkins, and cigarettes. Instead, people would travel only as far as their kitchens to shop.

There they'd be able to sit in front of a computer and purchase a week's staples, as well as such occasional needs as a garden hose, in 10 to 15 minutes. Perhaps 80 percent of suburban housewives, the authors suggested, "would never set foot" in the stores that supplied those products, "except possibly for guest tours."

If retailers were frightened by that prophecy, they needn't have been. Home shopping has yet to catch up with futurists' visions.

It is, however, coming a lot closer. Through computers, cable TV, and the two-way information service known as videotex, push-button purchasing has arrived technologically. What isn't known is how much consumers want to be armchair shoppers and how eager companies will be to invest in an unproven idea.

Shopping from home isn't new, of course. Aaron Montgomery Ward printed his first catalog in 1872. Electronic home shopping is unique, though, for the ease and immediacy it adds to browsing or ordering merchandise.

A sign that "teleshopping" has arrived is the roster of companies that have begun to dabble in it. Among large retailers and manufacturers are Sears, Roebuck & Co., J. C. Penney Co., Grand Union Co., General Mills Inc., Johnson & Johnson, ITT Corp., Federated Department Stores Inc., Dayton-Hudson Corp., and its B. Dalton subsidary.

"You've got important players in it," says Gary Arlen, publisher of a newsletter about electronic shopping and banking. "They can force the market to take shape."

Most of those companies have tested electronic shopping by participating in major videotex experiments that have been conducted since 1980 by Times Mirror Co., Knight-Ridder Newspapers Inc., and CBS Inc., the latter two in joint ventures with American Telephone & Telegraph Co. Although each test varied, all gave consumers access to a computer-and-TV hookup that provided text and cartoon-like still graphics. Services available included banking, shopping, and travel reservations, as well as news reports.

Fewer than 1,000 households were included in those three tests, and the sponsors are guarding details of the results closely, so it's difficult to determine how successful videotex home-shopping will be. Still, many of the companies involved say they're encouraged, especially for products now sold through conventional direct-marketing techniques.

In the Times Mirror Co. test in California, 53 percent of the 350 households made at least one purchase by videotex during a nine-month period. Two thirds of the 200 homes in Knight-Ridder tests in Florida shopped; the average order was $62. In a CBS test of 100 homes in New Jersey, reports a participating retailer, three $300 espresso machines were sold.

Harry Smith, a CBS vice president, says people used videotex more for browsing—"the equivalent of looking through a catalog or wandering through a mall"—than for placing orders. Those who made purchases went to the keyboard with a general idea of what they wanted. The medium, Mr. Smith says, "is a demand fulfiller instead of a demand creator."

The videotex trials also offered groceries, which aren't the sort of products now sold through direct mail or catalogs.

Although not as popular as durables among electronic shoppers, says a Times Mirror official, supermarket products sold surprisingly well.

Videotex has received most of the attention, but other forms of electronic salesmanship are being tried. Comp-U-Store, an electronic buying service with text but no graphics, has been available to personal-computer owners since November 1981.

Kirk Shelton, a Comp-U-Store executive, says that about 10,000 computer owners have paid $25 to join the service, which allows them to choose from 50,000 discounted brand-name products, including special markdowns listed in its "Databasement." Comp-U-Store also is used by some of 150,000 other computer owners who tap into it through three computer-information networks. Best-selling items include TV sets and stereos, cameras, and appliances.

Comp-U-Store is the largest home-shopping service to go beyond testing, but another one known as CompuServe also offers computer owners sporting goods, computer programs, flowers, and Godiva chocolates. Other lower-tech shop-at-home services use the telephone as the order-taker.

But Knight-Ridder's videotex service, with commercial operations in Southern Florida, is the one that national marketers are watching closest to assess home-shopping's prospects. In the joint venture with AT&T, the publisher expects to sign up 5,000 of 134,000 affluent homes there; subscribers will pay $600 for a special terminal and a monthly fee of $26. Times Mirror planned to start its videotex service in Orange County, California, in mid-1984.

Meanwhile, other tests are planned. A group of 20 U.S. and Canadian banks have disclosed plans for a year-long videotex experiment including home banking and shopping. J. C. Penney acquired its own videotex operation from a Minneapolis bank that had tested it among 285 farm families in Omaha, Nebraska, and Minneapolis.

Electronic Shopping: The Doubters

Electronic shop-at-home services may become large, profitable businesses someday. For now, though, the best way to profit from push-button purchasing may be as a management consultant touting it as a revolution that's imminent.

Decision Research Corp., for example, recently warned a meeting of food and drug executives that those who ignore electronic shopping "may find themselves stuck with products buried in a warehouse somewhere or, at best, gathering dust on the few retail shelves that are left." Management Horizons Inc., another consultant, predicted in 1981 that 20 percent of U.S. retail sales would be made electronically from homes by 1990 but now regards that estimate as "aggressive."

Booz, Allen & Hamilton Inc. made electronic shopping pay by running a two-year test of it, financed with $2.5 million from 28 sponsors. For $60,000, late comers can pick up a copy of the results, which project $50 billion in electronic retail sales by 1995.

A more restrained view comes from John Warwick, director of marketing for Times Mirror Co.'s videotex system, which provides transaction and information services to homes. While he is optimistic about videotex's prospects, he is skeptical about any revolutions in shopping. "The number of people who are going to change their behavior because of a technological change is small," he says. "To say that technology is going to make dinosaurs of retail stores is a little silly."

Sears, Roebuck and Co., which participated in a test of the Times Mirror system and another set up by Knight-Ridder Newspapers Inc. and American Telephone & Telegraph Co., also is cautious. "We feel there's great potential in this area," says a spokeswoman, "but any significant sales volume or participation by the public is sometime down the road."

One reason may be that, for many consumers, shopping fills time. "We are social creatures," says William Boehm, director of economic research for Kroger Co. supermarkets. "We do things in part because we enjoy social interaction."

There's also the limitation imposed by shopping from a TV screen that, with present technology, carries only text and unsophisticated still graphics. Although direct-mail marketers have proven that some products can be sold sight unseen, many cannot. As videotex experts often say of its mosaic graphics, "You can't sell a dress that looks like it's made out of Lego blocks."

Economic questions abound. National videotex systems will require substantial capital investments. Knight-Ridder figures that, by late 1984, it will have spent $26 million on its videotex venture.

It's also unclear whether consumers will spend $600 for a videotex terminal and $26 a month, the amounts Knight-Ridder will charge when it introduces videotex commercially in Southern Florida. In three videotex experiments by Times Mirror, Knight-Ridder, and CBC Inc., participating households didn't pay for the service.

Another potential problem, at least from a merchant's point of view, is how easy computerized browsing can make comparison shopping. Buyers may want to look around for the best deal, but sellers rarely encourage such behavior. Says Mr. Warwick of Times Mirror Co., "Merchants are going to figure out a way not to let that happen to them."

Many retailers don't see that as a problem for now, and some also maintain that videotex's limited graphics aren't an obstacle. In electronic selling, "colors and graphics get in the way," says Stuart MacIntire, who runs J. C. Penney Co.'s new videotex subsidiary.

Harry Smith, who is in charge of CBS's videotex trials, notes that videotex is a combination of computers and television. "It's the computer search that excites people," he says. To overcome videotex's visual shortcomings, J. C. Penney tested it in conjunction with the chain's regular catalogs.

Graphics could become more important if technologists figure out a way to transmit photographic-quality pictures or even full-motion video to subscribers' homes. In the meantime, home-shopping experimenters are developing merchandising techniques, such as quizzes and games, to lead customers to products and to spur impulse purchases. Because information in videotex can be updated at any time, some department stores have tested price reductions as a way to unload slow-moving inventory.

These issues and others will continue to be studied by videotex suppliers, manufacturers, and retailers who are convinced that electronic shopping will catch on eventually. For retailers, says John Harris, a retailing specialist at Booz Allen, electronic shopping could double profit margins by reducing inventory, fixed assets, and operating costs.

Mr. Harris and other analysts don't expect much more than shop-at-home tests until 1987, with sophisticated systems with full-motion video coming after 1990. Home banking is likely to arrive sooner than home shopping because the advantages for bankers are greater than for retailers.

Ultimately, some manufacturers may decide that they can cut out middlemen altogether and sell directly to consumers. The Institute for the Future, a California think tank, suggests that someday there will be "production on demand." A customer would tap an order on a home terminal, which then would direct an industrial robot to begin manufacturing the product.

Another possibility for the future: Electronic shopping will reduce the need for catalogs and mail solicitations. As a result, says a direct-marketing specialist, mailboxes crammed with junk mail could become a thing of the past.

Update

Electronic home shopping has turned out to be more difficult to implement than its enthusiasts had predicted. Both Times Mirror Co.'s Gateway and Knight-Ridder Newspapers Inc.'s Viewtron videotex services were shut down in early 1986. Neither service had signed up enough subscribers to justify the cost. However, other home-shopping services, especially those that didn't require special equipment and high monthly fees, continued to expand.

7

Selling Services

Marketing Money

Prudential-Bache Securities is getting scrappy. In its ad campaign for 1985, the brokerage firm takes on not one, not two, but three of its biggest competitors.

The TV commercial shows bulls charging through a restaurant and a stuffy men's club, while spoofing ad slogans for Merrill Lynch ("It's hard to make money these days just following the herd"), Smith Barney ("Old-fashioned techniques don't always seem to work anymore"), and E. F. Hutton ("Listening to yesterday's ideas isn't enough in today's financial markets").

"It isn't a slap," says Patricia Gates, director of advertising. "We tried to do it tastefully and with a sense of humor." Still, such brashness is unusual in financial-services advertising. The commercial, which replaces a sober ad featuring a pin-striped executive discoursing on "total financial planning," is a sign of the difficult times in financial-services marketing. Companies are spending record sums but struggling harder than ever to come up with truly creative ads that will make an impression on consumers. For TV commercials alone in 1984, expenditures rose to more than $650 million, from $556 million in 1983.

Many of the ads aren't hitting home, though. Video Storyboard Tests Inc., which polls consumers on which commercials they remember and like most, reports that only once in seven years has a financial ad made the top 10. That honor is held by American Express Co. for a credit-card commer-

cial featuring Dallas Cowboys coach Tom Landry surrounded by Redskins in an Old West saloon.

"Most financial advertising is dull or over people's heads," says Judith Langer, president of a market-research firm in New York. "Everybody is competing against everybody else with financial products nowadays, and a lot of these ads just blur."

It's not surprising then that Metropolitan Life Insurance Co. is using the "Peanuts" cartoon gang to make itself seem warmer and less institutional. Or that Paine Webber tries to get attention by having Jimmy Connors bat tennis balls around a brokerage office. Or even that Federal Home Loan Mortgage Corp. (Freddie Mac) has resorted to cuddly, white-bearded gnomes for its corporate symbol.

But skeptics wonder whether financial institutions will lose credibility by appearing too cute and lovable. Other insurance marketers are watching the Metropolitan Life campaign in particular to see if it attracts new customers or if, instead, consumers write off Charlie Brown and Snoopy as merely entertaining kid's stuff. The Freddie Mac gnomes might be seen as the financial industry's answer to the Pillsbury Doughboy, although the J. Walter Thompson Co. ad agency insists that cuteness hasn't been a problem.

The ads play on the "mythology of the gnomes of Zurich and the gnomes of Wall Street" who are supposed to be very savvy fellows on financial matters, explains Michael Lollis, a senior vice president at Thompson. Since the campaign began in 1984, awareness of Freddie Mac has increased, and people now view it as less stodgy and bureaucratic.

Humor in any form is risky in financial advertising. The conventional wisdom is that people take their money very seriously and won't entrust it to a company that clowns around too much. Bank of America tried humor once to advertise its traveler's checks, but the campaign was short-lived "because senior management didn't feel it was right," says Dawn Lesh, director of marketing research.

The Prudential-Bache commercial is actually little different from the comical way Wendy's regularly attacks McDonald's and Burger King. But critics of the ad say burgers and

IRAs are much different creatures. "Consumers are looking for meaningful information to help them make the best investment decisions," says Claudia Marshall, a vice president at Travelers Cos. "It doesn't make sense to position yourself against three competitors that aren't that well known themselves to the average person."

Even worse, knocking the other guys can backfire if it looks unfair to consumers. Financial institutions want to convey an image of integrity that will encourage consumers to trust them with their money, says Paula Pierce, a spokeswoman for McCollum/Spielman, an advertising research company. "This isn't the same as Anacin saying it's better than Bufferin."

For those reasons, comparative advertising continues to be rare among financial companies. Hibernia Bank in San Francisco does claim in ads that its new money-market account pays a higher rate than do five other California banks which are singled out by name. And although Dreyfus Corp. contends that the bull in its ad is merely a generic symbol for Wall Street, many people see it as a dig at Merrill Lynch. When the Dreyfus lion and a bull meet in the ad, the bull makes a swift retreat.

Prudential-Bache claims it has received positive reactions to its ad from both customers and its own brokers. The competitors who take their licks in the ad seem unfazed. Merrill Lynch believes all the bulls in other companies' ads reinforce its corporate symbol in consumers' minds. "I got a good laugh out of Pru-Bache's ad," says Bob Connor, Smith Barney's advertising manager. "But after you get through all the allusions to other brokerage firms, there's little room left in 30 seconds to say anything about yourself."

Banks Imitate
Packaged-Goods Strategies

Cynthia Miller's resumé doesn't read like a banker's. She has sold Imperial margarine for Lever Brothers; worked at Church & Dwight, the maker of Arm & Hammer Baking Soda, and helped develop Brush-On Peel-Off Mask, a skin care product from Helena Rubinstein.

But these days Mrs. Miller isn't peddling consumer products. She's a vice president at Citibank. As such, she's also a member of a growing new breed of marketing executives—those who have taken their packaged-goods experience to companies that are marketing neophytes. These executives are teaching banks, brokerage firms, retailers, rental-car companies, airlines, and others that their products and services can be sold like toothpaste.

"The banking business is going to be run by marketing people," predicts John Reed, a Citibank senior executive vice president. In addition to Mrs. Miller, 11 of the 40 highest-ranking managers who work for Mr. Reed in the consumer-banking division began their careers at such companies as General Mills, General Foods, PepsiCo, and Lever.

Executive recruiters agree that managers with that sort of experience are highly prized by non-packaged goods companies. Eugene Judd, president of a New York search firm that specializes in placing marketing executives, says he has seen "a tremendous increase in requests for people that come out of traditional packaged-goods companies." In

1980, he says, a fourth of his fees came from financial institutions.

Banks such as Citibank long had been adroit at wooing big corporate clients on golf courses or at lavish lunches. Retail customers, however, weren't courted aggressively because their dollars were in relatively small accounts. Then in the mid-1970s, Citibank decided to invest more than $200 million to pursue some of the $1.2 trillion in U.S. consumer deposits. The nation's second largest bank had to learn how to motivate consumers.

"We used to believe that, if you put a branch someplace, the customer sort of would just walk in," says Mr. Reed, who has spent his career in banking but picks up much of his marketing philosophy serving as a director of Philip Morris.

Packaged-goods executives, adds Mrs. Miller, "understand that consumers aren't to be trivialized. They have the money, and we have to cajole it out of them."

To do so, Citibank increasingly has relied on research, product development, and advertising techniques that would be routine at any large consumer-products company. "If we didn't have marketing people," says Mr. Reed, "we wouldn't know how to test."

When the bank wanted to know, for example, how well its customers would accept automatic teller machines, Mrs. Miller argued that a survey of consumers wouldn't be accurate because they hadn't ever used the machines. So a $250,000 simulated bank—complete with tellers and machines—was built in the basement of the Daily News building in New York. For the next two years, 2,500 customers there were observed regularly through one-way mirrors and sometimes were interviewed in small focus groups.

Her next assignment was to manage six money-losing Citibank branches on Long Island. Mrs. Miller, who had once helped design a perfume bottle for Helena Rubinstein, decided the offices were poorly packaged; they weren't visible to drivers passing by. The solution: installing automatic tellers in roadside kiosks with neon Citibank signs on top.

That change and others—including a course to help employees lose their Brooklyn accents—helped the six branches achieve a Citibank growth record.

Citibank's enthusiasm for packaged-goods techniques isn't shared by all bankers, some of whom note that the New York institution's retail-banking division has yet to turn a profit. "Just because you happened to work for Procter & Gamble or General Foods doesn't mean you'll be a superstar in banking," says Richard Rosenberg, vice chairman of Wells Fargo Bank in Los Angeles. "Many times you have a great deal to unlearn because you aren't experienced with a heavy regulatory environment."

A banker also must be both the manufacturer and retailer of his products. A packaged-goods marketer, in contrast, must rely on supermarkets, drugstore chains, wholesalers, and other third parties to distribute its products to consumers. Thus, bankers need additional skills, but gain by having more control of their products and the opportunity to load up customers with additional offerings.

In banking, brand loyalty is easier to cement because inertia prevents most customers from switching banks frequently; the first transaction is the hardest. Packaged-goods companies have an easier time making the first sale, which often is induced by coupons or price discounts; repeat purchases are more difficult.

"This business is more complex," says Citibank's Mrs. Miller. "I could probably tell you the basics of the cosmetics business in three hours."

Even Mr. Reed acknowledges that some packaged-goods companies, including P&G, don't interest him. Their alumni, he contends, are too dependent on support from corporate research, advertising and promotion departments, plus the time-tested procedures developed by large consumer-products concerns. "We've had people come to work for us who never got started," Mr. Reed says, "because they came in and waited for their boss to tell them what to do."

Adds David Joys, an executive vice president at Russell Reynolds Associates, a recruiting firm: "Many of our service-industry clients would love P&G in someone's background but would rather he'd worked somewhere else in between."

It Gets Nasty When Accountants Compete

KMG Main Hurdman, the ninth-biggest U.S. accounting firm, has a service that analyzes commercial ventures in outer space. Laventhol & Horwath, the 11th biggest, recently plugged one of its newsletters by offering potential subscribers cameras, clocks, and travel guides. Laventhol also owns an outfit called Index, which designs hotel interiors.

Is this any way to run an accounting firm?

As recently as the 1970s, accounting firms had only a handful of products—auditing, tax work, estate planning, and management consulting. And a clublike camaraderie prevailed: Most firms wouldn't be caught dead swiping a competitor's client. Because there was plenty of business to go around, firms sat back and waited for clients to come to them.

But the profession has been thrust into a new competitive world of survival. Corporate merger mania has shrunk the pool of clients. Rates for malpractice insurance have tripled. Firms now are scrapping for every piece of business by cutting auditing fees and branching into areas that often have little direct connection with accounting. And stealing clients has become a way of life.

"Five years ago if a client of another firm came to me and complained about the service, I'd immediately warn the other firm's chief executive," says J. Michael Cook, the chairman of Deloitte, Haskins & Sells, the nation's No. 7 accounting firm. "Today I try to take away his client."

Says Arthur Bowman, the editor of the *Public Accounting Report,* an Atlanta newsletter: "Today almost anything that makes money goes."

But the trend disturbs many in the profession, government, and the academic world. They worry that firms may get so cutthroat that they will fall down on what many see as their primary duty: independently auditing the books of publicly held companies. The biggest potential loser is the public, these critics argue.

"The increased aggressiveness of firms in selling their services is bound to lead to erosion in the quality of the audit," says Loyd Heath, a professor of accounting at the University of Washington in Seattle.

A House subcommittee headed by Rep. John Dingell, Democrat of Michigan, has been holding hearings on the accounting profession. The hearings were prompted by a belief that accounting firms had been too quick to give clean bills of health to banks, thrifts, securities firms, and other companies that subsequently collapsed. "We're very concerned that the more hats an accounting firm wears for its clients, the more the firm is in the client's pocket," says Michael Barrett, the subcommittee's chief counsel.

Clearly there is a revenue squeeze in the profession, and it is taking a human toll. Revenues at the eight largest firms grew a total of only 22 percent over the past two years, down from 40 percent in the preceding two-year span, according to Mr. Bowman's newsletter. The biggest gains since 1982 came from consulting fees, which rose 33 percent; accounting revenues were up only 14 percent.

Facing such conditions, Peat, Marwick, Mitchell & Co., the second-biggest firm, pushed out or retired 10 percent of its partners, an unprecedented bloodbath for a major firm.

"My boss doubled my quota (for new business) overnight," says a 50-year-old former Peat Marwick partner in the Midwest. "He made it virtually impossible for me to serve my current clients. I had to get out."

In 1983, David J. Charles, now 49, was asked to leave

the Miami office of Alexander Grant & Co. after 14 years with the 10th-largest firm. "I was told I wasn't marketing-oriented enough," says Mr. Charles, who now has his own practice. "I'm glad to be out of the big-firm rat race."

As competition to audit big public companies heats up, major accounting firms are trying to expand by acquiring smaller firms. Arthur Young & Co., the sixth-biggest firm, began doing business in Arkansas through an acquisition, and Coopers & Lybrand (No. 3) and Peat Marwick have sharply increased their Florida business that way.

Some small firms say they must merge to survive. In Tallahassee, Florida, May, Zima & Co. says it sent a "prospectus" profiling its business to eight major firms, hoping that one will make an offer. "Our revenues have flattened over the past year and we just can't compete with the big firms' financial and marketing resources," says John P. Thomas, May Zima's managing partner.

Big firms also are hiring sales specialists from other fields. Peat Marwick's William Goldberg, a former marketer of financial services for Continental Illinois National Bank & Trust Co., says that "peripheral services" around the audit can be used as a "marketing tool" to expand business.

Mr. Goldberg recently offered to review the tax returns of the top officers of United Bankers of Waco, Texas, a nine-bank holding company, for possible conflict-of-interest problems. "It's a great idea," says Matt Landry, United Bankers' president. "And it fits in with a new ethics policy we're drafting." He notes that Peat Marwick is charging only $100 to $200 per review.

But Jim Ainsworth, managing partner of Ainsworth & Lambert, a small firm in Commerce, Texas, isn't happy. Ainsworth & Lambert lost the auditing business of First National Bank of Commerce to Peat Marwick after the bank was acquired by United Bankers. However, Ainsworth & Lambert continues to do the tax returns of First National's top officers.

"Peat's has been pelting us with senseless questions about the tax returns that have nothing to do with conflict of interest," says Mr. Ainsworth. "It's simply a ploy to take all of First National's business away from us by trying to show we're incompetent."

Pettibone Corp., a Chicago-based maker of materials-handling equipment, recently switched to Arthur Andersen & Co., the biggest U.S. accounting firm, from Alexander Grant & Co., because of one of Andersen's consulting services. Grant had been Pettibone's auditor for 40 years.

"Andersen not only dropped our fee by 40 percent but helped us cut machine-tool set-up time at our biggest Chicago plant by up to 50 percent," says Roger Palmer, a Pettibone vice president. Pettibone has been suffering major losses over the past two years because of increased competition in its industry, and the production-time savings are "happy news," Mr. Palmer says.

Since 1980, Andersen has hired more than 600 engineers to complement its more than 1,000 accounting partners. "They're a big help in gaining an audit client," says William Hinkel, the Andersen partner in charge of the Pettibone audit. Mr. Hinkel says the plant study was part of Pettibone's audit package and "wasn't billed for separately."

Accounting executives insist that consulting improves the audit's quality. "It helps us know more about our clients," says William Gladstone, the chairman of Arthur Young. And Duane Kullberg, managing partner of Arthur Andersen, says consulting by firms is an "added dimension" that can only spur business and the economy. "The public is the winner, not the loser," he says.

But Eli Mason, managing partner of Mason & Co., says increased aggressiveness by big firms trying to lure away small firms' clients has brought "the law of the jungle to what once was a gentleman's profession; only the predators will survive."

Mr. Mason, who also is the chairman of the National Conference of CPA Practitioners, an organization of more than 1,000 small firms, recently complained to New York state regulators that Seidman & Seidman, the 12th-biggest firm in the country, was using false advertising to win clients from small competitors. He cited a Seidman advertisement in the *Westchester Business Journal* aimed at businessmen, that said small firms were "limited in their expertise and you've probably outgrown them already."

Seidman & Seidman says it will fight the charges. If the state finds a violation of professional rules, it can censure, fine, suspend, or expel a firm.

Big firms deny they are trying to push small ones out of business. But they speak with pride of beefed-up marketing efforts for clients of all sizes. Coopers & Lybrand has doubled the size of its marketing department to 80 people since 1980. It has been using Yankelovich, Skelly & White, a market-research firm, to query businessmen about such areas as planning for future growth and joint ventures.

"We want to project an image of knowing the businessman's problems so he will associate Coopers & Lybrand with solutions," says James Lafond, the accounting firm's national director of business development.

Since 1984, Arthur Young has hired marketers from Uniroyal Inc., the tire maker; Clairol Inc., the hair-products company; and Thomas J. Lipton Inc., the tea concern. "We're educating CPAs on how to close a sale for professional services slowly rather than using the hard sell," says Kenneth J. Wright, Arthur Young's director of marketing development. "Professional marketers are helping us learn how to sell our entire product line, using market research, demographics, positioning, and other innovations."

"The CPA, once versed only in double-entry bookkeeping, is adding the lexicon of Madison Avenue to his spiel," says Bruce Marcus, a former marketer for Arthur Young and Coopers & Lybrand who has just written a book on how to sell professional services.

Consulting has grown so varied that an accountant may be unaware of all the services at his own firm. That's why KMG Main Hurdman ran a two-day "trade fair" in Dallas for 500 partners to show them its complete line of 27 "products," including pension consulting, cost-sale analysis for auto dealers, and litigation support.

"The partners were so enthusiastic about the chance to learn everything we now offer that we're thinking of using videotapes of the fair as a marketing tool aimed at attracting new clients," says Sam Marks, the firm's marketing consultant. "We want to go out there and really do a selling job so potential clients will come flocking to us."

Says Donald Aronson, Arthur Young's director of marketing:

"Marketing is the new name of the game. The white gloves are off."

Hotels Wake Up
to Selling

In 1985 Marriott Corp. spent an estimated $16 million on a bonus program for frequent hotel guests, while Hyatt Corp., a direct competitor, was spending only about a fifth as much. Hyatt is putting most of its market muscle into nationwide print and broadcast ads, while Marriott is doing little of either. Concludes Darryl Hartley-Leonard, executive vice president of Hyatt, "One of us is making a terrible mistake."

Both companies are leaders of an industry that is just now learning to market its services after years of relative complacency. Traditionally, demand for hotel rooms has outpaced supply, but the past several years have brought hard times. Cities have too many hotels, occupancy rates are down about 7 percent since 1978, and room rates have nosedived. "I call it marketing by necessity—for survival," says Michael A. Levin, president and chief operating officer of Days Inns of America.

A plethora of marketing ploys has resulted, with some successes, some failures, and many "wait-and-sees." The experiments include concentrated direct mail, television and print advertising, aggressive expansion into new markets, and giveaways such as free airline tickets. "There is no set agreement on how to respond," says Gary Moss, a senior vice president of the advertising firm, J. Walter Thompson, which handles Hyatt's account.

Hotels pose special problems that have little to do with the industry's general lack of marketing experience. For one thing, hotels can't be moved or redesigned to suit rapidly changing customer tastes. Moreover, hoteliers don't get the second chance at selling that packaged-goods marketers often enjoy. Says Donald E. Hawkins, who studies the industry as a professor at George Washington University, "If you don't sell the product that night, it's over."

But even more troublesome is the lack of differentiation. "We all have happy people, we all have good facilities, we all have good service," says James Collins, senior vice president for marketing at Hilton Hotels Corp.

Further blurring the hotel market is a trend toward brand segmentation. Mid-priced Holiday Inns, for example, has introduced a budget product called "Hampton Inns," a high-priced urban hotel called "Holiday Inn Crowne Plaza," and two suites-only products, "Embassy Suites" and "Residence Inns," along with its casino hotels called "Harrah's."

The question is whether chains such as Holiday or Ramada Inns with a mid-price image can succeed in a high-priced market, or whether a more expensive chain, such as Marriott, will hurt its image with a lower-priced product. Proponents argue that entering new markets has become the only way to grow.

But some big chains aren't so sure. Hilton, which years ago built a small number of lower-priced hotels called Hilton Inns, is reluctant to segment further. "We've built up a certain level of expectancy for a Hilton customer," says the company's Mr. Collins. A less-expensive line of properties would hurt the image of the whole chain, he contends.

Additionally, hotels already have a difficult time developing consumer loyalty because of the large number of similar facilities; creating more lines may only add to customers' growing confusion.

Skillful advertising could be the answer to such difficulties, marketers say, but most companies' campaigns have only added to the problem.

"Nobody in the hotel industry, in my opinion, has really run any terrific ads," says Roger J. Dow, vice president for marketing at Marriott. His pet peeve is ads filled with buildings—what he terms "the edifice complex." Norman Tissian, president of Spiro & Associates, a Philadelphia-based company that does advertising and marketing consulting for hotel companies, says, "I'm sick and tired of ads with pretty girls, or that say, 'We give you the best service in the world.'"

In some cases, copying is the culprit. The industry has slim profit margins, and the hard times of the early 1980s have squeezed budgets even tighter. Robert W. Bloch, senior vice president for marketing at Four Seasons Hotels Ltd., remembers spending 10 percent to 15 percent of revenue on brand-related marketing when he was running General Foods Corp.'s Kool-Aid soft-drink campaign. Many hotel companies, he says, spend only about 1 percent to 2 percent on similar activities. Marketers say such companies often copy the marketing efforts of those that do the costly consumer research necessary to begin new campaigns.

Some lodging chains have taken bold gambles. Ramada Inns' "true hotel stories" campaign portrayed a businessman beset by things that can go wrong during a hotel stay. In one commercial, the hapless traveler misses his wake-up call, cuts himself shaving, then trips over a maid's cart.

Jerry Gelinas, Ramada's senior vice president for marketing, says the ads were popular with many guests, but franchisees balked at the way the industry was depicted. Some guests also felt Ramada was "overpromising" by suggesting such mayhem never happens in its hotels. Ramada says it is changing the campaign to make the commercials more "positive."

Marriott has gone out on a limb by dramatically reducing advertising to concentrate on its "Honored Guest" bonus program, analogous to the airlines' "frequent-flier" offerings. Marriott's Mr. Dow says he has "as many internal critics as external" because of the tremendous costs involved, but he says he is confident that the program will carry its weight by generating new business. He says the program allows Marriott to gather detailed information about its frequent customers and to offer, through direct mail, incentives to shop in Marriott's stores, eat in its restaurants, and stay in hotels where occupancy is lagging.

Yet competitors wonder whether the company is merely rewarding people who would stay at Marriott anyway. "We can't justify the cost no matter which way we work the numbers," says Hyatt's Mr. Hartley-Leonard.

Holiday Inns was the first chain to offer a bonus program, and its experience illustrates the risks and rewards involved. The chain got much more business than it expected, but it also underestimated the program's cost, says Ray Lewis, vice president for marketing, who won't provide details. Says Daniel R. Lee, an analyst at Drexel Burnham Lambert Inc., "A lot more people were qualifying for free rooms than (the company) thought," forcing it to begin "scaling back on giveaways."

Hotel marketers say they are learning from their mistakes. Marriott and Ramada, for example, studied Holiday's experience before designing their own bonus programs. There have also been some marketing successes, particularly in advertising. Marriott gets high praise for a campaign that featured its chairman and chief executive officer, J. W. Marriott, Jr., personally guaranteeing the quality of Marriott rooms. "That was very good," says Mr. Moss, who represents Hyatt. "We can't do that. There is no Mr. Hyatt."

Doctors Try a Dose
of Marketing

Roger B. Fenton wasn't in danger of having to drop out of medicine, but he wasn't seeing any growth in his practice either. The problem was the nature of his specialty, radiology. He had to depend on other physicians to send him referrals. Most people don't shop the Yellow Pages for X-rays.

Dr. Fenton, a Detroit osteopath, did what doctors are taught to do in puzzling cases. He called in a specialist, one he wasn't introduced to in medical school—a marketing consultant.

As a result, Dr. Fenton now markets his services directly to the public. He operates two well-advertised walk-in breast centers where a woman can go without a referral and get a complete breast examination for about $190. Two hours later she walks out with the results.

At first Dr. Fenton's colleagues were "shaking their heads." Now he gets a lot of calls from doctors who want to know how he did it. And he's thinking about opening a third office.

The days when a doctor could just hang out a shingle and expect a six-figure income are disappearing. So far the effect on earnings is still akin to a mild case of the sniffles, but the affliction promises to get worse, especially in urban areas.

The reason is in the numbers. More than half a million doctors are in practice in the mid-80s—up a third in the past decade—and their numbers continue to grow.

The prescription for ailing practices is often marketing, but the diagnosis and treatment aren't cheap. Consultant fees range from $2,500 to $5,000 a month, and research and advertising add to the bill.

The consultant Dr. Fenton called in is Ken Stern of Professional Market Builders, a Detroit marketing firm. Mr. Stern emphasizes the importance of research—focus groups, surveys of patients, and demographics studies.

His research for Dr. Fenton showed that women were confused and misinformed about breast examinations and breast cancer. Most didn't know how often they should get an examination, and many thought that the radiation from the exam was dangerous, when in fact, modern procedures are quite safe. Years ago, the American Cancer Society said a woman didn't need mammography until she was 50. Now physicians say no later than 40, but many women don't know that. He and Dr. Fenton decided that educational advertising would generate demand.

But Mr. Stern cautions that "nuances of each market determine how hard or soft to sell." And what's true for advertising also holds for other strategies, such as where to locate an office. For example, he found that patients in bustling Detroit like having their doctors' offices in shopping malls, while patients in more conservative Dayton, Ohio, don't.

Similarly, a group of Baton Rouge ophthalmologists found that their patients came from two distinct population groups. Sheila Jacobs, president of Healthcare Images, a firm that did the research, says one group was dominated by women 18 to 45, who make most of the medical decisions for their husbands and children. They were most concerned with getting the latest technology in eye care.

The other group was older people. "We found that they avoided surgery because they were afraid they wouldn't get good care and they were afraid of pain. Cost was the third consideration and convenience meant nothing."

So Ms. Jacobs designed two advertising campaigns. One emphasizes hi-tech; the other is a soft sell about being able to see your grandchildren again.

Sometimes the patients tell researchers what they could have told their doctors years ago. Patients want to be treated with dignity.

"What does your office look like?" asks Marilyn Benveniste, an Atlanta communications consultant who lectures doctors in marketing seminars. "Is the carpet clean? Are yesterday's Kleenex around the sign-in sheet? Does your waiting room look like a bus station?"

Mrs. Benveniste, whose husband is a dentist, tells physicians that a staff that smiles and genuinely cares about people brings in as many patients as an advertising campaign. "They've got to understand they're not the only person in town. That's old to business but new to medicine."

A Louisville-area ophthalmologist, Maurice John, recalls that it was considered unprofessional to take a management course when he was in medical school, "yet we're supposed to know how to deal with employees and run a business."

Dr. John has since taken a few business courses and has learned about marketing, though he still shies away from the word. He does "two or three hundred little things" that make his practice successful enough to support a 32-person staff and his own surgery center.

For example, he has video monitors in his office, so patients can watch films about eye care and surgery. And relatives who accompany a patient can watch the surgery live through cameras mounted in the operating room. The squeamish can select a movie from his entertainment library.

Dr. John does some big things along with the little things. He employs a public-relations firm, has a staff researcher and a community-service director who makes speeches and plans advertising. He has learned that a judicious use of technicians allows him to see more patients and still spend more time with each of them. He was the first doctor in the Louisville area to offer radial keratotomy, a controversial surgery procedure that corrects nearsightedness. He has advertised radial keratotomy on television.

For all that, he finds that patients are still his best source of referral. "We thank people for coming. My folks were big on 'yes, ma'am' and 'no, ma'am' and we push that in the office. Marcus Welby will never go out of style."

Dr. John concedes that his promotional efforts rankle some of his peers, who seem to want him to feel he is "doing something wrong." There are those who wonder about an inherent conflict between a doctor's role as a businessman scrambling for patients and as a healer.

One of those is Bryon J. Bailey, chairman of otolaryngology at the University of Texas Medical Branch in Galveston, who commented on the subject in the February 1985 issue of the *Journal of the American Medical Association.* Dr. Bailey fears that the physician's increased concern with marketing, advertising, and business management will distract from quality medical care. He wonders if competition will increase the incidence of unnecessary surgery and heighten conflict between specialties.

In the meantime, medical marketing doesn't seem likely to go away. Says Andrew Morley, an Atlanta physician who is collaborating on a book on the subject, "A good businessman has a good product. It's priced effectively and provides service. I don't have any problem with that. The days of the white-shoe, white-coat doctor who says 'Do as I say' are gone."

Selling God

Grey Advertising Inc. has applied the old soft sell to the Scriptures. A new public-service commercial promotes the Bible without ever mentioning God or religion. Instead, the New York ad agency's spot encourages people to view the Bible as a history book that can increase their appreciation of art, literature, and travel. "The history of Western Civilization begins in these pages. . . Come to the Bible to learn," actress Patricia Neal says as images of stained-glass windows flash on the screen.

The commercial was created for the Laymen's National Bible Committee, whose previous campaigns had stressed spirituality. "The committee tended to talk mainly to itself," says Sal Giacchi, the account supervisor at Grey. "We decided to reposition the Bible so it's more palatable to people who are turned off by organized religion."

Advertising the Bible is certainly a nobler assignment than trying to move Wheaties off the shelf. But in this secular age, some church groups are struggling much like packaged-goods marketers to convert nonusers to their product, whether it's the Bible or a specific brand of religion. The ads are slicker and less reverent than in the past, and they aren't confined to the religion pages of newspapers or to preachy, evangelical television shows. "You have to take risks and be provocative to get the customer's attention today," says the Rev. George Martin, executive director of the Episcopal Ad Project in Minneapolis. One of the proj-

The Episcopal Church welcomes you. Regardless of race, creed, color or the number of times you've been born.

Whether you've been born once or born again, the Episcopal Church invites you to come and join us in the fellowship and worship of Jesus Christ.
The Episcopal Church

Courtesy The Episcopal Ad Project, a ministry of St. Luke's Episcopal Church, 4557 Colfax S., Minneapolis, Minn., 55409

ect's print ads says: "The Episcopal Church welcomes you. Regardless of race, creed, color or the number of times you've been born."

The Episcopal Church's latest ad features Henry VIII and the message: "In the church started by a man who had six wives, forgiveness goes without saying." Mr. Martin expects flak from purists because it's not precisely correct to say Henry VIII started the church. "But we had a lot of fun with it," he says, "and the real message is forgiveness."

For television, religious advertisers increasingly are producing commercials with heart-warming, slice-of-life themes that might almost be confused with splashy ads for Kodak or McDonald's. In an ad for the Mormon sect, three muddy farm kids are having a water fight when their parents pull up in a truck. Instead of reprimanding the children, the father digs out his camera and snaps their picture. The jingle: "Don't let the magic pass you by."

Most Mormon ads deal with family values and don't proselytize; the church's name, in fact, is revealed only in the final three seconds. "But we hope people might feel more positively about our faith after seeing the commercials," says Gary Dixon, vice president of creative services at the church's ad agency. "We've had an image of being isolationists who are very solemn and think only about our own needs."

Some religious advertising is designed with the baby-boom generation in mind. Many of those people drifted away from religion in the 1960s and 1970s but now are settling down and starting families. The Saatchi & Saatchi Compton ad agency is preparing a public-service ad that depicts a parent teaching a child to ride a bicycle and advises, "You haven't given them everything until you've given them something to believe in." In a similar vein, an Episcopal ad shows two wide-eyed youngsters and asks, "Now that they know about Disneyland, isn't it time you told them about heaven?"

The more subtle the religious spiel, the greater the chance of getting a paid or public-service spot on television. "We encourage messages of an uplifting nature but won't allow anyone to promote doctrines or dogma," says Richard Gitter, a vice president at NBC. "Religion is a very personal, even passionate belief."

Grey Advertising had hoped its commercial portraying the Bible as a source of cultural enrichment would breeze through the clearance departments of all three major TV networks. But the agency is butting heads with CBS. The primary hang-up: all those stained-glass windows. "We only showed images of real people," Mr. Giacchi of Grey contends. "We purposely avoided any wings or halos." But among those people are King David and Jesus. "By our policy," a CBS spokeswoman says, "they are not secular."

Some churches believe personal contact is still the best marketing tool. But advertising has helped St. Luke's Episcopal Church in Minneapolis increase baptisms to 20 a year from 4. And the Central Church of the Nazarene in Flint, Michigan, attracted 28 visiting families one Sunday recently after running commercials supplied by the Nazarene central office.

The Nazarene commercials are the work of Rumrill-Hoyt, a New York ad agency whose biggest accounts include Bacardi rum and the New York lottery. "Not many agencies handle booze and gambling and a church that's against both of them," says Bill Hamilton, a creative director.

The commercials are parables based on true stories. One describes a retired schoolteacher helping a Vietnamese woman learn English, while another shows a pregnant unmarried woman finding comfort in the church. They are more blatant than some religious ads in that they invite people to make the Nazarene church "your home." Says Mr. Hamilton: "The Nazarenes have a very low profile, and we're trying to create an image of warmth and giving. Many people don't know that Nazarene refers to Jesus of Nazareth. They expect funny stuff like Holy Rollers."

8

The World Market

Searching for New Ideas Overseas

Browsing in a West German supermarket, executives from Minnetonka Inc. of Chaska, Minnesota, happened upon an intriguing product—toothpaste in a pump dispenser. This alternative to messy tubes hadn't yet reached U.S. shores, so Minnetonka quickly contacted Henkel, the German manufacturer.

Together, the companies brought the concept to America in the form of Check-Up toothpaste. Now, Colgate, Crest, and other major brands are being rushed out in pump form, too. "We make grocery shopping a regular part of our business trips to Europe," says Grant Wood, vice president of marketing at Minnetonka. "In this case, it helped give us a jump on our bigger competitors. We were like the tortoise beating the hare."

So much for Yankee ingenuity. In addition to pump toothpastes, U.S. marketers have looked abroad and found inspiration for such recent products as aseptic beverage cartons, hair-styling mousses, and body fragrance sprays. "The search across oceans and borders for new products is heating up," says Ervin Shames, president of General Foods Corp.'s international division. He adds that the energy shocks of the 1970s and the Japanese automobile invasion helped teach U.S. marketers and consumers "that we can't do it all, and that we can't necessarily do it best."

Facing sluggish growth in most consumer-goods markets, companies are racing to roll out new products that might net them a couple of extra market-share points. By copping an idea that has worked in another country, they can spare themselves months of research and perhaps millions of dollars. It's also a way to hedge against the high risk of new-product failure, says John Summers, director of new business development at Robin Hood Multifoods, a unit of International Multifoods Corp.

Whenever he travels abroad, Mr. Summers takes along an empty suitcase to load with samples. Lately, he says, "the cookie environment in the United Kingdom has been pretty interesting," and he has his eye on Scandinavian fiber-grain snack foods.

In a survey of senior marketing executives at a new-products conference in Canada in 1984, 86 percent said they deem foreign products a valuable source of ideas. But what is lacking at many companies is an "international intelligence" network. Product Initiatives, a new-product consulting company in Toronto, estimates that only 10 percent of companies have a regular system for tracking hot products.

Some companies subscribe to international new-product newsletters published in Britain and Japan; others use product-retrieval services that employ housewives to hunt for samples in grocery stores around the world. To satisfy reader demand, Dancer Fitzgerald Sample Inc., a New York ad agency, is adding a special international list to its *New Product News* bulletin.

Despite the keen interest, companies say they don't count on being able to duplicate the success of foreign products in the United States. Take tofu and soymilk from Japan. Both are struggling to find a niche in the United States. Food in tubes, likewise, hasn't caught on even though other countries sell everything from mayonnaise to caviar in what look like fat toothpaste tubes. "That's one of the great unexplained mysteries," says Norman Barnes, director of international marketing at Campbell Soup Co.

Gillette Co. brought out Body Flowers spray a year ago, but sales are weaker than in Europe. U.S. women view the sprays just as fragrances, whereas Europeans also use them as deodorants.

Carbonated Bubble Bath (Japan)

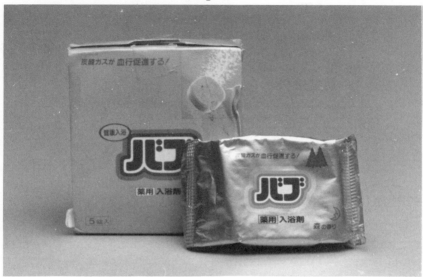

Plug-in Insecticide (Brazil)

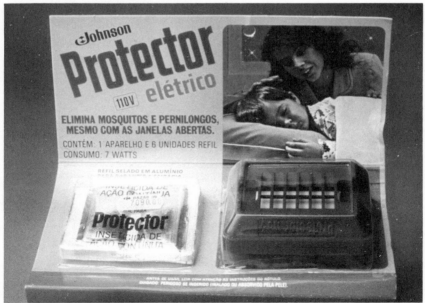

Photographs/products found by CAT*TRACK, a service of Product Initiatives.

Although it monitors the foreign competition closely, the Life Savers subsidiary of Nabisco Brands Inc. doesn't find confectionary products easily adaptable to the United States. "The cultural differences in food are vast," John Burke, manager of marketing research, says, noting that the popular hard candy flavors in Britain are currant and violet, and in South Africa, musk.

A new service will offer guidance on how well foreign products might fare in North America. Product Initiatives, the Toronto company, will select 50 new products quarterly and survey 400 consumers to measure their buying interest. In a pilot test, consumers gave high marks to such exotic offerings as a combination window cleaner/bug killer spray from South Africa and a Japanese carbonated bubble bath for reducing stress.

Such data could prove valuable because U.S. marketing executives tend to misjudge consumer tastes for foreign products. Many thought the British concept of selling yogurt and cereal in a two-section carton would be a hit. But in the pilot study, consumers were cool to the idea.

Sometimes, foreign products may simply need to be repackaged or repositioned. Consumer panelists frowned on an insecticide device from Brazil that could be plugged into an electrical outlet. The package showed a sleeping child, and the thought of a chemical wafting for hours through a child's bedroom was unnerving. Similarly, consumers didn't go much for champagne ice cream from France. The flavor wasn't the problem. Rather, people objected to the gimmicky plastic champagne bottles the dessert came in.

Most market researchers agree that Americans are becoming a ripe audience for innovative foreign products. People travel more and have more cosmopolitan tastes. They also want to have more fun at the supermarket. Although consumer panelists hooted when Product Initiatives showed them disposable men's underwear from Europe, they said they would love to be able to try such products. "They want pushing a shopping cart to be an adventure," says Edward Ogiba of Product Initiatives. "Too often, it's a drudgery."

Can World Brands
Cross Borders?

If advertising agencies had their way, multinational companies would all be racing to develop "world brands" that
could be marketed the same way around the globe. "As you
expand brands across continents, you keep getting bigger
economies of scale and more power," says John O'Toole,
chairman of Foote, Cone & Belding Communications Inc.

But multinational companies still have reservations
about attempting to create world brands despite such well-
known success stories as Coca-Cola and Marlboro cigarettes. Sweeping theories about world brands leave out
some important differences among countries, they reply.
And while some things like soft drinks have been successful
in many countries, executives find the obstacles much
tougher with other products.

Mark Sloan, European planning director for General
Foods Corp., wishes it were true that the world brand concept worked consistently. "It would save a lot of time," he
says. Instead, he finds it necessary to keep tailoring products to different national markets.

But differences from country to country are moderating,
says Prof. Theodore Levitt of the Harvard Business School.
He has become the high priest of the global-brands movement and is a frequent consultant to the major advertising
agencies.

As international communication increases, consumer
tastes become more similar around the world, Prof. Levitt

says. Smart companies save costs by operating "as if the entire world were a single entity," he adds. The benefits from this strategy "make the multinational corporation obsolete and the global corporation absolute," he maintains.

Big U.S. ad agencies such as Young & Rubicam Inc., Foote Cone & Belding and Doyle Dane Bernbach International Inc. agree with the global strategy idea. World brands are marketing's "most important development since television," a New York advertising executive declares. Another advocate is Europe's biggest agency, London-based Saatchi & Saatchi PLC.

Some cynics say that the biggest beneficiaries of global marketing are the major ad agencies. At Saatchi & Saatchi, global campaigns have fueled much of the agency's rapid growth in the past few years. When it won the British Airways account in 1982, it developed uniform television commercials that now appear in 34 countries with only the voice-over changed for each market. (In the United States, it is referred to as the "Manhattan Landing" commercial.)

These ads amount to a "British Airways campaign for Saatchi & Saatchi," says a London management consultant. The British ad agency doesn't like the criticism, but it has become more subdued about its global strategy. It concedes that "if you do dull advertising," no worldwide approach can compensate for it.

At Unilever PLC, the Anglo-Dutch food and detergent company, executives say it takes patience to cash in on a gradual merging of national tastes. Standard preferences are more common in detergents and soaps than in foods, they add. Unilever's Jif brand liquid soap sells well across Europe, but its margarine has different names and styles in each country. And Unilever says its Italian-style ice cream had to be modified for France even though sales were good elsewhere in Europe. The reason: a French belief that if it wasn't French, it wasn't worth eating.

In technology as well, international companies find global strategies can be hit and miss. Stand-alone products such as heart pacemakers can easily be sold the same way worldwide, says an ITT Corp. official. But telecommunications equipment has to function within the local phone system, and it would be naive to ignore national differences, the official adds. Personal computers, too, are being sold with plenty of variations. Acorn Computers PLC, a British personal-computer maker, plays up technical specifications in ads for the highly competitive British market but puts more emphasis on how easy its machines are to use in ads for the German market.

Commonly cited as a company with a successful global strategy is Levi Strauss & Co., the San Francisco blue-jeans maker. That amuses Rudolf Deutekom, head of Levi Strauss's European operations, because a few years ago the strategy started to go awry when the Swedes stopped buying jeans.

At first, Levi Strauss figured Sweden was an oddity. But with the U.S. market for ordinary jeans fading as well, the company moved into the broader market for casual clothes in those two countries, even selling clothing without the Levi name attached.

Then other European markets also cut back on jeans buying. So Levi Strauss is experimenting with different kinds of casual clothes, including a range of tops, trousers, and matching outfits, in France, Germany, and Italy. At such times as these, Mr. Deutekom says, it is essential to know how to switch between a global and a multinational strategy.

Caveats for Global Marketers

Grey Advertising Inc., which has done global marketing for such products as Revlon's Flex shampoo and BankAmerica travelers' checks, suggests three questions companies should ask themselves about selling products in other countries. A negative answer to even one indicates that a single global marketing strategy probably would flop:

Has the market developed in the same way from country to country? Grey notes that Kellogg's Pop-Tarts failed in Britain because toasters weren't used widely. The continued popularity of clotheslines in Europe similarly meant little demand for fabric-softener sheets used in dryers.

Are the consumer targets similar in different nations? Canon found that in advertising 35mm cameras in the United States, it had to appeal to people who are fearful about complex technological products. Many Japanese consumers, on the other hand, seek sophisticated, high-tech products.

Do consumers share the same wants and needs around the world? In the United States, General Foods Corp. successfully positioned Tang as a substitute for orange juice at breakfast, but discovered that in France people drink little orange juice, and almost none at breakfast. General Foods had to create a totally different advertising approach promoting Tang as a refreshment for any time of day.

In a survey of big multinational companies, Grey found that half favor a world ad campaign. About 60 percent of the respondents are centralizing their advertising management, and 75 percent believe that hiring one agency to handle all international marketing would be ideal. About 71 percent still employ more than one agency, however.

The companies surveyed also say they are encountering resistance from the managers of their overseas offices who view global marketing as a threat to their autonomy. "The whole idea has been oversimplified by some people," says Barbara Feigin, an executive vice president at Grey. "There's not a simple answer for every company and every brand in every single country."

Playing by
International Rules

When General Mills Inc. decided to advertise Action Man soldiers in West Germany, it wasn't a simple matter of changing the language in its commercials. The company had to film an entirely different TV spot to tone down the violence. Instead of holding machine guns and driving tanks, the toy soldiers could be shown on German television only if they were unarmed and seated in jeeps rather than tanks.

In Austria, where companies aren't permitted to use children in commercials, some advertisers have resorted to hiring dwarfs and showing animated drawings of kids instead. And the Marlboro cowboy has been sidelined altogether by stiff regulations in Britain. The reasoning: Heroic figures in cigarette ads might have special appeal and encourage people to start smoking.

Such restrictions have become a nettlesome fact of life for advertisers as more countries regulate the content of ads and as companies step up their international marketing. The maze of government regulations makes it difficult to create a universal ad campaign that can work in dozens of countries. "You have to be infinitely more creative and flexible now to make advertisements that can be used in a number of places," says Edward Roncarelli, president of the multinational business group at the Foote, Cone & Belding ad agency.

At the J. Walter Thompson ad agency, executives point to a 30-second Kellogg cereal commercial produced for British TV to show how much regulations in Europe alone can sap an ad. References to iron and vitamins would have to be deleted in the Netherlands; a child wearing a Kellogg's T-shirt would be edited out in France where children are forbidden from endorsing products on TV. And in Germany, the line, "Kellogg makes their cornflakes the best they've ever been" would be axed because of rules against making competitive claims. After the required changes, the commercial would be about five seconds long.

Lately, there has been a push in particular to restrict ads for cigarettes, children's products, liquor, and pharmaceuticals. "It's really a thicket for drug companies to pick their way through," says James Adler, director of Saatchi & Saatchi Compton Worldwide, an ad agency. "Some countries don't allow analgesic ads at all, some refuse comparative ads, and others won't allow companies to mention whether doctors recommend the product." Doyle Dane Bernbach, another ad shop, notes that a Panadol ad lost much of its selling power when the Singapore government required the headline to be watered down to, "Panadol relieves headaches."

The International Advertising Association has formed a global commission on product marketing that hopes to head off more government rules by encouraging advertisers to regulate themselves. Some companies blame the regulatory trend on the growing influence of consumer advocacy groups in some countries.

Nationalistic policies also are curbing advertisers' freedom. More countries now are requiring local production of at least a portion of TV commercials to build fledgling film industries and create more jobs. "These rules wreck the economies of scale for big companies like Revlon," says Anthony Thurston, vice president and general manager at Grey Advertising Inc.'s international division.

In one Revlon commercial for Jontue perfume, a young woman trips through a pastoral estate filled with deer and peacocks and gets scooped up by a man on horseback. The ad has a fantasy feel to it, with little sense of time or place. Still, Revlon ended up spending an extra $100,000 to film nearly identical versions in Australia and Colombia. Both countries refused the U.S. ad.

Some companies try to hold extra production expenses to a minimum by flying film crews from restrictive foreign countries to a commercial shooting site in the United States. Often, such people get paid for just standing around with their hands in their pockets, but their unions and government officials seem appeased nonetheless.

It's becoming especially tough for cigarette companies to find legal ways to keep their brand names and images before the public. "The situation is getting absolutely ridiculous," complains Robert Barocci, president of the international division of the Leo Burnett Co. ad agency. He says that in Britain, where the Marlboro cowboy is outlawed, Philip Morris couldn't even show a chuck wagon and a lit camp fire in its ads. That would indicate that the cowboy was lurking nearby.

The United States, of course, has its share of government and TV network regulations: Cigarettes can't be pitched on TV at all, and actors in beer commercials aren't permitted to guzzle the brew on camera. "But in the area of children's products, the United States is an advertiser's paradise compared with many countries," says Christopher Campbell, international marketing director at the Parker Brothers subsidiary of General Mills.

The other countries' aim is to protect kids from exploitation. For instance, candy companies must show a toothbrush in their ads in the Netherlands. And in France, Mr. Campbell says, he can spend a maximum of just $130,000 a year per toy on ads.

Parker Brothers plays it safe by using animation and showing only the hands of children playing with games or turning the pages of books. It also avoids celebrities believed to have some influence over children. "In the United Kingdom," says Mr. Campbell, "we would violate the rules if we used someone like Captain Kangaroo or Mister Rogers in a commercial before 9 P.M."

Gillette Travels to the Third World

Gillette Co. discovered a while back that only 8 percent of Mexican men who shave use shaving cream. The rest soften their beards with soapy water or—ouch!—plain water, neither of which Gillette sells.

Sensing an opportunity, Gillette introduced in Guadalajara plastic tubs of shaving cream that sell for half the price of its aerosol. Today 13 percent of Guadalajaran men use shaving cream, and Gillette is planning to sell its new product, Prestobarba (Spanish for "quick shave"), in the rest of Mexico, Colombia, and Brazil.

Tailoring its marketing to Third World budgets and tastes—from packaging blades so they can be sold one at a time, to educating the unshaven about the joys of a smooth face—has become an important part of Gillette's growth strategy. The company sells its pens, toiletries, toothbrushes, and other products in developing countries. But despite Gillette's efforts to diversify, razor blades still produce one third of the company's revenue and two thirds of its pre-tax profit.

The market for blades in developed countries is stagnant. "The opportunities on the blade side really lie in new geography," says Rodney Mills, an executive vice president for Gillette's international business. "In the Third World, there's a very high proportion of people under 15 years old. All those young men are going to be in the shaving population in a very short time."

Courtesy the Gillette Company

Few U.S. consumer-products companies that compete in the Third World have devoted as much energy or made as many inroads as Gillette, which draws more than half its sales from abroad. Since the company targeted the developing world in 1969, the proportion of its sales that come from Latin America, Asia, Africa, and the Middle East has doubled to 20 percent and the dollar volume has risen sevenfold.

Gillette has had a strong business in Latin America since it began building plants there in the 1940s. Fidel Castro once told television interviewer Barbara Walters that he grew a beard because he couldn't get Gillette blades while fighting in the mountains.

The company's push into Asia, Africa, and the Middle East dates to 1969, when Gillette dropped a policy of investing only where it could have 100 percent-owned subsidiaries. That year, it formed a joint venture in Malaysia, which was threatening to bar imports of Gillette products. The company has added one foreign plant nearly every year, in such countries as China, Egypt, Thailand, and India and, Mr. Mills says, is now looking at Pakistan, Nigeria, and Turkey.

The company always starts with a factory that makes double-edged blades—still popular in the Third World—and, if all goes well, expands later into production of pens, deodorants, shampoo, or toothbrushes. Only a few ventures have gone sour: A Yugoslav project never got off the ground, and Gillette had to sell its interest in Iran to its local partners.

In a few markets, Gillette has developed products exclusively for the Third World. The low-cost shaving cream is one. Another is Black Silk, a hair relaxer developed for sale to blacks in South Africa and now being introduced in Kenya.

More often, Gillette sells familiar products in different packages or smaller sizes. Because many Latin American consumers can't afford a seven-ounce bottle of Silkience shampoo, for instance, Gillette sells it in half-ounce plastic bubbles. In Brazil, Gillette sells Right Guard deodorant in plastic squeeze bottles instead of metal cans. "It's a poor man's aerosol," says David Waldron, Gillette's Latin American marketing manager.

But the toughest task for Gillette is convincing Third World men to shave. The company recently began dispatching portable theaters to remote villages—Gillette calls them "mobile propaganda units"—to show movies and commercials that tout daily shaving.

In South African and Indonesian versions, a bewildered bearded man enters a locker room where clean-shaven friends show him how to shave. In the Mexican one, a handsome sheriff, tracking bandits who have kidnapped a woman, pauses on the trail to shave every morning. The camera lingers as he snaps a double-edged blade into his razor, lathers his face, and strokes it carefully. In the end, of course, the smooth-faced sheriff gets the woman.

In other places, Mr. Mills says, Gillette agents with an oversized shaving brush and a mug of shaving cream lather up and shave a villager while others watch. Plastic razors are then distributed free and blades—which, of course, must be bought—are left with the local storekeeper.

Such campaigns win few immediate converts, acknowledges Robert King, director of international marketing, planning, and administration. Migration of peasants to the city does more to boost Gillette sales. "If you slog around in the field all day, there's not much incentive to shave," he says. "If in the next generation, you move into the city and the older son gets a job as a counter clerk, he'll probably have to shave if not everyday, then every other day."

Only recently has Gillette begun to ease a policy of never using its prime trademarks—the Gillette and Papermate names, for instance—in countries where it owns less than 100 percent of a venture. The drawbacks of the old practice became obvious several years ago when Gillette began sponsoring the World Cup in soccer and posting its name on stadium walls that are seen on television around the world.

"All of those messages are wasted in markets where the Gillette name is not being licensed," Mr. Mills says.

China:
Four Approaches

When Fluor Corp. opened its office in Peking back in 1978—one of the early American companies to do so—its officials knew they would need staying power.

"We never had any illusions," says Fluor Chairman David Tappan. "It's a long-term opportunity, a long-term potential." It was a good thing they felt that way; the company, he says, has been putting more money overall into all its projects there than it has been taking out.

Now that China has embarked on a major business push, Fluor thinks the cash is going to start flowing back out, and the company is forging ahead. "We've decided . . . to significantly increase the time, manpower, and effort devoted to China," says Mr. Tappan. In early 1985 Fluor signed a big petrochemical joint venture contract there.

No one knows for sure whether doing business with China henceforth really is going to be easier or more profitable than in the past. But scores of American companies are starting to think—like Fluor—that it's time to try harder to find out.

The number of U.S. companies' Peking representative offices spurted by 20 percent in 1984, to over 140. One U.S. commercial officer says his business-seeking visitors have doubled since 1984. Adds an American lawyer there, "If my firm lets loose every client who wants to do China business, I'll be dead tomorrow."

Herewith are the experiences of four major U.S. companies that have started major ventures recently to cash in on the business push.

1. When Gould Inc. Vice Chairman David Simpson arrived in Peking in October 1984, to open his company's first office there, he was feeling a sense of urgency. Ten days earlier, China had announced a dramatic new market-oriented policy. Do-business fervor was in the air.

"My gut feeling is an enormous rush to get into the door before it closes," he said after the celebratory banquet. "The faster you get in, the better." He was thinking of the competition, not political reversals. "If you don't get through the gate, you'll be locked out," he said.

The lure for Gould, which makes computer equipment to regulate industrial processes, is China's huge, aging industrial base. One of China's major goals is to upgrade and modernize as many of its million factories as possible. "If they're all prepared to upgrade, then the spending power is enormous," Mr. Simpson concludes.

Still, he admits, the actual size and growth of the market for Gould's products is hard to estimate. "We haven't got a figure for the China market," he says. "But it's big."

Gould isn't staking the shop on that feeling, though. It isn't investing any capital, concentrating instead on licensing Chinese factories to produce Gould products. In 1984, it signed one $12 million licensing agreement, two more are on the way, and its Peking office is sifting through prospects.

Right now, sales of Gould's computers, either directly or in systems being installed in Chinese factories by other companies, represent just a tiny fraction of Gould's sales, which in 1983 totaled $1.32 billion. Still, says Mr. Simpson, "It's the biggest opportunity we have worldwide because it's brand new. It's virgin territory."

2. Otis Group Inc. President Francois Jaulin was looking over his shoulder en route to the China market. A Swiss competitor, Schindler Holding AG, had set up shop in Shanghai back in 1980. And the Japanese had invaded. Elevators in luxury hotels rising throughout China increasingly bear names like Mitsubishi and Hitachi.

China was installing 5,000 elevators a year in 1985. Chinese officials predicted that within 10 years demand would grow to 10,000 a year. Otis, a unit of United Technologies Corp.—which accounts for 20,000 of the 100,000 elevators sold in the world each year—figured it couldn't let China slip away.

"I can't miss the train with competitors in the Pacific and me not having access to the source," Mr. Jaulin said as he came to sign a joint venture to build elevators in Tianjin.

Under an interim agreement approved in 1983, Otis sold 100 elevators and escalators here, and since has sold some more. But China is pressing to build at home. "It would be crazy to assume China is going to import elevators forever," Mr. Jaulin said.

In 1985 Otis had seven of its own employees working in a Chinese factory, helping upgrade production of the 600 elevators a year the factory makes, and working toward turning out at least 2,000 a year after 10 years. The Chinese company is profitable, but Mr. Jaulin doesn't expect to take out any profits for years. Because of China's urge to hang onto foreign exchange, the joint venture will have to make its own foreign exchange-generating sales to get money for Otis to take home.

Mr. Jaulin said the venture will make its "best efforts" to export 25 percent of the factory's output within three or four years. But clearly his mind is on the China market. "Every country wants to export half its production," he says. "But if we did that, the sea would be full of elevator parts."

3. For Nabisco Brands Inc., the China market has an age-old attraction: the lure of a billion mouths to feed.

"This is a great market," says William Seidler, a Nabisco senior vice president who helped negotiate a joint-venture contract under which Nabisco and a Chinese company will jointly build a factory in Peking to make Ritz crackers. Within 100 miles of the plant, he says, are millions of people who need convenience food, who spend a lot of their disposable income on edibles, and who like baked goods. "It's mind-boggling in terms of potential," he declares.

Nabisco is starting out small. The total venture is valued at $8.8 million. The 6,000-ton annual capacity, one-production-line plant the company plans to build is "tiny" compared with operations in other parts of the world, Mr. Seidler says. In the United States, its smallest plant has three production lines; the largest, 20.

But the sense of huge promise is present. As the company was discussing how to plan its contractual commitment to export, officials decided not to make the pledge in terms of a certain percentage of sales. Instead, it promised to export a certain number of tons of crackers—between 300 to 900 tons a year at first. "If this thing grows as fast as we hope it will, 5 percent of sales will flood the world," says Mr. Seidler.

4. Fluor Corp. opened its China office and signed its first contract back in 1978. It has stayed there through a number of Chinese reversals, including one that cost it a major venture. After 18 months and 235,000 worker-hours of engineering work by Fluor, China canceled a plan to build the world's largest copper mine.

In the fall of 1984, Fluor entered a major joint-venture engineering project with a Chinese petrochemical company to upgrade existing oil refineries and contract for new ones. Fluor won't discuss financial terms of the contract.

As Mr. Tappan has been telling other business executives in speeches over the past few months, the company bases its positive view of China partly on political factors. The year "1984 will go down as a very significant year for U.S.-China trade relations," he says, noting the visit of Chinese Premier Zhao Ziyang to the United States, the visit of President Reagan to China, and China's participation in the Olympics in the United States.

Also, Fluor's operations there seem to be changing for the better. This year, says Mr. Tappan, "It's the beginning of the reverse" into a positive cash flow.

9

Corporate Strategies

P&G Rivals Try to
Beat the Leader

Long before most companies ever bothered with such things as consumer research, a former manager at Procter & Gamble Co. remembers heading to work for nine months with one brand of deodorant under his right arm and another under his left.

At the end of each day, he would report to a small office where a researcher would sniff to see how each product was holding up. "We always said only guinea pigs need apply at that company," the former P&Ger recalls. "P&G tested everything imaginable."

Such stories are typical of Procter & Gamble, whose reputation for thoroughness is just one reason many regard it as the nation's premier marketing company. Its long dominance of the household-products industry is another. With its record of creating such well-known products as Tide detergent, Crest toothpaste, and Pampers disposable diapers, the Cincinnati giant has often seemed in a different league from its rivals.

Recently, however, Brand X has been striking back. No longer behind in marketing sophistication, P&G's competitors have been waging increasingly tough battles in some of its most critical markets. Colgate may be on the verge of passing Crest. Tide is under pressure from Wisk. And Pampers' market share, which reached 75 percent a decade before, was down to less than 33 percent in 1985.

The competitive onslaught reflects improvements in the

opposition more than failure at P&G. Nevertheless, as the company's rivals have become sharper, they also have been finding chinks in P&G's armor. Being called into question are such bedrock marketing practices as brand management, network television advertising, and test marketing.

"The old disciplines haven't been as successful as they were in the past," writes Cliff Angers, a senior vice president at Ogilvy & Mather, in a report on P&G to clients of the New York ad agency. One result: For the first time in more than three decades, P&G expects to report a decline in profit for the fiscal year ending June 1985.

Although its executives rarely publicly acknowledge even the existence of any rivals, P&G's own actions testify to the heightened competition. In recent years, it has taken such uncharacteristic steps as launching products without test marketing, introducing brands that don't exhibit any quality advantage, and experimenting with image advertising.

P&G officials, however, deny that the company has ever faced weak competition. "None of our competitors have ever been pushovers," says a company spokesman. He adds that one reason P&G seems to be fighting tougher competition these days is that it has gone into new markets and is now battling the likes of Coca-Cola Co. and other savvy marketers.

Nevertheless, while P&G officials say they fully expect to make up lost ground, some marketing experts and competitors believe they are witnessing the end of an era in the packaged-goods business. "Procter & Gamble probably will never be as dominant as it was in the past," says Laurel Cutler, vice chairman of Leber Katz Partners, a New York ad agency. Emboldened by his company's inroads against P&G in the diaper market, Darwin Smith, chairman of Kimberly-Clark Co., vowed to shareholders that the company would "continue making life miserable for Procter & Gamble."

To an extent, P&G has been a victim of its own success. As companies have put more emphasis on marketing, many have raided P&G's ranks for talent. A directory of P&G alumni lists hundreds of former executives now at such companies as Bristol-Myers, PepsiCo Inc., and Warner-Lambert. When P&G re-entered the feminine hygiene market in 1984, two of its top three opponents—Johnson & Johnson and Tambrands Inc.—both were headed by past Procter & Gamble executives. The third—Kimberly-Clark—had a P&G alumnus in charge of the division responsible for that business.

But P&G's competitors no longer merely copy its system. Geared to selling blockbuster brands to legions of shoppers with similar tastes, the classic P&G mass-market system worked best when the preferences of its customers were more homogeneous than they are today.

Essentially, that system called for entering a market slowly, studying all the angles, and then launching a clearly superior product with a huge advertising blast. Selling a better brand, in turn, meant that P&G usually could charge a higher price, which helped fuel its extensive research activities and big ad budgets.

But in a faster-moving and less stable market, the super-cautious approach can easily backfire—a fact that P&G executives acknowledge and say they are trying to remedy. Kimberly-Clark, for instance, owes part of its success in diapers to beating P&G to nationwide sales of a product with refastenable tabs. The two companies actually had begun testing the product improvement at about the same time. While P&G took time to make sure it had the tabs just right, Kimberly-Clark raced into the market and began capturing sales.

Edwin Shutt, Jr., president of Tambrands Inc., estimates his company was able to develop and market its highly successful Maxithin panty shields in half the time it would have taken at P&G, where he once worked. "Here you have to only go through a few layers to get something approved," Mr. Shutt says. "At P&G it was more like seven or eight."

By improving their technical skills, the opposition also has been making it increasingly difficult for P&G to stick to its policy of selling only the best-quality products. For years, it has taught its executives that a brand must demonstrate in a blind test that at least 55 of 100 consumers prefer it over the closest competitor. However, achieving noticeable superiority in something like a toothpaste or deodorant is a difficult task. And even when it happens, it often doesn't last. When P&G first developed its new Duncan Hines cookies, for instance, the product reportedly had one of the highest blind-test scores in company history. But by the time the cookies were selling nationwide, Nabisco, Frito-Lay, and Keebler all had introduced their own versions, eliminating any taste advantage.

P&G has since sued all three of the competitors in Delaware federal court, alleging they violated its patents. Meanwhile, P&G executives, while agreeing that product quality has improved at its competitors, still maintain P&G brands are the best.

Scores that measure superiority also have become less meaningful as markets have become more fragmented, with dozens of brands offering different advantages to suit different consumer tastes. In such a market, even a product that was outscored 90 to 10 by the leading brand theoretically could become a best seller if the same 10 percent also stuck with it against other brands.

Moreover, such long-time rivals as Colgate-Palmolive Co. and Lever Brothers Co. often have shown more skill at selling products that have less tangible consumer benefits. Colgate, for instance, has moved within striking distance of P&G's Crest by doing a better job with pump dispensers. As a result, industry officials say Colgate's share of the market is within one-half a percentage point of Crest and still gaining.

"Procter sometimes hurts itself by giving the consumer too much credit," says a former executive. If they think something is junk, "they won't touch it even if it becomes the next big seller." P&G officials agree that they tend to ignore products that they consider faddish.

Competitors cite just that sort of rationale as a possible explanation of why P&G avoided making a serious effort in the liquid detergent market, where Lever's Wisk has captured nearly a 40 percent share.

The difficulties of maintaining any product advantage

also have undermined P&G's historical strategy of slapping premium prices on its brands. Lever Brothers saw an opening in the fabric-softener market in 1983 because of the high prices P&G was charging for its Downy brand. Entering with Snuggle, a brand priced at about 15 percent below the P&G product, Lever was able to quickly capture a share of the business.

For similar reasons, competitors say they have forced P&G away from its practice of spending 60 percent of its marketing dollars on advertising, which is better for building long-term franchises, and 40 percent on promotion, which is better for short-term results. Although P&G won't discuss its ad budget, industry officials say that because of constant day-to-day price battles, the company recently has had to pour more money into promotion, thereby raising its costs.

Many of P&G's rivals also have been moving away from the brand-management system it has been using since the early 1930s. In its classic form, brand management assigns the responsibility for a brand to one executive, who coordinates all business decisions that affect it. Within certain constraints, the job is to build sales of that product as much as possible, even in competition with other company brands.

But just as politicians often try to broaden their appeal by moving closer to center, brand managers are sometimes tempted to do the same with the product for which they are responsible. In a mass market, that might be good. But in a highly fragmented product category, a company is usually better off if each of its entries aims at its own distinct audience.

"The big problem P&G has had in diapers is that its two products, Luvs and Pampers, are too similar," says a former executive. "You have to wonder if that would have happened if Procter wasn't still sticking to its traditional system."

As P&G's rivals have come closer to matching its strengths, their own strong points have worked even more to their advantage. The most noticeable has been the powerful ties of some companies to the wholesale and retail buyers, an area where P&G has traditionally been weak. Although Procter is scrambling to catch up, companies like General Foods and Pillsbury enjoy long-standing good will. For years, they have cultivated relationships through such steps as conducting studies to help the trade do its business more efficiently.

As P&G has increasingly been beaten in the market-place, even companies that were self-proclaimed imitators of its system have been changing their ways. Once an equally deliberate and cautious mass marketer, Campbell Soup Co. a few years ago began breaking out of the P&G mold. Emphasizing a far more entrepreneurial approach, it began fragmenting its market segments and targeting more of its new products at selected groups. Following its new system, the company has been the leading introducer of new products since 1980.

"There was a time here when you would frequently hear people asking 'Is that what P&G would do?'" says Marty Buchalski, general manager of Campbell's refrigerated-foods division. "You don't hear that so much anymore."

Riunite: Selling Wine Like Soda Pop

Wine snobs may turn up their noses, but one of the unheralded marketing successes of the past decade is Riunite wine. Described by a large New York retailer as a "lollipop wine," it is sweeter, fruitier, fizzier, lower in alcoholic content and—at about $3 a bottle—less expensive than the drinks that might please oenophiles.

But that hasn't hindered Riunite. In 1980, 9.1 million 2.4-gallon cases were sold in the United States, up 35 percent from 1979 and almost equal to total French and German wine sales in the United States in 1980. Outselling its closest imported competitor three-to-one, Riunite accounts for nearly one fourth of all imported table wine consumed.

Still, John Mariani, chairman of Villa Banfi, the importer and marketer of Riunite, admits to some anxiety. "I feel like a student going into final exams," he says. Mr. Mariani's test: mounting competition, notably from Coca-Cola, which is introducing a line of wines as a direct rival to Riunite.

Mr. Mariani's strategy for maintaining Banfi's growth: continuing Riunite's heady ad spending, promoting a second, similar line of wines, and adding higher-priced classier ones. "When Coke says it's going to stop Riunite," Mr. Mariani says, "that's a lot of malarkey." His 1981 sales goal for the brand is 11.5 million cases, up 27 percent from the prior year.

Much of Banfi's success comes from imitating Coca-Cola,

April is National Riunite Tasting Month. Have a little Riunite on us.

We're telling millions on network TV, in magazines and in newspapers to go buy a little Riunite (187 ml.) from you and send the bill to us! Profit from our April foolishness!

It's America's first ever coast-to-coast wine tasting and the Riunite is on us! Riunite is telling the world to taste a little Riunite and get up to the full purchase price back from us. Or your customers can get a $1.25 refund from Riunite when they buy a 750 ml., 1.5 L or 3 L size!

Bonus! Every refund will arrive with a $2 bonus! $2 worth of money-saving coupons on 750 ml., 1.5 L or 3 L sizes of Riunite. Bonus profits for you!

April will be a history-making month for the wine industry, for Riunite and for you! What better time to stock, display, and feature America's best loved imported wine—Riunite!

A complete "Riunite on Us" Display Kit is ready now. Be sure to order yours today from your Riunite Distributor.

What's better than Riunite on ice? Riunite on us! A little Riunite can make you a lot of money in April!*

Riunite

Miller Brewing, and other beverage mass-marketers. Their lessons: Spend millions on advertising to create brand identities, utilize the economies of scale that come from selling large volumes, and most of all, remember that Americans like their drinks sweet and cold.

"The only difference between Riunite and Coca-Cola," says John Gibbons, a Pace University management professor and consultant to Banfi, "is that one has alcohol and the other doesn't."

Lately Banfi even is telling consumers to look at Riunite as an alternative to Coke. "We no longer think of ourselves competing exclusively in the wine market," says Sandy Jamieson, marketing director. "The refrigerator, not the wine cellar, is the place to store Riunite, right next to the orange juice, beer, and soft drinks."

To accomplish that, Banfi is banking on an ad budget of $14 million, two thirds of it for TV commercials, and a 6.3-ounce bottle nicknamed the "cutie." The company hopes to win acceptance for the bottle at restaurant salad bars, fast-food outlets, airlines, and sports events; it also will push the smaller size in supermarkets.

Mr. Mariani counts on such tactics to push Banfi's 1981 U.S. sales to a record $225 million, many times more than its sales in the late 1960s, when it was a small New York importer that specialized in wines popular in the city's Italian neighborhoods.

Unlike other importers of that time, John Mariani and his younger brother Harry didn't want to wait until Americans' tastes in wine caught up to Europeans'. "It was becoming fashionable to drink wine," recalls Frank Gentile, Banfi's senior vice president, "but a lot of people didn't like the taste of the wines the industry was trying to force them to drink."

They did like sweet wines, though, particularly cold duck, Asti Spumante, sangria, and Portuguese rose. Finding an Italian grape cooperative that made a sweet Lambrusco wine that they thought would satisfy American palates, the Marianis began importing it in 1969. Another important feature of the wine: It didn't need aging, a process that tied up capital, so Riunite could be priced at $1.99 a bottle.

Immediately successful, Riunite continued growing and confounded skeptics who said the wine would be a short-lived fad, as cold duck had become. Many Riunite buyers were first-time wine-drinkers who later branched out to other types, increasing the total demand for wines.

"Banfi has contributed a great deal to our industry," says Jack Battipaglia, a major New York retailer. "It catered to the masses, but those masses eventually became the classes." With increased sales came more competition, chiefly from Cella and Giacobazzi wines. Similar in price and character to Riunite, they were the next-best-selling imports in 1980, with volume of about 2.3 million cases each.

Those competitors helped expand the market for low-priced wines, says John Mariani. He hopes Coca-Cola will do likewise with its Taylor Lake Country Soft. Like Riunite, it is sweet and has about 9 percent alcohol content, compared to about 12 percent in traditional wines. It also will be advertised heavily.

Regardless of whether Coke's wine increases the size of the market or takes share from Riunite, Banfi is diversifying for part of its future growth. The company has invested in two wine operations in Italy and one in California.

A product from one of those ventures is Bell'Agio, a new wine comparable to Riunite in price and appeal but, because of its grapes, different in taste. In traditional marketing terms, Bell'Agio will be a "flanker brand"—close to the parent in most respects but different enough to appeal to consumers who don't buy Riunite, thus adding to Banfi's sales and deflecting competition.

The other wines from those investments will be higher-priced vintage wines to add to those Banfi already imports. As Americans become more familiar with wine, says Mr. Mariani, demand for more sophisticated wines will increase. Banfi, he hopes, will be ready to fill those needs.

Update

Riunite hasn't reached Mr. Mariani's sales goal of 11.5 million cases a year, instead peaking at 11.3 million cases in 1984. In late 1985, Villa Banfi faced a serious setback when it had to recall 1.2 million cases of Riunite that were suspected of containing trace amounts of a nontoxic chemical. A separate wine scare in 1986 over the adulteration of various wines was expected to hamper the brand's sales and reputation, even though Riunite wasn't implicated.

Villa Banfi's plans for Bell'Agio, its "flanker brand" to Riunite, didn't live up to expectations. Sales of Bell'Agio were only 500,000 cases in 1985, although a similar-tasting version of Riunite, known as Riunite D'Oro, has gained acceptance.

Chattem Gets Big with Small Brands

If John A. Patten hadn't died suddenly in 1915, at age 48, prosperity might have come sooner for Chattem Inc. A believer in thorough distribution and advertising, Mr. Patten dispatched his patent-medicine salesmen by horse and buggy to backwoods general stores, and he painted barn roofs with a genteel slogan for his alcohol-laced menstrual cramps remedy: "Are you a woman? Take Cardui."

But Mr. Patten's death marked the start of nearly 60 years of hibernation for Chattem. Profits in 1959 were lower than in 1919; Black Draught laxative, the product on which the company was founded in 1879, was still its biggest seller 90 years later. "We'd be a big company today if John Patten hadn't been succeeded by a banker," says Alex Guerry, his grandson and Chattem's chairman since 1959.

A bit late perhaps, but this little Chattanooga company finally is strutting its stuff. It has taken dud brands from the likes of Gillette Co., American Cyanamid Co., and SmithKline Beckman Corp. and made them into winners. Chattem's sales—$78.9 million in the year ended May 1982 had grown at a compounded rate of 18 percent a year since 1976. Profits from continuing operations—$4.4 million in fiscal 1982—had advanced 22 percent annually.

There's no unusual marketing genius at work, though. Chattem simply is small enough to appreciate small brands. "Something that isn't worth the time of day to a big company," says Mr. Guerry, "is important to us."

One such product is Sun-In, a peroxide hair lightener acquired from Gillette in early 1974. With only $500,000 in annual sales, it was almost a nonentity at Gillette, which had revenue then of $1.06 billion. Tiny Chattem pumped in ad money and Sun-In sales quadrupled within three years. In 1982 they were at the $4 million level.

Other acquisitions benefited from careful market research. A mud-pack facial cleanser named Mudd originally was pitched to teen-age girls with the slogan "Mudd zaps zits." Chattem found instead that women were better prospects and, within seven years, annual sales jumped to $3 million from $90,000.

The company also has chosen its products carefully, nimbly sidestepping much larger foes in cosmetics, perfume, analgesics, and hair coloring. When American Cyanamid was auctioning its broad line of Corn Silk cosmetics in 1977, for example, Chattem only picked up a powdered makeup for oily teen-age complexions, thus staying clear of Revlon Inc. and other cosmetics giants.

Likewise, Chattem bought Love's Baby Soft fragrances from SmithKline because they were popular with teen-age girls, a group most other perfume marketers overlooked. Chattem's small corner of the analgesic market is Pamprin, a remedy for menstrual pain and the company's only major home-grown product.

Chattem's strategy, as its managers are fond of repeating, is "to be big in small markets." That philosophy is carried out as well in the industrial chemical division, which accounts for just over half the company's revenue. Its specialty chemicals—including buffering agents for Bristol-Myers Co.'s Bufferin and ingredients in Warner-Lambert Co.'s Rolaids and Schering-Plough Corp.'s Di-Gel antacids—have few competitors.

More recently, though, Chattem's ambitions swelled as it tried to triple the size of its $36 million consumer-products division within four years. The company hunted for more products to buy, including some with sales of up to $20 million, and may even acquire, or merge with, another small consumer-products concern.

At the same time, Chattem is redoubling its efforts behind Pamprin. Another version, Maximum Cramp Relief Pamprin, is being backed with a $4.5 million ad campaign that compares the analgesic to Johnson & Johnson's Tylenol, which Chattem research found was used by more women than either Pamprin or rival Midol. Expectations are for Pamprin, which had fiscal 1982 sales of $8.5 million, to triple in dollar volume within three years.

The company also wants to develop its own new products, a talent it has conspicuously lacked. An attempt to add a Mudd moisturizing cream flopped, and Chattem executives regretfully recall other more promising new-product ideas that weren't pursued.

An odorless salve for sore muscles is one of the ideas that never went past a Chattem bull session. Thompson Medical Co., on its own, introduced one under the name Sportscreme, prompting Chattem's chief financial officer to later scribble in the margins of a Thompson annual report, next to a passage about Sportscreme: "We are a day late and a dollar short."

As it has grown, Chattem has attracted executives from Bristol-Myers, Avon Products Inc., A. H. Robins Co., and other big-name marketers. The latest catch is the marketing vice president of Revlon's Norcliff-Thayer division. The lure: a company where committees are few, meetings brief, and decisions quick. Says Howard Ottley, a Merck & Co. alumnus now at Chattem, "We're servicing our customers rather than our management."

Fiscal 1982 was difficult for Chattem, though. Pretax profits rose just 1 percent on a 5 percent sales gain, due to a consumer-products slump and $1.5 million spent on the Pamprin introduction. The company also bumped into larger competitors; Gillette, which sold it Sun-In, clipped Mudd sales with a new facial cleanser named Aapri. Economic conditions also have made it tough for Chattem's chemical business, especially for products it sells to the housing and auto industries.

Still, Chattem hasn't wavered from its goal of 20 percent average annual growth over the next several years. The company's followers on Wall Street say they like that ambitious course, as long as it doesn't lead to any serious gaffes. "This isn't like Procter & Gamble where, if one or two brands flop, it'll wash out," says a U.S. Trust Co. analyst. "At Chattem there's no room for mistakes."

L'eggs Proves a Hard Act to Follow

If women will buy pantyhose in supermarkets, why not lipstick and nail polish too? Or so Hanes Corp. figured when it introduced L'erin cosmetics in 1977. Heady with the success of its seven-year-old L'eggs hosiery, the first brand in that industry to be marketed outside department stores, Hanes saw plenty of similarities in cosmetics.

Maybe Hanes should have thought more about the differences. If it had, it might have learned sooner that the beauty trade can be ugly indeed for a newcomer.

L'erin annual revenues had yet to top $30 million in 1983—L'eggs reached $150 million by its sixth birthday—and the brand accounted for only about 5 percent of the $1.1 billion of cosmetics sold through food, drug, and mass-merchandise stores. L'erin had just begun to make a small profit—mostly through Hanes's cutting costs, including advertising—after accumulating about $30 million in losses.

"We knew this business would be tough," concedes Jack Ward, a L'eggs veteran who now runs the L'erin division, "but it's been a lot tougher than we'd ever imagined."

He continues to be optimistic about the struggling venture's prospects, as does Consolidated Foods Corp., which acquired Hanes in 1979. Despite persistent cosmetics-industry rumors that Consolidated Foods will pull the plug on L'erin, a company spokeswoman says L'erin is expected eventually to reach a corporate goal of a 30 percent pretax return on investment.

When Hanes began studying cosmetics in 1975, there was reason for optimism. The industry, although dominated by Revlon Inc., was growing. Most sales were of higher-priced goods distributed through department stores, so there seemed to be opportunity for a low-priced brand carried by supermarkets and other mass-market outlets.

Noxell Corp.'s Cover Girl and Schering-Plough Corp.'s Maybelline had low price tags but hadn't yet accomplished much in food stores, where L'eggs had been so successful. Hanes already had an armada of 1,000 trucks delivering egg-shaped L'eggs cartons to retailers. A few cases of cosmetics would fit along easily.

What the pantyhose salesmen at Hanes apparently hadn't realized, though, was that they had entered a business unlike any other. Many retailers wanted cosmetics shipped to warehouses, not stocked on store shelves by Hanes's field crew. Although L'erin sold its products on consignment, some chains preferred the higher margins.

Nor had L'erin anticipated the need for a steady flow of new lipstick and polish colors. Color—not discounts, as Hanes believed—sold cosmetics. And by farming out its production to other manufacturers, L'erin raised its costs well above competitors'.

L'erin also blundered, says Mr. Ward, when it "listened to the consumer too much." The women interviewed by Hanes described their ideal cosmetic in functional, not emotional, terms: it was one they could wear all day without much upkeep. As a result, L'erin advertising was logical but dull. The slogan, delivered by a plain-Jane model in an ordinary setting: "Put your face on and forget it."

By late 1980, L'erin began to recognize its mistakes, "any one of which would have killed a less well-funded company," says Suzanne Grayson, a marketing consultant who helped with Hanes's original cosmetic plans. Executives were recruited from Revlon, Max Factor, and other cosmetics companies. Retailers no longer were required to take L'erin on consignment or by direct-to-store delivery from Hanes trucks. Packaging was spiffed up.

To keep up with the latest colors, L'erin polled the textile manufacturers and clothing makers that set styles. L'erin established its own research and development lab to cook up formulas that reduced ingredient costs by 20 percent or more. The company also cut costs by making its own lipsticks and nail polish in a converted Hanes hosiery factory in Winston-Salem, North Carolina.

There was also a new ad agency and campaign. More glamorous—and more expensive—models were hired; their clothes became more fashionable. Music was added to commercials. Little intrigues were set up: In one ad, a man and woman rendezvous on a train. The new slogan: "Let L'erin do the talking."

But even as L'erin was improving almost every aspect of its business, competitors were moving faster. By the time L'erin was available nationally in mid-1981, Cover Girl and Maybelline had become aggressive rivals.

L'erin now is carried by about 25,000 stores, fewer than its competitors and about half the number Mr. Ward wants. Its most successful outlets are supermarkets, where the brand accounts for about 14 percent of total cosmetics sales.

Drugstores sell five times as many cosmetics as food stores, though, and L'erin has only about 2 percent of the drugstore market. "You can't make it in this industry," says a competitor, "without making it in drugstores." The recession hasn't helped either. Retailers have trimmed inventories, and cosmetics sales generally have stopped growing, at least temporarily.

L'erin appears to have little chance any time soon of becoming a winner like L'eggs, whose annual revenue is about $340 million. Consolidated Foods Chairman John H. Bryan Jr. may have been correct in 1979 when he predicted that L'erin would become profitable within three years. He was a bit too optimistic, though, when he also said that 1982 would be the year the cosmetics enterprise would "turn into a swan."

Update

Hanes gave up on L'erin in August 1983 when it sold the cosmetics line to a small beauty-care company.

Cadillac Chases the BMW Crowd

In 1959 Harold Cohen of Shawnee Mission, Kansas, became a loyal Cadillac customer, trading in his plush Sedan de Ville for a new model every subsequent year. In 1985, though, he traded his Cadillac for something entirely different—a Lincoln Town Car, Ford Motor Co.'s big luxury sedan. "Cadillac threw a smaller car at me," complains the 66-year-old salesman, who has just ordered a 1986 Town Car.

Losing old customers like Mr. Cohen wouldn't be so bad for Cadillac if it could attract new buyers like Julio Mori. But Mr. Mori, who bought a new Saab last year and is thinking of buying another one, didn't even consider a Cadillac, even though he could easily afford it. "I'm not an old man," bristles the 33-year-old Chicagoan. "I want to enjoy driving, and that means performance rather than comfort."

Cadillac, the luxury-car division of General Motors Corp., is walking a tightrope these days, without much success. Its eight-year program of making its cars smaller hasn't weaned many younger buyers from their Audis, BMWs, Saabs, and Volvos. But it has alienated some longtime customers who bewail the loss of their traditional Cadillac behemoths. "Cadillac is losing some older buyers of luxury cars but still isn't attracting many younger ones," says Edsel B. Ford II, the Ford Motor heir who heads marketing for Ford's luxury Lincoln line.

So Cadillac is introducing two restyled, peppier 1986 models that it hopes will finally excite younger buyers. And in a rearguard action, it recently decided to continue making an old-fashioned king-size car that it had planned to drop. But Cadillac officials concede they don't have any quick solutions. "You develop an image over an 83-year period and it's hard to change," says Gordon Horsburgh, Cadillac's director of marketing.

Not that Cadillac isn't trying. The average age of Cadillac buyers peaked at 58 in 1984, but dropped to 57 in the 1985 model year. That bit of progress, however, is tempered by another statistic: Cadillac's share of the total new-car market dropped to 2.8 percent from 3.2 percent in 1984. That translated into lost sales of some 40,000 cars, for a division that sold 311,000 cars in 1984.

"We aren't especially proud of that 2.8 percent," says John O. Grettenberger, the GM vice president who heads Cadillac. "But competition in the luxury end of the market is proliferating rapidly."

Indeed it is. While Cadillac remains the single top-selling luxury car in the United States by far, its share of that desirable market segment dropped to 22.6 percent in the 1985 model year, which ended September 30, from 28.5 percent in 1980. During the same period, highbrow imports, almost all from Europe, soared to nearly 31 percent of that market from less than 25 percent. And the competition is getting tougher. Honda, whose Accord isn't really a luxury car but attracts many affluent young buyers, is about to launch its up-scale Acura division in the United States with two luxury models for the spring of 1986.

What worries Cadillac is that it isn't attracting the young buyers the Europeans are snaring. The average BMW buyer is 38; the average Audi buyer 43. But the average buyer of Cadillac's supposed import-fighter, the compact Cimarron, is 48 years old. The Cimarron, which debuted in 1981, is relatively low-priced (at a base price of $13,128 compared to $26,756 for the top-of-the-line Seville), but has produced more yawns than sales. In fact, it's Cadillac's slowest-selling model.

"Imports are getting too large a share of young, high-income buyers," says Mr. Horsburgh. "Yuppies have an image of a Cadillac as like their father's car—big and ostentatious. It isn't their bag."

Cadillac began making its cars smaller—what automakers call "downsizing"—in 1977. It had scheduled the Fleetwood Brougham, Cadillac's sole surviving rear-drive giant, for extinction.

That gave Ford's Lincoln-Mercury division an opening. It began heavily advertising its own giant, the Town Car at $20,764 (base price). It posted a 50 percent sales jump in the 1985 model year to a record 116,015 vehicles.

A chastened Cadillac now says it will continue the Fleetwood Brougham "for a couple years at least," and will give the 1986 version a larger engine. "The market clearly said don't phase it out," says Mr. Grettenberger. "We'll be very aggressive again in 1986 on our rear-drive car."

That may address one problem. But Cadillac still has a lineup of front-drive cars that look so much like those of its sister divisions—Buick and Oldsmobile—that even some GM dealers call them "GM generic." Lincoln recently tweaked Cadillac's nose with a television commercial showing confusion as a man asks a valet for "the black Cadillac, please." The car pulls up but a second man says, "Excuse me, I believe that's my Buick." The farce continues with an Oldsmobile until another man asks for his Lincoln Town Car, and gets it right away.

The commercial has touched a nerve at Cadillac. "You wouldn't find GM or Cadillac doing that," says Cadillac boss Mr. Grettenberger. "I don't think anybody ever benefited from knocking the other guy." Besides, say Cadillac officials, the new Eldorado and Seville have features to appeal to younger buyers; the 1986 Eldorado accelerates from zero to 60 miles per hour two seconds faster than the 1985 model.

But some Cadillac dealers complain that the styling of both new models is simply a variation on GM's boxy, wedge-shaped body. "The new Eldorado and Seville are going in the right direction, but they aren't as different as we would have liked," says Rob Mancuso, a Cadillac dealer in Barrington, Ill. "We want our own cars. We want people to be able to look at a car from a block away and tell that it's a Cadillac."

The dealers may get their wish, but they'll have to wait a year. Cadillac plans to introduce as a 1987 model the Allante, a two-seat luxury coupe whose body will be built in Italy by Pininfarina S.p.A. before being shipped to the United States for final assembly.

At a price expected to be upwards of $50,000, the Allante won't be a big seller. But Mr. Grettenberger says it will provide "an umbrella for the brand."

Meanwhile, some Cadillac dealers are making changes of their own. Mr. Mancuso has stopped hiring stale car salesmen and instead wants "fresh, young, educated people" who can relate better to young buyers. Once he hires them, he says, he sends them out to shop for imports "to see how those other salespeople sell."

Such moves might attract buyers like Mr. Mori, the young Saab owner, but it won't happen soon. Although Mr. Mori bought his Saab at a Cadillac-Saab showroom, he gave the Cadillacs nary a glance. "I might consider a Cadillac when I'm older," he says. "Until then I want to drive something that I really enjoy."

Sparks Fly between Scripto and Bic

Ever since smokers started flicking their Bics in 1973, disposable lighters have all looked pretty much alike and fetched about the same price. Now, in a drive to become the leading U.S. marketer of throwaway lighters, Scripto/Tokai is spicing things up with a "family of lighters."

"We don't look at lighters as just cheap functional products to replace matches," says Richard Brett, vice president of sales and marketing. "Consumers today want more choice in lighters just as they do in many other products."

He likens Scripto's line to the ice-cream assortment in the supermarket freezer case. For the budget-minded consumer who buys store brands of ice cream, there's Mighty Match, a clear plastic lighter that retails for 49 cents. Scripto figures shoppers who go for national ice-cream brands such as Sealtest might prefer its 69-cent silver-and-gold Ultra Lite model. And the company's Haagen-Dazs version is the fancy new 99-cent Electra, featuring an electric ignition that operates more smoothly than the old standard flint and sparkwheel.

This segmentation strategy is part of Scripto's heady plans to topple Bic Corp. as king of the hill in the $270 million U.S. disposable lighter market. Scripto was acquired in 1984 by Tokai Seiki Co. of Yokohama, Japan, which as the world's largest producer of lighters (about 90 million a month) is determined to become No. 1 in the United States as well. Its target date: 1987.

With only 24 percent of the American market, Scripto must work fast. Currently, Bic claims about 55 percent of the 450 million lighters sold each year. "It's going to be quite a battle, but I really don't think Scripto can win," says Claes Wennerth, president of Universal Match Corp., which sells lighters under the Feudor brand. "Bic makes a quality product, and its distribution system is far superior to anyone else's."

But already Bic is smarting from more intense price competition. For instance, Scripto is pushing a package of four lighters for a dollar and distributing 20 million cents-off coupons. Even more irritating for Bic was Scripto's recruitment this spring of Jack Paige, a former marketing vice president at Bic. He says he is filling in his new bosses on how Bic thinks and how it became the market leader. "I was attracted to the Scripto people partly because they reminded me of the hungry young guys I worked with at Bic in the 1970s," says Mr. Paige. Back then, Bic took on Gillette Co. in a David and Goliath battle that finally forced Gillette to abandon its unprofitable Cricket lighter business in 1984.

With the catchy "Flick Your Bic" ad campaign, Bic forged ahead of Gillette at a time when lighter sales were hot. Now, as cigarette consumption lags, lighter sales are rising only 5 percent a year. Still, industry executives see room for growth; they believe only half of U.S. smokers regularly use lighters instead of matches.

Like Scripto, Bic and other companies are trying to boost their market share with more specialized lighters. Bic's first new model since it entered the disposable lighter market, the Bic 2000, is a miniature lighter that industry sources believe will appeal mostly to women. That launch will follow Scripto's introduction of a line of lighters imprinted with cornball but popular expressions like "Let's get foolish" and "Lack of sex causes insanity."

A small company in Denver, meanwhile, is trying to crack the market with a lighter that doubles as a breath freshener spray. There's also a new model called Surefire that has a "wind guard" device and promises to protect the flame in gusts up to 40 mph.

But it takes much more than clever products to score big in the lighter business. Scripto is struggling both to bolster its weak distribution system and to become a household name among consumers. The company budgeted $5 million for advertising in 1985, which it says is more than the entire lighter industry spent on ads during the previous six years. Scripto will need that much and more to make a dent in Bic's reputation. "The Bic name has become a generic like the Frigidaire and Victrola names," says Arnold Benjamin, purchasing director of Metropolitan Distribution Services, a wholesaler of tobacco, candy, and sundry products. "People often will say, 'Give me a Bic,' instead of 'Give me a lighter.'"

For its TV campaign, Scripto hired actors Jerry Stiller and Anne Meara to engage in an off-camera comedy routine. He keeps blowing out a pair of candles to spark a little romance; she keeps relighting them with an Electra. Although the dialogue is humorous and gets viewers' attention, critics say the ad fails to make a compelling sales pitch. "Scripto should be hitting women harder with the message that its lighter is easier to operate," says Mr. Benjamin. "The thing women hate most about lighters is getting their fingers black and breaking their nails."

More important than advertising is a strong merchandising team that can get eye-stopping displays near cash registers. "The space at checkouts is becoming very competitive with more lighters, candy, batteries, magazines, and cigarettes all fighting for room," says Keith Koski, Bic's marketing manager.

Scripto is expanding its sales force by 60 percent in 1985 and adding 100 merchandisers to monitor store displays. In the past, no one regularly made sure that store racks were kept well stocked with Scripto lighters. "Lighters are an impulse purchase," says Mr. Brett, Scripto's top marketing executive. "Two weeks without any products on display can really hurt."

Update

By the first quarter of 1986, Scripto said its share of the
disposable lighter market had grown to 30 percent. It cited
new products and a fortified sales force as the major factors
in the gain and said the increase came largely at the expense of the Cricket line.

Smokestack Firms Try Sophisticated Selling

Salesmanship at AmCast Industrial Corp. used to involve little more than what company officials referred to as "chasing smokestacks"—a description for the process of driving from one customer to the next to make sales calls. But that phrase isn't used much anymore at the Dayton, Ohio, parts maker, which used to be known as Dayton Malleable Inc. AmCast, like a lot of other Rust Belt companies, has had to change its ways.

No longer are its sales representatives mere glad-handers, skilled at wining and dining purchasing agents in hopes of getting a share of available orders. Today, they are college graduates with metalworking backgrounds, who not only deal with buyers but with customers' engineers, marketing specialists, and manufacturing personnel as well. The purpose: to get involved early on in the business plans of potential customers.

The changing strategy at AmCast is part of what some sales experts see as a revolution in industrial marketing. "Smokestack industries are realizing the need to be involved in the customers' decision-making process," says Richard G. Hodapp, president of Managing Process Inc., a Cincinnati marketing firm. Once a supplier gets order specifications, it's too late to do anything but react, Mr. Hodapp says.

Aggressive industrial marketing isn't totally new. For years Timken Co., in Canton, Ohio, has designed bearings to meet customers' needs rather than waiting for them to place orders. But new technology and increased competition are pushing more industrial concerns into sophisticated marketing.

Trucking deregulation, for instance, is spurring Cleveland's Leaseway Transportation Corp. to use computers to show customers how to haul goods more effectively and cheaply. Leaseway beefed up its marketing department to 20 people, from just two in 1981. In the past, Leaseway simply hoped that customers such as General Motors and Sears Roebuck would prosper, because "the more they sold, the more we hauled," says Chuck Lounsbury, vice president of sales and marketing.

The Big Three automakers have also given impetus to the new marketing methods, partly because they are asking suppliers to share more of the research and development costs associated with engineering new autos. To be able to provide for those needs, car industry suppliers have had to become a lot more knowledgeable about technological trends—both in terms of what the auto companies are likely to want and in terms of what areas the supplier might be best able to address.

Thus, by learning about the handling and performance characteristics GM wanted for its redesigned Corvette, Goodyear Tire & Rubber Co. was able to go to work on new tires that eventually won it a contract with GM.

A closer look at some of the changes at AmCast illustrates how some of the new industrial marketing strategies can work. Like many old-line companies, AmCast had been set in its ways. At the close of the Civil War it began shaping iron parts for horse-drawn buggies. Then it evolved into an automobile parts maker. "We were known as The Malleable," says Leo W. Ladehoff, chairman and president. "It was like being known as The Obsolete."

AmCast's sales representatives for years called on customers who bought iron castings as a commodity—by the ton. Of six salesmen in 1979, only one was college-educated. Each drove his own car. "We found that when they left the office they were just racking up mileage expenses to pay off new cars," says a company official. The company didn't have a WATS line. Salesmen waited for customers to phone in orders.

Major changes began at AmCast in 1979 and 1980 when the company cut its cast-iron business in half in response to automakers' demand for lighter metals. It also decided to double its capacity to cast aluminum parts and get into finished-metals businesses. Since then it has tripled its sales force and begun working more closely with its customers—both to learn more about their needs and to show that it can help develop better designs.

Now, says Thomas Amato, AmCast's vice president of finance, "when we target a customer, we want to get in bed with them." By working closely with GM engineers, Am-Cast officials helped design a new aluminum disk brake. The result: a contract from the automaker that resulted in $3.5 million of brake-part sales in the fiscal year ended August 31, 1984.

A key to AmCast's marketing is its computer-controlled casting. Until 1981 it made parts on a trial-and-error basis, just like foundries always had. "You never knew whether you had a good part until the end when it was inspected, machined, or X-rayed," says Oral K. Hunsaker, head of research and development. "It was a black art."

Now AmCast's process resembles a science. It got an Apple computer to memorize casting temperatures necessary to make parts that rarely have cracks, pores, or weak spots.

Its high-quality castings helped AmCast land a $4 million contract to make sporty aluminum wheels for Pontiac's Fiero and other orders. AmCast expected to sell $20 million of aluminum wheels in 1985.

Loctite 'Listens' to
the Marketplace

A comely model in a bikini or tight-fitting T-shirt: She's a staple of industrial advertising. She's also irrelevant, uncommunicative, and the symbol of what's wrong with the way some industrial marketers sell their products.

A company that doesn't fit that pattern is Loctite Corp., which is demonstrating how consumer-goods marketing techniques can be applied to a product as prosaic as a putty-like adhesive for repairing worn machine parts. Results have been impressive: In the first seven months after the chemical's introduction, Loctite retailers sold $2.2 million of it. Traditional industrial marketing methods, Loctite estimates, would have yielded sales of only $320,000.

The adhesive's name—Quick Metal—and almost all of its other features result from the sort of careful research and planning most often associated with consumer products. "In the past we'd make a product in the lab and then say, 'Now how are we going to sell it?'" says Richard Thompson, Loctite senior application engineer. "The difference here is that the marketing preceded the chemistry."

That approach—finding what potential customers wanted and then designing a product to satisfy them—might seem obvious, but it hasn't been for many industrial marketers, including Loctite. Quick Metal's predecessor, for example, was similar in function but didn't sell well. Carrying the uninformative name of RC 601, it was a runny green liquid packaged in a plain red bottle. It was difficult to use, and its target consumers—equipment designers—often were reluctant to try unproven materials.

Loctite's use of consumer marketing techniques is part of "a definite trend," says John Quelch, a Harvard Business School assistant professor, who has written a case study about the company. He says the sophistication of industrial marketers is increasing because of rising costs of personal sales calls, increased competition, and the migration of consumer products marketing executives to industrial concerns.

Jeffrey Fox, Loctite's vice president of marketing and the prime mover behind Quick Metal, is one such executive. A Harvard MBA and a veteran of five years at Heublein and two at Pillsbury, he joined Loctite in 1976. The company was growing rapidly (sales for the fiscal year ended June 1980 were $199.3 million, compared with $20.3 million a decade earlier) but its industrial products were "under-marketed," says Mr. Fox.

Quick Metal got its start in early 1979, when Mr. Fox and other Loctite marketing executives began looking for ways to revive RC 601. Instead of depending on its own chemists and sales experts to design a new product that the market might not want, Loctite asked customers what they were looking for. "You have to have ironclad control of your ego," says Mr. Fox. "We listened to the marketplace with big ears."

Even before Loctite chemists went to work on Quick Metal, the company's ad agency, Mintz & Hoke, was helping to plan the new product. After six weeks of interviews with about 20 equipment designers and production engineers and 40 maintenance workers, Loctite devised its strategy.

The choicest market: maintenance workers, who are more likely than equipment manufacturers to try an unfamiliar product. "When the production line is down, the maintenance worker can buy anything anywhere that he feels will put the line back into production," noted a May 1979 company memo.

If Loctite had marketed Quick Metal with a more traditional approach, advertising and promotional materials would have described the adhesive as a "non-migrating thixotropic anaerobic gel" and cited its various physical properties. Instead, says Mr. Fox, "we wanted to cut through the cryptic jargon and get into the basic benefits for the customer." One slogan now in use: "keeps machinery running until the new parts arrive."

The company wasn't shy about pricing Quick Metal; a 50 cc. tube retails for $17.75, resulting in an 85 percent gross margin for the manufacturer. "The competition might have priced it at half as much," says Mr. Fox, who defends the price by pointing out that one tube can eliminate 800 hours of machine downtime.

To fire up its workers, Loctite awarded hockey tickets to those who answered "Loctite, home of Quick Metal" when a "mystery caller" telephoned. Others who collected business cards from prospective customers or found new uses for Quick Metal were entered in drawings for color TV sets and hockey tickets.

The hoopla culminated during a five-day period, dubbed Quick Metal Week, when Loctite set up a bank of WATS lines at its Newington, Connecticut, headquarters. Daily calls of encouragement went out to the 695 branches of the independent distributors who sell Loctite products. Those who sold the most won prizes of $100 or $1,000.

The result: In addition to selling more than 100,000 tubes of Quick Metal in one week, Loctite developed detailed information about its sales force, improved morale, and boosted the sale of the company's other products. But some distributors weren't impressed; one in Florida said Quick Metal Week "didn't stimulate me one bit and seemed like a waste of money."

And Loctite's attempts to add sophistication to its marketing didn't work with some customers. A potential buyer told an Elizabeth, New Jersey, saleswoman that, if she'd show up braless in her Quick Metal T-shirt, he would purchase 50 tubes. She did, and he did.

National Enquirer Craves Respect

The *National Enquirer* might headline this column: "An Anguished Man's Desperate Plea—I Want To Be Loved." It's about a newspaper that has 14.6 million readers, $130 million in annual revenue, and an unsatisfied owner who craves respect.

The paper is the *National Enquirer* itself, and the man is Generoso Pope, Jr. Shunned for 30 years by General Motors, Procter & Gamble, Sears Roebuck, and other blue-chip advertisers, in 1982 he began to make an all-out attempt to change their minds about his publication. The sales pitch, according to an executive of the paper, is "You may not like the *Enquirer,* but 14 million people do."

Here's what it's up against: "Our clients don't want to be associated with the stuff they're writing about," says the buyer for a New York ad agency. The advertising head at a packaged-goods concern explains, "When you're talking to product managers who are Harvard Business School graduates, they say, 'Nobody reads that at my club.'"

Persuading them otherwise, says Mr. Pope, is a "matter of education." His teaching aids include free subscriptions for the wives of advertising executives, testimonials from the likes of Bob Hope and Billy Graham, and piles of demographic research. To deliver his message, Mr. Pope has hired the ex-presidents of Newsweek and Liggett & Myers Tobacco, the former Detroit ad sales chief for CBS-TV, and a retired Johnson & Johnson marketing executive.

National Enquirer cover, April 22, 1986

NATIONAL

ENQUIRER

65¢

April 22, 1986   30586-2   LARGEST CIRCULATION OF ANY PAPER IN AMERICA

WILD DALLAS CLIFFHANGER

Sneak Preview: J.R. Faces Death — Here's What You'll See

Chilling Interview With Man Who Sat Next to the Bomb

'My Seat Was Sucked Out of the Hole — The Man Next to Me Vanished'

Liz: It's Love Again — George Hamilton Plays Cupid

Tony Danza to Wed Gal Who Kept Him Waiting For 2½ Years

WORLD EXCLUSIVE

Meanwhile, the tabloid also is trying to double its recent sales of more than 5 million copies per issue (each copy has about three readers), a weekly volume second only to *TV Guide*. The means: a television advertising campaign with a budget—$30 million for 1982—comparable to the ad spending of Pepsi-Cola, Crest toothpaste, or Polaroid cameras.

Such lofty goals may be the product of Mr. Pope's entrepreneurial enthusiasm (in 1971 he predicted that the *Enquirer*'s circulation would reach 20 million by 1976), but he says his ambitions are modest in comparison to the risk he took in 1968. Then, the *Enquirer* was a lurid publication (sample headline: "Madman Cut Up His Date and Put Her Body In His Freezer") that got most of its circulation of 1 million from newsstand sales.

Looking for a larger market, Mr. Pope purged the paper of blood and gore and began promoting it to food and drug chains. The effort was much like the current plan to enlist national advertisers. Free subscriptions were given to the wives of food-store executives and endorsements from Hubert Humphrey, Barry Goldwater, and Joan Crawford were collected in a film narrated by newscaster Chet Huntley. Retailers were promised 22 percent of the paper's cover price.

Today the *Enquirer* is stocked by 170,000 supermarkets and drug stores, and its circulation is growing. Even a recent increase in the cover price—to 65 cents from 45 cents—didn't affect *Enquirer* sales. "None of this could happen," brags Mr. Pope, "unless you have a product people want."

He insists that the new ad campaign and sales drive were in the works before actress Carol Burnett won a libel suit against the paper last year. Still, he acknowledges, one of the campaign's purposes is to gain prestige. "National advertising would be very good for the image of the *Enquirer*," he says, not to mention additional profit.

Unlike most publications, which derive at least half of their revenues from advertising, the *Enquirer* collected only

12 percent of its total 1981 revenue from ads. Most were mail-order pitches for such products as wrinkle creams, biorhythm charts, diets ("I lost 16 pounds in one week"), and seeds that grow 6½-pound tomatoes.

Replacing those advertisers with big-name companies, which pay $26,500 for a full-page color ad, could increase the paper's revenue by 25 percent or more. Cigarette companies now are the only national advertisers that regularly buy full pages.

The *Enquirer*'s new sales squad has drawn up a list of 20 prospects to work on during the coming months; most are automobile companies, large retailers, distillers, brewers, food concerns, and marketers of household-cleaning and personal-care products.

The sales squad will be equipped with reams of data about *Enquirer* readers, supplied by an independent research service. They're above-average consumers of Charmin toilet paper, Tupperware, Coppertone suntan lotion, and Chef-Boy-Ar-Dee spaghetti. More than 7 million of them are smokers, 4.7 million are working women, and 7.5 million are teenagers.

If that sort of data, plus the paper's relatively inexpensive ad rates, aren't enough, the *Enquirer* also is conducting a study of what its readers think of the publication and how much of it they believe. With a similar study conducted among Madison Avenue executives, the *Enquirer* hopes to persuade a reluctant ad buyer not to treat it any differently than other media. "He doesn't watch 'Laverne and Shirley,'" says Ralph Gallagher, the paper's advertising director, "but he spends a lot of money on it."

Arthur Sloat, the former tobacco executive who joined the *Enquirer* last month, expects to sign up 8 of its targets within a year and all 20 within two years. Many outsiders aren't as sure. "I think it's a crazy idea," says Lawrence Epting, an executive at Ted Bates Advertising and one of the marketers Mr. Sloat sought for advice before taking the *Enquirer* job. "The paper carries with it such an incredible aura from the past. It's a difficult thing to change."

Mr. Pope, who has invested more than $1 million in his sales drive, remains unperturbed by such sentiments. "We have to do it on an individual basis," he says. "If we were to crack Procter & Gamble, I think a lot of companies would follow."

Update

By continuing to shed its old editorial image and add more service and human-interest stories, the *National Enquirer* has succeeded in attracting blue-chip advertisers, including several Procter & Gamble brands that Mr. Pope wanted most of all. Starting a weekly food column helped lure advertisers like Kraft, Campbell Soup, and Nabisco. The *Enquirer* carried 354 pages of national advertising in 1985, compared to 251 in 1983.

References

The following articles have been reprinted by permission of *The Wall Street Journal*, © Dow Jones & Company, Inc.

1

1. "Prisoners of the Past," Ronald Alsop (March 24, 1986).

2. "American Express Is Gearing New Ad Campaign to Women," Bill Abrams (August 4, 1983).

3. "Firms Still Struggle to Devise Best Approach to Black Buyers," Ronald Alsop (October 25, 1984).

4. "Firms Try New Ways to Tap Growing Over-50 Population," Ronald Alsop (August 23, 1984).

5. "Liquor Concerns Are Creating Fresh Ads for Baby Boomers," Ronald Alsop (June 21, 1984).

6. "Liggett Tests a New Cigarette Developed for Hispanic Tastes," Ronald Alsop (July 12, 1984).

7. "Teen-Age Girls, Alas, Are Big Consumers—But Poor Customers," John Koten (November 9, 1984).

2

1. "Fixing a Snack: The Public Doesn't Get a Better Potato Chip without a Bit of Pain," Janet Guyon (March 25, 1983).

2. "Exploiting Proven Brand Names Can Cut Risk of New Products," Bill Abrams (January 22, 1981).

3. "Fisher-Price Banks on Name, Design in Foray into Playwear," Ronald Alsop (August 2, 1984).

4. "Novel Barclay Pitch Fires Up Sales for Brown & Williamson," Bill Abrams (April 30, 1981).

5. "Careful Study, Good Product Making AMC's Alliance a Hit," Bill Abrams (April 21, 1983).

6. "Coke's Flip-Flop Underscores Risks of Consumer Taste Tests," Ronald Alsop (July 18, 1985).

7. "Charles of the Ritz Discovers What It Is that Women Want," Bill Abrams (August 20, 1981).

8. "Jell-O's Revival Shows Sales Can Grow with Older Products," Bill Abrams (September 11, 1980).

9. "Ten Ways to Restore Vitality to Old, Worn-Out Products," Bill Abrams (February 18, 1982).

3

1. "Admen Say 'Brand Personality' Is As Crucial As the Product," Bill Abrams (August 13, 1981).

2. "More Firms Try to Associate Corporate Names with Brands," Ronald Alsop (September 6, 1984).

3. "Jaded TV Viewers Tune Out Glut of Celebrity Commercials," Ronald Alsop (February 7, 1985).

4. "Real People Star in Many Ads, but Are They Really Credible?" Ronald Alsop (May 23, 1985).

5. "Comparative Ads Are Getting More Popular, Harder Hitting," Bill Abrams (March 11, 1982).

6. "Ad Agencies Jazz Up Jingles by Playing on 1960s Nostalgia," Ronald Alsop (April 18, 1985).

7. "If Logic in Ads Doesn't Sell, Try a Tug on the Heartstrings," Bill Abrams (April 8, 1982).

8. "Companies Look to Weather to Find Best Climate for Ads," Ronald Alsop (January 10, 1985).

9. "Ad Directors Fuss over Foods As Much As over Live Models," Ronald Alsop (July 11, 1985).

4

1. "J&B Scotch Scuttles Old Ads to Put Kick into Stagnant Sales," Bill Abrams (September 18, 1980).

2. "To Stir Up J&B Scotch Sales, Ads Hype Its British Heritage," Ronald Alsop (October 17, 1985).

3. "Why Revlon's Charlie Seems to Be Ready to Settle Down," Bill Abrams (December 23, 1982).

4. " 'Ring around the Collar' Ads Irritate Many Yet Get Results," Bill Abrams (November 4, 1982).

5. "New Alka-Seltzer Ads Revert to the Humor of Heartburn," Ronald Alsop (November 7, 1985).

6. "Dr Pepper Is Bubbling Again after Its 'Be a Pepper' Setback," Ronald Alsop (September 26, 1985).

7. "More Direct Approach to Dying Enlivens Ads for Life Insurance," Bill Abrams (January 29, 1981).

8. "New Prudential Ads Portray Death as No Laughing Matter," Bill Abrams (November 10, 1983).

9. "Spreading the Word: How ITT Shells Out $10 Million or So a Year to Polish Reputation," Bill Abrams (April 2, 1982).

5

1. "Packaging Often Irks Buyers, but Firms Are Slow to Change," Bill Abrams (January 28, 1982).

2. "Color Grows More Important in Catching Consumers' Eyes," Ronald Alsop (November 29, 1984).

3. "More Firms Use '800' Numbers to Keep Consumers Satisfied," Bill Abrams (April 7, 1983).

4. "Companies Seek Ways to Put Coupons Where They'll Count," Ronald Alsop (August 8, 1985).

5. "Aggressive Use of Warranties Is Benefiting Many Concerns," John Koten (April 5, 1984).

6. "Diamonds and Furs Help Sell Broadway Theater in Sun Belt," Ronald Alsop (February 14, 1985).

7. "Companies Cram Ads in Stores to Sway Shopping Decisions," Ronald Alsop (August 22, 1985).

8. "How a Much-Ballyhooed Advertising Idea Failed to Fly and Enrich Hopeful Investors," Bill Abrams (August 26, 1982).

6

1. "Retailers Exert More Influence in Selling of Packaged Goods," Ronald Alsop (April 25, 1985).

2. "Selling to the Poor: Retailers that Target Low-Income Shoppers Are Growing Rapidly," Hank Gilman (June 24, 1985).

3. "Food Giants Take to the Mails to Push Fancy Product Lines," Ronald Alsop (February 28, 1985).

4. "Discount Drugstores Thriving with Tricky Buying Strategy," Bill Abrams (March 17, 1983).

5. "Book Chains Look for Big Author, Great Cover, and Sometimes, Merit," Steve Weiner (June 27, 1985).

6. "Electronic Shopping Awaiting Consumer, Corporate Support," Bill Abrams (June 16, 1983).

7. "Electronic Shopping Is Called Imminent, but Doubts Persist," Bill Abrams (June 23, 1983).

7

1. "Firms Liven Up Financial Ads, but Will Cuteness Sell IRAs?" Ronald Alsop (February 21, 1985).

2. "Marketers Start to Help Banks Recognize Gains from Selling," Julie Salamon (September 3, 1981).

3. "Total War: CPA Firms Diversify, Cut Fees, Steal Clients in Battle for Business," Lee Berton (September 20, 1985).

4. "Once-Complacent Hotel Industry Is Forced to Learn How to Market," Steve Swartz (November 29, 1985).

5. "Doctors Find a Dose of Marketing Can Cure Pain of Sluggish Practice," Ed Bean (March 15, 1985).

6. "Advertisers Promote Religion in a Splashy and Secular Style," Ronald Alsop (November 21, 1985).

8

1. "U.S. Concerns Seek Inspiration for Products from Overseas," Ronald Alsop (January 3, 1985).

2. "Ad Agencies and Big Concerns Debate World Brands' Value," George Anders (June 14, 1984).

3. "Efficacy of Global Ad Projects Is Questioned in Firm's Survey," Ronald Alsop (September 13, 1984).

4. "Countries' Different Ad Rules Are Problem for Global Firms," Ronald Alsop (September 27, 1984).

5. "Gillette Keys Sales to Third World Tastes," David Wessel (January 23, 1986).

6. "U.S. Firms Rush through China's Open Door," Amanda Bennett (April 8, 1985).

9

1. "For P&G's Rivals, the New Game Is to Beat the Leader, Not Copy It," John Koten (May 1, 1985).

2. "Selling Wine like Soda Pop, Riunite Uncorks Huge Market," Bill Abrams (July 2, 1981).

3. "Stressing Neglected Markets, Firm Ends Its 60-Year Slump," Bill Abrams (August 19, 1982).

4. "Hanes Finds L'eggs Methods Don't Work with Cosmetics," Bill Abrams (February 3, 1983).

5. "Cadillac Wants to Attract Younger Buyers but Its 'Old Man' Image Gets in the Way," Paul Ingrassia (November 18, 1985).

6. "Sparks Fly in Scripto's Battle to Dump Bic as Lighter King," Ronald Alsop (May 2, 1985).

7. "Smokestack Industries Adopt Sophisticated Sales Approach," Gregory Stricharchuk (March 15, 1984).

8. "Consumer-Product Techniques Help Loctite Sell to Industry," Bill Abrams (April 2, 1981).

9. *"National Enquirer* Starts Drive to Lure Big-Time Advertisers," Bill Abrams (March 18, 1982).